Lifelong Learning
in action

This book is dedicated to my granddaughter, Charlotte, aged 6 years and my grandson Adam, aged 6 days, who will stand to benefit most from the implementation of the ideas and actions contained in its pages. May they, when the time comes, be able to contribute to harmony, understanding and peace in the world as a result.

Lifelong Learning
in action

Transforming Education in the
21st Century

NORMAN LONGWORTH

KOGAN
PAGE

London and Sterling, VA

First published in Great Britain and the United States in 2003 by Kogan Page
Limited

120 Pentonville Road   22883 Quicksilver Drive
London N1 9JN   Sterling VA 20166–2012
UK   USA
www.kogan-page.co.uk

© Norman Longworth, 2003

ISBN 0 7494 4013 9

British Library Cataloguing-in-Publication Data

A CIP record for this book is available from the British Library.

Library of Congress Cataloging-in-Publication Data

Longworth, Norman.
  Lifelong learning in action : transforming education for the 21st
century/Norman Longworth.
      p. cm.
Includes bibliographical references (p.   ) and index.
  ISBN 0-7494-4013-9
  1. Continuing education--History. 2. Adult education. I. Title
  LC5215.L572 2003
  374--dc21
                                    2003004775

Typeset by Saxon Graphics Ltd, Derby.
Printed and bound in Great Britain by Clays Ltd, St Ives plc

Contents

CONTENTS

Foreword by Sylvia Lee, President of World Initiative on Lifelong Learning

This book's title says it's about 'lifelong' learning. The term suggests something linear, but it's far more; it's lifelong, lifewide, and lifedeep. There is no term that captures this three-dimensionality (four in many people's minds) and we are left, as we so often are, with a term that fails to fully express something profound.

Perhaps the linear thinking implied by the term is part of our problem. We have a tendency, especially in the Western world, to build 'silo' structures and models, series of activities and programs deliberately designed to be aligned and parallel – and therefore to never meet!

What Norman is promoting in this and his earlier books is breaking down the silos, and not only acknowledging, but embracing, the notion of integration – whole heartedly and whole mindedly.

Schools and education should not exist in silos, but, for far too long, they have. Certainly there have been vast efforts recently to integrate school and business, but integrating two of the silos without the rest hasn't solved the problem, and may have made it worse. The schools themselves remain detached from their communities, and we have schools in many parts of the world in which administrators and teachers seem to view their role as preparing our children for the world of work. Certainly that is a critical component, but the enormous emphasis on career has often excluded, or at least marginalized, other critical areas such as the arts, citizenship, and personal quality of life. Communities and societies encompass far more than work. The Native American Medicine Wheel, in which life is only in balance when its physical, mental, emotional, and spiritual components are in balance, offers an old-world model for a new-world environment. Many other ancient models echo this theme – Taoist principles among them. The more modern silo model results in one component operating at best in isolation from, at worst in competition with, the other components.

Communities and societies are complex, organic entities. They are ever-evolving and every molecule is inextricably linked to every other molecule. Changing one affects all the others in some way, large or small. School must not only believe in, but live, this ideal – be an integral part of the learning society, not just an entity within it. And if they live it, they can do no other but teach it, through both curriculum and example.

In this book, Norman shares his deep understanding of the problem together with some roadmaps for practical solutions. He shows how those maps are local, national and global in essence. Although in Part 2 he concentrates on the nature and role of schools in a lifelong learning world, Part 1 is a tour de force of that world as we know it. It provides case studies, diagrams and highly readable descriptions of the basic fundamentals of lifelong learning in that easy knowledgeable style which has characterized his earlier books. It is not only essential reading for our educators, administrators, and politicians but also for anyone with an interest in understanding how this movement will fundamentally change the world we all live in for the better.

Sylvia Lee
Edmonton, Alberta, Canada

Preface: a time for action

My grandfather was born in the 1880s, a time when the world order was pretty well set in Victorian concrete. Britain ruled the waves, the Queen was undisputed head of an empire made affluent by its industry and its overseas possessions, and less than half of his countrymen could read, mostly, but not exclusively, the male half. Local events were all – in the absence of radio, television and readable news-papers, the world was a million miles away, a territory to be dealt with by politi-cians and those born to deal with those sorts of things. After leaving school at the age of 13 he went to work as an apprentice in a cotton spinning factory. He and my grandmother raised a family of three boys and two girls in a small back-to-back, two-up, two-down house in Bolton in the North-west of England. Today Bolton is a part of Greater Manchester – in those days Manchester was 11 miles away in another world of strangers and unknown and unwanted problems.

His eyes were first opened to this other world during the First World War, when he, like so many of his generation anxious to escape from the clogging poverty and intractable problems of the industrial North of England, enlisted, and he found himself dodging the bullets to carry the wounded and the dead from the grim battlefields of Ypres and Passchendaele in Belgium.

Unlike so many of his compatriots, he survived, a little wiser and a lot deafer, and resumed his job as a cotton spinner. He walked the three miles to work every morning and home every evening because there was no other way to get there that he could afford. He did more or less the same job day after day for 40 years. He doffed, he cocked, he tended and he span the fine cottons for which Bolton was known throughout the world – and he learned how to do this from sitting with Nellie for two days before being let loose on his own spinning machine. The noise in the spinning shed was loud and uncompromising and did little to alle-viate the deafness he had contracted in the trenches.

Despite all this he was a superb pianist who could play without music any of the tunes from the shows of the 1880s when he was born, to the 1920s, when everything became new-fangled and immoral. He acted as choir-master to the local Unitarian church choir, took in a few free piano pupils, including myself, and was known for his patience, his enquiring mind and his exceptional musical talent. During the Second World War, he and my grandmother lost two of their sons in action. He died at 65, a relatively average age for that period, from a lung disease caused by the floating fibres in the atmosphere of the cotton shed. The cotton industry of Bolton more or less died at the same time. There was no causal effect from these two events, simply it transpired that cotton could be spun much more cheaply elsewhere in the world. Today of course he would not have had a job – there is only one cotton mill in Bolton. The industry no longer exists.

My father, the eldest and the surviving son, was born in 1907. While grand-father was away at war he became the acting head of the family, a position not conducive to success in the elementary and primitive education systems of the day. By the time he became of working age it was the Great Depression and he was unemployed for a long period. When he was finally offered a job with an insurance agent, because he was good at sums, he kept it for the whole of his life. Every day in summer and winter he would get on his bicycle and cycle from house to house, come fair weather or foul, and believe me, the weather in the North-west of England is mostly the latter, over a radius of some 30 miles, collecting the insurance premiums from his customers. In 1953 he was given one year to live because his lungs had been damaged by the constant drenchings he had received over the years. So he bought a car with his meagre savings, did the job with that and died 30 years later at the age of 77.

He never read much – not because he couldn't, but because it gave him no pleasure to do so. But he was a natural mathematician who, in different days, might have made something of that aptitude. He was also a superb pianist who could play without the benefit of music any piece of music written before the 1960s, when music became new-fangled and immoral. He never trained or retrained. Although he travelled often in his later years, he never left the shores of England. His advice to me was 'Join the co-op, tha'll never be out of a job and they'll pay thee a good pension when tha's finished.' Of course I ignored him in a way that would not have been acceptable 30 years earlier. Today of course he wouldn't have had a job himself – insurance is done in a different way now – and the co-op went bust about 30 years ago.

Let's skip a generation and come to the present day. I have a neighbour, Luc. He's a French farmer aged 36. Like me, he lives in the Conflent, a demi-paradise in the South of France under the surveillance of Mount Canigou, the sacred mountain of the Catalans. He is a peach farmer like his father before him. His trees yield deep luscious peaches and nectarines, the best you have ever tasted – large golden orbs of sweet nectar which play a symphony on your taste buds and turn your eyes inwards with every bite. He's presently trying to diversify into pears and cherries. He owns about 40 acres of land in the valley where we live. He's angry. Over the past five years he has seen his income drop by 50 per cent, and half the peaches he grows are thrown into a valley up the mountain. Partly it's because there is an overproduction of peaches in the area – hence his efforts to diversify. Partly it's the mediaeval marketing system by which a farmer assumes that if he grows it someone will pay for it, even if that's only the government. Partly it is that 40 acres are no longer sufficient to sustain his family in the style to which they have become accustomed, and partly it is the intense competition from other parts of Europe. And of course all of this is the government's fault.

There are another 40–50 Lucs in our valley. They are all proud to be peasants – they know no other calling – and more than half of them will not be able to sustain a living in the next ten years.

I am, by contrast, despite the best efforts of my grandfather, a lousy pianist who needs the music as an aid to memory. Unlike my father and grandfather, I am now in my seventh career, having worked as a statistician in the RAF, as a teacher in schools, as a systems analyst, marketing manager, project manager and education developer in industry, as a professor in university, as an administrator in professional associations and, for the past ten years, as an author, project manager and adviser in the harsh, competitive world of educational consultancy. I've had at least ten jobs. I read avidly, sing passably in a choir, write boring books and excruciating poetry, play variable golf but a little better tennis and hope to be able to afford to retire in another 50 years' time, by which time I will be 110.

The point of this rather long-winded introduction to the book is to emphasize what most people already know and experience – that the world is changing more rapidly than we could ever imagine, that this change is accelerating, and that it is this which is driving every agenda, including the educational one. My granddaughter was born just six years ago today, and my grandson just six days ago. They will both be alive until somewhere near the end of this century, and few can predict with any certainty what will come to pass during that period. Already, since Charlotte was born, the number of people in Europe having access to e-mail and the Internet has grown from about 5 million to more than 100 million and it is rising exponentially every day. In my small village of 300 souls in the South of France, I was the only person with a computer in 1996 – even the *Mairie* didn't have one. Now I know of 30 people – and probably more – with computers there (and still the *Mairie* hasn't got one!). Add to that the vastly increased use of mobile phones, car-phones, fax machines, voice mail, mobile offices – all of them making demands on our time and our patience and our ability to communicate meaningfully with our families. The oases of tranquillity where one can escape the burdens of a thrusting world are diminishing with equal rapidity.

Maybe I'm unusual in my multiple careers. But I am a product of my era and my grandchildren will be a product of theirs. But also in every city and rural area there are tens of thousands of Lucs – people who expect to be employed for a lifetime, don't ever expect to be retrained – don't ever want to change – and don't ever want to go back into learning – mostly because of bad experiences the first time round. And that is a recipe for social disaster, unless we are prepared to do something drastic and radical about it.

Arthur C Clarke, the British science fiction writer, wrote this in 1963: 'Everyone', he said, 'will need to be educated to the standard of semi-literacy of the average university graduate by the year 2000 – this is the minimum survival level of the human race.' We can see what he's getting at – it's just that he got his timescales wrong.

Charles Handy in *Managing the Dream* quotes the equation ½ × 2 × 3 – meaning that those multinational industry leaders he interviewed expected to release half their workers and pay the remainder twice their current salary to produce 3× the productivity. It has been predicted that today's school-leavers will have many careers – not just jobs, over their lifetimes, and that more than 50 per cent of the jobs they will be doing don't yet exist. But one thing is certain – they will be knowledge jobs, intellectually more demanding and almost certainly involving interaction with computers far more sophisticated than those existing at present. Mindpower is replacing manpower.

There is another reason why educational systems have to produce a steep increase in intellectual ability. The new participative democracy demands that citizens be asked to make judgements, and even vote, on subjects about which they know very little – the desirability of cloning animals and human beings, nuking your enemies, eugenics, genetic engineering, GM foods, the European single currency and other great moral and economic questions of the day. The intellectual processes to be gone through in order to provide sane answers to such deep philosophical questions, previously the domain of university researchers after three years' careful study, are not exactly the stuff of educational policy at present. A curriculum based on the development of personal skills and competencies would be much preferable to the present system of testing the ability to memorize facts and dates. Climbing the learning ladder shown in *Making Lifelong Learning Work*, and reproduced in Figure 0.1, entails an upward movement from the information–obsessed educational world into the higher realms of knowledge, understanding and insight – no matter that the distance between the rungs is wider, and even though the top rung of wisdom may be beyond our capabilities.

A quotation from the booklet written by Sir Christopher Ball for the Kent region of learning puts all of this succinctly: 'We belong to the first generation that knows for certain that it doesn't know what the future will be like.' And the humility inherent in that quotation should be what drives learning for the future.

Most governments in the developed, and many in the developing, world are now pinning their hopes on 'lifelong learning' as a means of adding ingredient *x* to their educational menu. But quite what this term means differs from country to country, from organization to organization and from person to person. Part 1 of this book is therefore an attempt to get to the heart of lifelong learning, to spell out the profound implications it will have on all providers and people in education, business and industry and society at large, and to explain how an amorphous and intangible philosophy can become an action-based set of practices which will transform the way we do things and the way we see things. Part 2

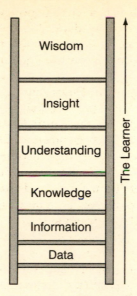

The Learning Ladder

Personal Voyage from Data to Wisdom

Figure 0.1 The learning ladder

concentrates on the neglected impact of lifelong learning in schools, until recently regarded as peripheral, but in reality the most crucial organizations for the development of lifelong learning skills, attitudes, values and knowledge that there can be. Let the action begin.

Part 1

Key concepts of lifelong learning for the 21st century

A brief history of lifelong learning and its major features

Where we are now, where we are going to and why we are making the journey in lifelong learning. A map of the 12 major differences between education and training and the lifelong learning future with examples from places that are already implementing good practice.

Chapter 1

Learning is for people – an introduction

Visions

As the 21st century unfolds, humanity finds itself at a crossroads. The writer Dee Hock puts it thus:

> As the old millennium departs and leaves behind a thousand years of conflict, ignorance, discord and division, we find ourselves at a crossroads in the development of human society.
>
> Before us lies a beguiling vision of the regeneration of our unique individuality, of a precious liberty of thought and conscience, of unselfish contribution to the betterment of community and the life of others, and of a mature, open-minded sense of ethics more advanced than life on this planet has ever known.
>
> The insights, the infrastructures and the tools to encourage learning throughout life, and to unlock the vast creative potential in each one of us, are now moving into place. They can help us to revitalize a new harmony with nature, with each other and with the concept of a divine intelligence, however we may define it.

In a sense, such visionary declarations articulate what many of us may want to believe about the times we live in: an image of a glorious future through lifelong learning; a rebirth of creativity, of culture, of imagination, of invention, of partnership; the notion that finally we have the tools and the vision to enable human beings to realize their own enormous potential for good. It is indeed a beguiling vision.

And it contrasts strongly with the evidence we see around us. The increasing violence in inner cities, the occasional acts of genocide when pathological dictatorship or tribal hatreds spill over into brutality, the abomination of the destruction of the New York twin towers, the growth of fundamentalist ignorance and suppression of rational thought in many religions – they all point to an

3

unprecedented erosion of human values rendered all the more appalling by the use of ever more sophisticated weapons of communication and oppression.

But at least it presents a stark choice. Both scenarios are possible, as are a hundred more in between. And the only thing preventing the achievement of the desirable outcomes has to be rooted in the persistence of poverty and the chronic lack of education in more than half the world. It will not be solved by the manufacture and application of more weapons of destruction. H G Wells was correct when he said that 'the whole of human history is a battle between education and catastrophe'. Those of us immersed in a lifelong learning culture can all sense that the new millennium brings with it the opportunity for a new beginning. But we can all see, as well, the scale of the task ahead just to make it happen, perhaps starting in our own communities and branching out from there with new understandings, new persuasions, new insights, new wisdom.

Thanks to inter-governmental organizations – UNESCO, OECD, APEC, the Council of Europe, The European Commission and others – and some of the more enlightened liberal democracies, the lifelong learning movement is now rampaging around the whole world, from Europe to South Africa and from North America to Japan, like a benign educational plague. It is the future – and it is not before time.

Why lifelong learning?

In *Lifelong Learning*, written nine years ago, Longworth and Davies suggested eight reasons why lifelong learning is particularly appropriate for this age. But nine years is a long time in a lifelong learning world. While some are still as relevant as on the day they were written, it is time to update the rest to take into account the changes in the meanwhile:

- *Fundamental global demographics* – in the rich developed world, ageing, more mobile, more multicultural and multi-ethnic societies which could release high inter-racial and inter-generational social tensions and a reduced investment in welfare programmes through a fall in working, and an increase in retired, populations. By contrast, in the poorer parts of the world a massive population growth exacerbating already chronic shortages of resource and education and condemning vast numbers of people to live at subsistence level and below unless ameliorative projects are initiated. To avoid the worst effects of both these scenarios, a high emphasis will need to be put on fundamental lifelong learning principles and a use of the new development and delivery technologies.
- *The pervasive influence of television and the media on the development of peoples' thoughts, ideas and perceptions.* Television has an enormously powerful effect on people. Where it is in the hands of those who would use it as an instrument of propaganda, whether raw or subtle, as happens in both poor and rich coun-

tries, it can be used to foster hatred and intolerance. Where it is used purely as an instrument of entertainment, it can, through trivialization and ignorance of real issues, have an equally insidious effect on the ability of people to make informed choices. As an occasional, independent, instrument of education it could be used to transform nations into dynamic, well-educated and flexible lifelong learning societies.

- *Environmental imperatives* – the depletion of the world's resources and the need for renewable energy, the destruction of ecosystems and the demand for sustainable development. There is a crucial need to educate continually all the world's people in environmental matters as a basis for the survival of species on earth and to be inventive and innovative about how environmental information is kept constantly in the forefront of popular consciousness. In other words, the need for a lifelong learning approach to a lifelong survival issue.

These are issues affecting every society and they propagate a view of lifelong learning as a global phenomenon, entirely consonant with the reality of governmental perceptions. The efforts of international governmental agencies have offered some hope that it may be used to improve the lot of the developed and developing world alike, even though responses and actions will be very different. Other issues, mainly affecting the advanced industrial nations, include:

- *New developments in all branches of science and technology*, on the one hand offering a variety of new opportunities for organizational and personal growth and on the other stimulating a questioning of basic values. Both of these have important implications for lifelong learning. At one level, science and technology have helped to improve material standards of living in many parts of the world. Their spread into other communities, other societies, other countries in the developing world will help achieve growth and improve health and education, though there are fundamental environmental implications that need to be addressed in so doing. It augurs a massive increase in learning in order to understand and use technology wisely.
- *The explosion of information and knowledge through the use of the Internet and communications technology.* This has multiplied manyfold the information and knowledge available to us and transformed our way of living, working and communicating. At the same time the speed at which these changes have taken place has outstripped the capacity of many people to cope easily with it. The wealth of information and the technology of handling it have made possible greater personal decision making, and, paradoxically, through its sheer volume reduced the likelihood of this being informed and balanced. Technology can empower or enslave, and learning is the key to its benevolent use.
- *The need for both industry and people to remain innovative and flexible in order to retain high employment* – the migration of work in the advanced nations towards high-skill, high-technology, high-added-value service industries. This renders much semi-skilled and unskilled work obsolete, increases the need for lifelong

education and training to a high standard in all sections of the population and promotes the development of innovative work-related programmes to offset potential social unrest.

- *Increasing individualization and the breakdown in parts of Western society of religious and family structures* which traditionally have provided meaning and fulfilment to most people. More focus on personal development in order to realize and release creative human potential leads to the need for the further development of educational structures based on understanding, tolerance and contribution to the community.

The individual and the community

It is perhaps the last of these that focused minds and mindsets on lifelong learning at the time. The 'triumph of the individual' was one of the key ideas behind Naisbitt's ten 'Megatrends', first published in the 1980s and repeated for the 90s. It was a document to be found on the tables of many industrial leaders. But since that time raw individualism has become less fashionable. 'There is no solitary learning: we can only create our worlds together', say Ranson, Rikowski and Strain. 'The unfolding capability of the self always grows out of interaction with others. It is inescapably a social interaction.' And they are right. While the onus is still, and always will be, on the individual to decide on his/her learning, there has come to be a realization that other people and other organizations may have a key part to play too. The watchword for today is 'community' in every meaning of that word, whether it is a geographical entity as in a learning city or a learning region, or a community of people with a common sense of purpose or interest, as in a religious or a tribal community.

For Jan Visser, for example, the notion of a learning environment is much more than providing the tools to enable people to learn. 'For learning communities to emerge and evolve,' he says, 'and for members of a learning community to participate in a flexible manner and to move between them, we need to conceive of more holistic concepts in which such restricted learning environments are only a part.' He sets individuals into an integrated learning environment which includes the whole gamut of political, social, psychological, cultural, educational and environmental factors as both influences and resources from which they can draw. Whatever the scenario, it seems that cooperation is replacing competition in many walks of life, and the power of the new synergy of aspiration that it engenders will be demonstrated frequently in subsequent pages.

The growth of lifelong learning

There was, of course, already activity before the 1980s. UNESCO's Fauré Commission Report, published in 1972, was considered by many to be one of the most important educational reform documents of the second half of the 20th century. Among many other things it proposed:

- the development of human skills and abilities as the primary objective of education at all levels;
- support for situation-specific learning in the context of everyday life and work so that individuals could understand, and be given the competency, creativity and confidence to cope with the urgent tasks and changes arising throughout a lifetime;
- the creation of the sort of learning society in which independent learning is supported and provides an essential part of the continuum of learning as people move into, and out of, education during their lives;
- the involvement of the community in the learning process and the wider social role of education in understanding conflict, violence, peace, the environment and how to reconcile differences.

Again we see an overall focus on individual responsibility for learning, albeit with a supportive role for the community. The concepts were further refined and developed in papers by Paul Lengrand and A J Cropley under the auspices of the UNESCO Institute of Education in Hamburg. In these, lifelong learning became a key concept for the survival of mankind, perhaps echoing Arthur C Clarke's dictum in *Prelude to Space*, 'Everyone will need to be educated to the level of semi-literacy of the average university graduate by the year 2000. This is the minimum survival level of the human race.' Science fiction writers often show remarkable percipience about the future of mankind but have a tendency to underestimate the time-scales.

A similar theme was taken up by the Club of Rome report of 1979, 'No Limits to Learning'. In this seminal document, following its 'Limits to Growth' report which took the world by storm in 1973, a broad-based mobilization of the creative talent inherent in all human beings was considered to be the only way to allow them to understand, adapt to, and make progress in an increasingly complex world.

The Organization for Economic Cooperation and Development (OECD), too, has long been a strong supporter of a lifelong learning approach, though initially under the name of 'recurrent education'. Its own landmark report 'Recurrent Education: A Strategy for Lifelong Learning. A Clarifying Report', produced in 1973, was well received by governments, higher education and NGOs alike. Recurrent Education concerned itself principally with post-compulsory and post-basic education and with preparation of the individual for a life of work. In practice, however, it acknowledged that work and learning are synergistic. Attitudes and values built up during the early learning process are important during the total life-span of an individual and have a profound effect on total human development, including learning for leisure, during retirement and within the community. Among OECD's recommendations at the time were:

- the promotion of complementarity between school and adult education, with the emphasis on personal development and growth;
- increasing the participation of adults in tertiary education by recognizing the value of work experience and 'opening up' the universities;
- extending the provision of formal adult education to a wider audience;
- abolishing 'terminal stages' in the formal education system so that all programmes lead on to other programmes.

Here we see the first modern signs that learning is considered to be a holistic process in a holistic world. Complementarity and seamlessness may seem to be obviously desirable now, but in the fragmented and specialist world of the 1970s it was not evidently so. The transition from education to learning entails a much wider definition of the way in which people acquire and synthesize knowledge, and a consequent fusion of responsibility for educational provision from many sources, but we have a long way to go before the empires so carefully built up in a specialist world yield to the new imperative of connectedness.

In the more materialistic Thatcher and Reagan-dominated Western world of the 1980s lifelong learning thinking became less fashionable, though there were pockets of activity in Europe and the Far East, much of it based on the need to train, retrain and renew in industry. At the same time in Europe in the middle 1980s the Industrial Advisory Committee to the European Commission made the comment: 'The information revolution is rendering much previous education and training obsolete, or simply irrelevant. Intellectual capital is depreciating at 7% per year which is a much higher rate than the recruitment of new graduates. On these grounds alone it is necessary for industry to develop and adopt systems of continuing education and training to update existing staff.' And still this was not enough.

Two years later the Council of European Rectors and the European Round Table of Industrialists complained that: 'Although the systems and standards of training and education in Europe are evolving to meet pressures on them, the changes are not wide, deep or fast enough to keep up with the pace of change in knowledge and technology.' But it was in the 1990s that the major thrust for lifelong learning took place. The renaissance was again led by UNESCO and OECD, though other international governmental organizations such as the European Commission and the Council of Europe will also want to claim some credit, as well as some of the innovative initiatives in Japan and Australia.

Fast forward with lifelong learning

The UNESCO-sponsored Delors report on Education for the 21st Century was published only months after the 1996 OECD ministerial conference on lifelong learning. The four pillars of 'The Treasure Within' – 'Learning to do, Learning to be, Learning to understand and Learning to live together' – put the needs and demands of the individual once more at the centre of this quadrumvirate as the focus of educational activity. 'Lifelong Learning for All', OECD's flagship justification for lifelong learning, resulted from the 1996 conference of Ministers and provoked a great deal of national governmental activity in this area. For example, from 1998, the UK produced Green and White Papers on the subject as well as a flurry of recommendations, initiatives, reports and exhortations. Finland has produced its national lifelong learning strategy, the appropriately named 'The Joy of Learning', and other countries, the Netherlands, Sweden, Ireland and Denmark among them, have also produced similar national plans.

Meanwhile, the European Commission was declaring 1996 to be the 'European Year of Lifelong Learning' and preparing a White Paper on the subject, closely pursued by the European Round Table of Industrialists which collaborated with the Council of University Rectors to produce its definition of 'the learning society'. In the same year, Longworth and Davies published their book *Lifelong Learning*, spelling out its implications for schools, universities, business and industry, teacher training and the community at large.

Since that time the number of words, actions and initiatives has seemed to proliferate geometrically. The EU Lisbon Summit in March 2000 produced for Europe the strategic target of 'becoming the most competitive economy in the world capable of sustainable growth, with more and better jobs and greater social cohesion, through the development and promotion of a comprehensive lifelong learning strategy'. As a result the Commission organized a number of policy input seminars, the results of which were published in a 'Memorandum on Lifelong Learning for Active Citizenship in a Europe of Knowledge' in December 2000. It boldly states:

> Lifelong learning is no longer just one aspect of education and training; it must become the guiding principle for provision and participation across the full continuum of learning contexts. The coming decade must see the implementation of this vision. All those living in Europe, without exception, should have equal opportunities to adjust to the demands of social and economic change and to participate actively in the shaping of Europe's future.

The memorandum went on to recommend five community-related objectives which are broadly paraphrased as:

- to provide lifelong learning opportunities as close to learners as possible, in their own communities and supported through ICT-based facilities wherever appropriate;
- to build an inclusive society which offers equal opportunities for access to quality learning throughout life to all people, and in which education and training provision is based first and foremost on the needs and demands of individuals;
- to adjust the ways in which education and training are provided, and how paid working life is organized, so that people can participate in learning throughout their lives and can plan for themselves how they combine learning, working and family life;
- to achieve higher overall levels of education and qualification in all sectors, to ensure high-quality provision of education and training, and at the same time to ensure that people's knowledge and skills match the changing demands of jobs and occupations, workplace organization and working methods;
- to encourage and equip people to participate more actively once more in all spheres of modern public life, especially in social and political life at all levels of the community, including at European level.

High ideals like this, carried over into the Commission's definitive policy paper 'Realizing a Europe of Lifelong Learning', both mirror and update the recommendations of the Fauré Commission some 30 years earlier.

Lifelong learning and the information revolution

Such a potted history cannot possibly do justice to the many people and organizations which have contributed to the lifelong learning debate over the past 30 years. However, even in a new millennium, and despite this plethora of animated vigour and the unanswerable case for lifelong learning, the debate still lies largely in the hands of academic educationists and politicians. The message that lifelong is 'lifelong' (from cradle to grave), that learning is 'learning' (and learner-focused), and that it is for everybody has not yet reached the vast majority of people targeted as the new generation of learners. Even for the vast majority of teachers in schools, lifelong learning is as remote a concept as was the idea of universal education to 18th-century society.

And yet the case is undeniable. The convergence of information, communication and broadcasting technologies into what has become known as the knowledge society is one of the major determinants of the need for lifelong learning. In Europe the European Commission is investing some billions of euros in opening it up – it is, rightly, perceived to be crucial to the economic future of nations, of regions, of cities. In North America its equivalent – the 'Smart Cities' movement – pours vast amounts of technology into every aspect of its major cities

– so that citizens can receive education, entertainment, shopping, banking services through computers at home.

Effective use of the technology itself is also a large part of the answer. But, after years of rapid development, there is coming to be a realization that this alone cannot solve problems of human development. There needs to be an equivalent movement towards a 'learning society' – that is, in the words of the European Round Table of Industrialists, 'a society in which everyone is empowered and enabled to develop his or her own human potential'. Without it, vast numbers of people can become alienated from a fast-changing technological society.

The European Council of University Rectors agrees. The indiscriminate use of technology does not always liberate. In their excellent booklet (see ERT/CRE) – 'Creating the Learning Society' – they suggest that 'The Information Society… must be completed and matched by a Learning Society, if we do not want to fall into an over-informed world and a valueless culture based on "zapping" and a "patchwork" superficiality'. And they are right. It isn't just academic doom-mongering. Sound-bite television already exists in many advanced countries anxious to spare their audiences the in-depth analysis which would cut into the entertainment schedules. It won't create informed citizens with 21st-century skills – learning how to learn, how to make critical judgements, how to tell the difference between good, bad and indifferent, how to communicate intelligently, to be flexible, adaptable and tolerant to other creeds and cultures, and to make a contribution to their city and to the well-being of others.

What is lifelong learning really?

And so we come back to lifelong learning. But what does it mean? Any phrase which has become so overused is inevitably accused of being amorphous, vague, meaningless, intangible, motherhood, apple pie – all things to all people. And so it is, until we can find a definition which leads to action. So let us start with the words themselves. Lifelong learning is what it says it is:

- It is *'lifelong'*. As Jan Comenius said, it is from 'cradle to grave'. It is not simply relevant to the adult part of our lives, and not only related to continuous professional development or the acquisition of skills and competencies for the workplace, though governments inevitably put the emphasis on the economic advantage to be gained by the fact of more people learning. There is much more to it than that. Between the ages of 0 and 5 we learn to perform the most wonderfully complicated tasks with no formal education whatsoever. Communicating our needs, speaking, imagining, learning to read, to enumerate, sometimes even to write – they represent a major intellectual achievement which almost everyone masters. Research also tends to show that those senior citizens who stay learning and keep their minds lively are less likely to suffer from debilitating diseases like Alzheimer's and senile dementia.

- It is also '*learning*' and that is one of the most important, and most misunderstood, words in the lexicon. It means doing things in a different way, creating an out-and-out focus on the needs and demands of the learner; giving learners the tools and techniques with which they can learn according to their own learning styles and needs. It is not teaching, not training, and not even education in its narrow didactic sense. It has a much wider scope. It has a social, economic, political, personal, cultural and, of course, educational meaning in its widest sense.

  Learning means giving ownership of learning to the learner him or herself and not to the teacher – a 180-degree shift of emphasis and power from provider to receiver. It moves teaching from the concept of 'the sage on the stage' to the idea of 'the guide at the side'. And it means using the tools and techniques which hopefully switch people back into the learning habit – personal learning plans, learning audits, creative learning partnerships, mentoring, electronic networks and the information and communications technologies in general.

All of these aspects will be expanded in later chapters, but the other major difference between education and training and the lifelong learning paradigm is that lifelong learning is, as OECD reminded us, for all. It is not only for the educational élites, those already switched on to learning, the career-minded expanding their economic possibilities. In the long run lifelong learning excludes no one. If the focus is indeed on the needs and demands of the learner, it is also for the switched-off kids from the housing estates, the drop-outs from school, the people in mental or physical prisons everywhere.

It is for the cybergrannies of Craiglockhart in Edinburgh, where an enterprising community officer took some portable computers into an elderly ladies' lunch club and transformed their lives. They communicate with third-age people from the USA, New Zealand and Canada, such that it is now difficult to get them to eat their lunch. And so successful was this experiment that it has bred 'modem mums', 'digital dads', techno-tots and so on. Technological literacy is thriving in the community centres of Edinburgh.

From education and training to lifelong learning

If Dee Hock, quoted above, is correct, this is a turning point in history. In the developed world we are changing from a system we have called 'education and training', which has served us well in the late 20th century, but which is also a system in which teachers and learning providers make courses available to those who need them on the basis of what they, the learning providers, think they need. As often as not it is answering questions that people are not necessarily asking. The replacement is a system of lifelong learning in which everyone is targeted, which is continuous throughout life and which is focused entirely on the needs and demands of the learners themselves. Those nations, cities and organizations which don't make this huge shift in their thinking will risk both economic decline and social instability. This is the essence of this book. It will reinforce these concepts with quotations, examples and case studies where lifelong learning really is making an impact on the lives of people and communities.

Lastly, to return to the theme with which this chapter first started, the following are extracts from an article in the *Swindon Evening Advertiser*, 23 July 2001, entitled 'Spirit of Swindon':

> Swindon's city status bid will be a turning point for our town. And it won't be because we have spent thousands of pounds on producing a glossy booklet, nor will it be because of our outstanding economic achievements. But it will be the Spirit of Swindon which wins the day. Who can forget that leaked report from the Home Office, when our town's city status bid was criticized for being too materialistic and lacking the most important element of all – the spirit. Although our bid presented strong evidence of an exciting and economically booming town, it seems that concentrating too much on our economic success story may have been our downfall. After all, who would want Swindon to be a city based on material and economic growth alone?
>
> In his book *The Earth is but One Country*, John Huddleston says that today's cities can become in some instances, a hell on earth, a sad contrast with the ancient dream of the city as the centre of refinement and culture, the pride of civilization. In that same book Huddleston describes some of the all too familiar spiritual sicknesses suffered in big cities.
>
> - The majority of the poor feel they have no stake in society.
> - Many of the citizens find their only satisfaction in their job and the rest of their lives is a desert.
> - A growing disenchantment with the rat race.
> - The boredom and frustration of private life producing a reliance on sedatives, psychiatrists, sex, alcohol/drug abuse.
> - Reliance on the above leading to increased crime.
> - The collapse of social morality.
> - The crumbling away of respect for all forms of authority, which includes the young increasingly despising and ignoring their parents and teachers.
>
> The *Evening Advertiser*'s inspirational Spirit of Swindon campaign will ensure that we get a more balanced bid this time round – a people's bid, driven by the spirit of the people of this town. Only if we get this bit right can we avoid the pitfalls suffered by other cities. The bid for city status may help us develop that essential spiritual dimension which will transform Swindon into a truly prosperous city, where prosperity will be understood to mean both economic and spiritual well-being. In any case, whatever dimensions we deem important for Swindon as a city, surely it can only be achieved through wide ranging consultation which the *Evening Advertiser* could spearhead. If this is undertaken, it is very much our hope that this consultation will focus around issues that will bring meaning and fulfilment to the lives of the people of Swindon.

So even if for some reason we fail in our bid to be recognized as a city, but have actually achieved a balance between material and spiritual development, we may well have earned the accolade of following in our forebears' footsteps, and once again be seen as truly pioneering and visionary people who put the Spirit back in Swindon.

As it happens, Swindon's bid was unsuccessful, but it wasn't for a lack of innovative thinking.

Chapter 2

Decisions, decisions, decisions! Educational decision making

The transition from education and training to lifelong learning

Throughout the latter half of the 20th century the needs of society, industry and citizenship have been dominated by the paradigm of an education and training system whose limited objectives were geared to ensure as full employment as possible and to promote economic growth. In its later stages this was barely sufficient for a society in transition from an industrial to a post-industrial model. A large number of people have been left on the fringes, mostly through lack of awareness and motivation rather than of opportunity. Such a system can go only so far before social instability is created, and many countries are already experiencing the signs of social break-up, from unrest within the housing estates in major cities to the growth of Far Right protest movements in Europe, North America and the Pacific Rim. Dissatisfaction is in the air and an inclusive system of learning for all is one of the strategies that all countries must adopt in order to cure it.

The OECD is well aware of this. In 'Lifelong Learning for All', its three major rationales for the introduction of lifelong learning concepts into the educational systems of liberal democracies included social stability as well as economic growth and personal well-being. The European Commission, too, voices its opinion in a memorandum on lifelong learning. 'Most of what our education and training systems offer,' it says, 'is still organized and taught as if the traditional ways of planning and organizing one's life had not changed for at least half a century. Learning systems must adapt to the changing ways in which people live and learn their lives today.'

Educational decision making

So what are the major movements in educational and social practice and what actions need to be taken to make them reality? This chapter looks at educational decision making in the face of change and examines examples of how they are taking root in some places. The first concerns the very basis on which educational decision making takes place and is shown in Figure 2.1.

Education and training C20th	Lifelong learning C21st	Action for change
Educational decision making is rooted in a 20th-century mass education and training paradigm	Decisions are made on individual learning needs, demands and styling of all citizens of all ages, aptitudes and abilities	Find the barriers to learning and dismantle them. Develop and market a strategy based on lifelong and lifewide learning for all

Figure 2.1 Decisions to break down barriers

As most of us have experienced, the classrooms of the 20th century were places where we succeeded, failed or, in the case of many, got by. Emotional, social, cultural, personality and environmental factors were either unseen or ignored in the interests of delivering a mass result from within a group system. Those who could not cope fell by the wayside or, if they were particularly dogged, caught up later on. The teacher's and lecturer's task description from the educational decision-maker was to educate as many as possible to a particular standard, determined by external experts. Those above it would have passed, those below would be deemed to have failed – and as for those who refused to play the game or didn't fit (which could include some very bright individuals who saw the futility or the flaw in the system), well – they were often omitted from the system.

Learning styles counted for nothing since there was only one delivery method, usually that of teacher presentation with follow-up exercises. The system could not cope with particular learning needs or demands. Reluctant learners remained reluctant learners, though, in some circumstances, people with learning difficulties were identified and given special treatment.

Of course this is a caricature. Many dedicated teachers interpreted these guidelines in their own particular way and, as they were trained to do, treated children and students as individuals. Many went even further and set up their one-person support systems for those unable to cope with the requirements. But in the end they were, and still are, working within a massified system in which the objective is to teach people to jump the particular hurdles set up by the educational planners.

This wasteful, failure-creating system should not be allowed to continue, even within the constraints of budgets and logistics. As we shall see, it does not create people who want to learn throughout their lives and it engenders emotional, educational and cultural difficulties, impelling the creation of other, much larger, budgets elsewhere and in later life, for example in law and order and social services. What may seem to be an economic way of developing as many successful students as possible is, in the big picture, wasteful and often degrading.

Public attitudes to learning

Take this example from Glasgow, City of Learning. In 1999 the City Development Association commissioned some research into people's attitudes to learning – it also tried to predict current and future learning, and to discover why people learn, how people want to learn and how aware they were of the learning opportunities.

The results were interesting to say the least. Seventy per cent of respondents agreed that self-development is important, 90 per cent said they enjoy learning new things (they didn't say what) and 82 per cent were quite adamant that learning was very or fairly important to them personally. And while 83 per cent were very aware that learning would be increasingly important in the future, only 18 per cent thought it very likely that they would participate in taught learning activity in the coming year. Another 18 per cent might – or might not – while 63 per cent thought it unlikely that they would participate at all in learning.

It doesn't take a highly academic mind to recognize that there is something very strange going on here. Perhaps the answer is that Glaswegians don't like going to college and prefer to study on their own. Unfortunately this is not true either. The next question addressed this issue and found that a good 68 per cent were doing absolutely nothing at all in this area.

This conflicts violently with the real need in Glasgow or any other city. We have already seen how a changing world leads to a need for renewed learning, leads to employability, leads to employment and leads to prosperity if that's what we want. And it is difficult to believe that people in Glasgow actually want to live in poverty, temporally and spiritually as well as corporeally. Nor is it acceptable to stay with the status quo, because the future prosperity of the whole city depends on a learning workforce; the social stability of the city depends on a literate and learning population; and the health and welfare of every citizen depends on every citizen acquiring the skills and competencies to live in an increasingly complex world.

Why this aversion to learning? Of course the survey tried to find out some answers and discovered such things as the fact that 40 per cent of Glaswegians believed that schools did not prepare them for a learning life, that 50 per cent of people received no support from their employers, and that only 29 per cent thought that classroom learning was an efficient way to learn.

This is the result of a massified, failure-oriented educational system of education and training. It creates a great number of people, in cities, towns and regions all over the developed world, who are not learning in spite of the many opportunities that exist. While Glasgow has now made impressive efforts to correct this situation, the problems of low learner motivation continue to tax the efforts of educators in many of the world's cities.

The syndrome is reinforced by the survey made for the Fryer report in the UK, which came to the conclusion that:

- in Britain – only 1 adult in 4 describes him/herself as a learner;
- 1 in 3 has taken no part in education or training since leaving school;
- at any one time only 14% of employees are taking part in job-related training;
- one-third of employees say their employer has never offered any kind of training;
- only 5% of the workforce has obtained an NVQ;
- over 40% of 18-year-olds are not currently in any kind of education and training.

Breaking down the barriers

Figure 2.1 also suggests the action to be taken to combat such deliberate ignorance. Finding the barriers can be done at institutional, local government or governmental level. Some suggested ones identified in the European Commission's TELS project are as follows (in results order):

- poor family culture of learning;
- low aspiration – perception of learning as not important enough;
- lack of finance to participate in learning in large numbers of people;
- low self-esteem – learning is for others, not the likes of me;
- bad childhood experience of learning;
- learning providers not geared to the needs of learners;
- poor information services attracting people to learning;
- distance from educational provision for large numbers of people;
- lack of local crèche provision for parents;
- lack of facilities for the disabled in educational establishments;
- lack of facilities to study at home for large numbers of people;
- perception that the benefits system discourages learning.

These tend to suggest that the major barriers are in the minds of people, but that there are other important issues, such as lack of finance, lack of opportunity and the attitude of learning providers, which could profitably be addressed. They demonstrate that educational decision-makers in both local and national government and in the learning providers need a strategy which goes far beyond the production of nice statistics and encouraging charts and diagrams. It needs to be an all-encompassing strategy to address the marketing issues which attract a wider and more committed audience and to examine the elements which make up lifelong and lifewide learning for all.

Such a strategy would base itself much more on the individual, following the trends described earlier. It would look at the major components of lifelong learning. The first obligation would be seamlessness from cradle to grave as recommended by the European Round Table of Industrialists and described in Chapter 1. It would be based on the requirement to give every individual a learning pathway throughout primary, secondary and tertiary education, working life and retirement, tailored to suit learning, earning and discerning across the lifewide spectrum of his or her life.

But there is much more to it than that! The second obligation is to respect the word 'learning'. In Chapter 1 we said that this is a concept that is 180 degrees from education, training and instructing. The stimulus comes from the two-way flow of ideas, concepts, topics, imagination, vision and creativity when the learner is intimately involved with the learning. It is not, as in so many classrooms, a process of opening up the lid, pouring it in and then testing whether it has stuck there or leaked out. It is a continuation of what we did in the first five years of our lives before we ever set foot in the formal education system, creating our own motivation and using the new tools and techniques which the system can give us to understand progressively more complex topics.

The third obligation of the educational decision-maker is to ensure that it is for everyone. That it takes into account learning styles, learning difficulties, learning needs and learning interests. That will entail positive discrimination and effective marketing to engender a massive increase in learning activity right across the cultural, social and financial spectrum. That this will have to be paid for is sure but there are many promising initiatives, tools and techniques to make this less onerous and more of an investment in the future. In any case the price of ignorance and inaction is much higher in the long term.

Recognizing the need

But one can now see a glimpse of recognition that some governments are addressing the issues. In Australia, the Northern Territory Curriculum Framework sets inclusivity as one of its goals, attacking the problems at root. 'All learners irrespective of culture, disability, socio-economic background, geographical location and gender,' it says, 'must be given the opportunity to access a widely ranging and empowering education. Learners' backgrounds, interests, prior understandings experiences, learning styles and rates of learning should be valued and considered.' The European Commission's policy document 'Realizing a European Area of Lifelong Learning' sets three fundamental principles for education systems in member states:

- the centrality of the learner;
- equality of opportunity;
- high quality and relevance.

Its memorandum sets an aim 'to build an inclusive society which offers equal opportunities for access to quality learning throughout life to all people, and in which education and training provision is based first and foremost on the needs and demands of individuals'.

And again: 'most of what our education and training systems offer is still organized and taught as if the traditional ways of planning and organizing one's life had not changed for at least half a century. Learning systems must adapt to the changing ways in which people live and learn their lives today.'

Governments in Japan, Britain, the USA, Canada, the Netherlands, Finland and many others have written such words into their policies for education, though not all of them have implemented strategies to make it happen.

Learning organizations

An equally imaginative movement is taking place in business and industry. Anita Roddick, Managing Director of the Body Shop, asks: 'So how do you educate employees away from a values system of endlessly increasing affluence to one in which values are community, caring for the environment, and personal development?' She then provides an answer: 'Answer, you empower them. Empowerment means that each staff member is responsible for creating the organization's culture. This is a true adventure.' And empowerment is indeed the guiding principle behind the movement in industry towards establishing 'learning organizations'. The larger companies, especially, have recognized that their survival depends on a workforce that will constantly renew its knowledge and practice in order to stay current with developments in its own field. And it goes further than that. In a fast-changing world which renders individual jobs frequently redundant, companies will often require their own people to retrain rather than employ new recruits. Thus there is a continuous process of learning and re-learning throughout every operation of the business, and this extends to Mrs Roddick's affirmation of company values and culture.

Such fine words from government and industry need to be followed up with action in the places where it makes a difference to the way in which individuals become active learners rather than 'teaching objects'. There is no reason why the concept of a learning organization should be confined to industry and business. Indeed a look at the characteristics of a learning organization shown in Figure 2.2, an updated version of the European Lifelong Learning Initiative classic shown in the Longworth and Davies book, will confirm that many organizations can qualify for this description.

Ten indicators of a learning organization

1. A learning organization can be a company, a professional association, a university, a school, a city, a nation or any group of people, large or small, with a need and a desire to improve performance through learning

2. A learning organization invests in its own future through the education and training of all its people

3. A learning organization creates opportunities for, and encourages, all its people in all its functions to fulfil their human potential
   - *as employees, members, professionals or students of the organization*
   - *as ambassadors of the organization to its customers, clients, audiences and suppliers*
   - *as citizens of the wider society in which the organization exists*
   - *as human beings with the need to realize their own capabilities*

4. A learning organization shares its vision of tomorrow with its people and stimulates them to challenge it, to change it and to contribute to it

5. A learning organization integrates work and learning and inspires all its people to seek quality, excellence and continuous improvement in both

6. A learning organization mobilizes all its human talent by putting the emphasis on 'learning' and planning its education and training activities accordingly

7. A learning organization empowers ALL its people to broaden their horizons, in harmony with their own preferred learning styles

8. A learning organization applies up-to-date open and distance delivery technologies appropriately to create broader and more varied learning opportunities

9. A learning organization responds proactively to the wider needs of the environment and the community in which it operates, and encourages its people to do likewise

10. A learning organization learns and relearns constantly in order to remain innovative, inventive, invigorating and in business

Figure 2.2 Characteristics of a learning organization

Each one of these has serious implications. They confirm the usefulness of a learning organization charter applicable to all institutions. They affect the way every learning provider, every business and every individual sees things and the way they do things. One industrial example is described by the Campaign for Learning. LGG Charlesworth in the UK manufactures engineering components.

Although now a holder of the valued 'Investors in People' kitemark standard, it recognizes that this, allied to a continued investment in new machinery and enlightened management, was still not enough to guarantee continued survival in a competitive marketplace. The last piece of the jigsaw lay in the continuous learning of all its employees. Its experience in working with schools and colleges in enterprise programmes persuaded it of the value of one-to-one learning in acquiring new skills and so it has installed a programme by which experienced staff coach and mentor less experienced ones. This, together with individual development programmes for every employee and an individual recognition programme, has resulted in much greater commitment to company growth and output.

There are many other facets to a learning organization and some of these are shown in Figure 2.2, but its essence is the importance of learning in the achievement of goals for any organization, be it a school, a college, a university, or a public or private sector workplace. What follows in Part 1 explores what the implications of lifelong learning are and how some organizations are addressing them.

Written on the walls of an adult education college in Australia are the words 'Not learning? Maybe it's our fault? Contact 236 8907 to discuss in confidence how we can help you fulfil your potential.' That is a good start. A strategy which can encompass that sort of courageous self-analysis in both people and organizations, and put into practice the support that would make it work, would be a real breakthrough into a lifelong learning outlook.

Chapter 3

Whose learning is it anyway?
Ownership and motivation

Einstein once said: 'It is the supreme art of the teacher to awaken joy in creative expression and knowledge.' And most of the world's great teachers, from Socrates to Plato to Erasmus, Seneca and Comenius, recognized that learning comes primarily from an inner desire to learn, and not from the outer desire of the teacher or the examination board. It has not always been so. The Calvinistic notion that wisdom is inherently evil, and that therefore adults should direct, control, and ultimately limit children's learning in order to keep them innocent, has, unfortunately, pervaded our education systems since the 17th century. Figure 3.1 highlights this important key to lifelong learning, that is, the movement from the learner as a receiver of education determined by others, to the learner as a customer taking ownership of his or her own learning.

Education and training C20th	Lifelong learning C21st	Action for change
Ownership of the need to learn and its content is with the teacher	Learner, as customer, rules. As far as possible, ownership of the need to learn and its content is given to individuals	Involve in-service teachers in strategies to empower learners. Train a team to run lifelong learning seminars in every learning provider

Figure 3.1 The ownership of learning

The Fryer report, 'Next Steps in Achieving the Learning Age', suggests that 'professionals should not seek to impose their own conception of learning needs on communities. Successful learning should relate closely to people's own developing sense of their needs. It should chime well with the rhythms and exigencies of their own circumstances and be evidently fit for purpose and of a guaranteed high standard.'

The ownership of learning must be one of the most significant, and occasionally contentious, issues in the field of lifelong learning. The suggestion that learners can be given a choice about what they need and want to learn is, in some circles, barely acceptable at an adult level and certainly undesirable and unworkable in schools. The idea of the learner as customer with control over what he/she buys into is not one that has hitherto been attractive to learning providers. After all, are not they rendering a service by accepting him/her into their institution and providing the opportunity and the facilities to learn in the first place?

Such attitudes are typical of an education and training world, though they are beginning to break down as the new century unfolds and as lifelong learning concepts and methods take hold. Ownership does not always mean that the learner decides the content of the curriculum, though his/her assent to it would be a step in the right direction. At the very least, it *can* mean that the learning is the subject of an accord between the teacher/lecturer and the student, and that the teacher/lecturer has at least made some effort to justify to the student the need for a particular content, the insights and new knowledge it will give, and the way(s) in which it will be learnt. Such a compact increases commitment and motivation on both sides, and gives the learner a clear idea of the why, the who, the when and the how of the learning. At a more advanced level, and with the use of lifelong learning tools described in Chapter 4, learners will become much more able to diagnose their own learning requirements and styles and take action to satisfy them.

Learning styles

The identification of different learning styles is also a key issue in the ownership of learning. We do not all learn in the same way, at the same speed or with the same objectives, and nor should we be expected to do so. The UK Campaign for Learning suggests that there are four types of learners:

- *activists*, who like to learn by doing and favour an active participation in the learning process;
- *reflectors*, who like to learn by watching others and to think about things before they act;
- *theorists*, who want to understand the theory and have a clear grasp of what it means before they act;
- *pragmatists*, who want practical tips and techniques from someone with experience before acting.

It recommends some flexibility between the four styles. But more profound research into this phenomenon distinguishes between individual perception styles (reacting to the physical environment), information processing styles (the way we sense, think, solve problems and remember) and personality patterns (focusing on attention spans, emotions and personal values). All three are important but one of them tends to be more dominant than the other for different individuals.

There are, for example, those who try to see a word when spelling, while auditory learners might experience it as a sound and tactile learners would need to write it down to test how right it seems. Yet others have a different style of talking and listening – some using gestures and body movements as opposed to those who talk little and listen quietly but effectively. To some, visualization comes easily, while others relate to sounds or have difficulty in seeing the detailed pictures inside their heads. Concentration and memory levels differ, some seeing faces but forgetting names, while others remember names but cannot visualize faces. Visual learners absorb things well through pictures and diagrams, auditory learners might prefer to read and study, and tactile learners need active learning methods. It would be rare if a learner conformed completely to one method, but every learner has a dominant learning style.

And yet traditional education and training structures seem to make the assumption that every learner learns in the same way or that one style is preferable to another. And there is more. Some brilliant scientists, thespians and surgeons are known to be dyslexic, but have managed, through early detection and remedial treatment, to beat the system which says that incorrect spelling demonstrates low intelligence. Research into the functions of the different hemispheres of the brain – the left brain as a word-oriented and logical centre and the right with a more emotional and picture-dominated focus – has extended our knowledge of how people think and why they think in particular ways.

Howard Gardner's research into multiple intelligences, described more fully in Chapter 8, enhances our knowledge of preferred learning styles and preferences. More recent research into emotional and spiritual intelligence pushes back the frontiers still further. Some people are motivated to learn in classroom environments, others in front of a computer screen and yet others by reflection in front of a book or study materials. And yet attempts in the media and educational circles to measure intelligence quotients (IQ), discredited as long ago as the 1960s, show how education can become stuck in a time warp. The fulfilment of human potential is mobilized much more by external factors such as motivation, the availability of learning choices, ownership, sensitive teachers and lecturers, and the learning environment. The individualized approach to learning, taking all these, and other, factors into account, allows for such diversity.

Learning centred on the learner

Certainly the European Commission's memorandum on lifelong learning recognizes such diversity and supports an individualized approach to accommodate it. 'Everyone,' it says, 'should be able to follow open learning pathways of their own choice, rather than being obliged to follow predetermined routes to specific destinations. This means, quite simply, that education and training systems should adapt to individual needs and demands rather than the other way round.'

It is supported by the OECD. 'Lifelong Learning for All' suggests '"individual pathways to learning", open-ended and interconnected learning targets within a system of personal learning plans and individualized assessment methods. This would allow learning to take place in a variety of environments – at home, in school, in specially designed centres.'

Certainly, the application of such strategies and skills in schools is especially desirable. Markkula and Suurla suggest, 'It is in very early childhood that learning principles and attitudes are adopted... If a person learns to learn in early childhood the capacity for learning will be tremendously enhanced... Earlier, no one could picture a 3-year-old child capable of using a computer to acquire new knowledge in the way children do today.' The Finnish national lifelong learning strategy reflects such a sentiment by emphasizing the individual child's ability to learn as the first, and most crucial, pillar of lifelong learning.

However, such ideas, while now becoming more popular in industry and university education, pass many of the schools and teachers by. Learner-centred education has received a hostile press in some countries, partly because efforts to introduce it in the late 1960s suffered from a shortage of teachers capable of understanding its requirements, and mainly because traditional attitudes to learning proved more difficult to break down than expected. Few schools try to explain the curriculum, its content, its message, its meaning and its advantages, to their pupils. There are exceptions. In Birmingham in the UK, experiments on target-based learning in schools are yielding at worst a reduced drop-out rate, and at best an increase in motivation and results. The Nordic countries of Europe, and schools in parts of Australia, are also active in learner-centred education. Mawson Lakes School near Adelaide uses all the resources in the community to deliver education to its children. One is as likely to see a grandmother sharing a mathematics lesson there as a child learning Indonesian via a television link to Djakarta. In its mission description it states:

Educational services at Mawson Lakes will have two complementary functions:

- To serve the needs of learners at Mawson Lakes by offering advice and advocacy on their behalf with providers, brokering in services, diagnosing the needs of learners, offering learning strategies and plans, and, in general, providing a pathway between Mawson Lakes learners and the global learning marketplace.

- To serve the community and advance the concepts of the learning community and its culture of continuous improvement by promoting learning opportunities, reporting on the nature and extent of learning at Mawson Lakes, encouraging and assisting individual learners, families and groups of learners [eg an occupational group, an age group or a group with a special need or talent] to learn.

Other schools are embracing such forward-looking, student-centred attitudes. For example, the Mankaa School, in the city of Espoo, with which Mawson is twinned in the exciting Pallace project (see Appendix 1), devotes every tenth day to a 'virtual working day' in which all children are given the freedom to develop their own learning, studying whatever they want to study and wherever they want to study it. The ownership process starts early in the city of Espoo. Tommila reports:

> The Friisilä day nursery emphasizes individual attention to the children's needs as individuals in the group, and it emphasizes that childhood has to be considered as a whole. Day care is infant education in which the pre-school for 6-year-olds serves as an important bridge between day care and the school. The day nursery cooperates with the local school. The objective is that the children develop healthy self-esteem and control of their own life, in other words, we give instructions for life. In the compilation of the curriculum, cooperation with the parents and the children themselves was especially important. When it was ready in 1999, the curriculum had become a 'learning plan', emphasizing the child's point of view, with the child's possibilities to learn through experiences as its starting point.

This plan has received international attention. It resulted in a new approach to teaching in the early years, emphasizing project work and paying particular attention to the learning environment. Nor is it static. The process continuously unfolds new elements and challenges, making this perhaps the only day nursery working as a true 'learning organization' in the sense that we have described it in Chapter 13. And of course the lessons learned are being replicated in schools dealing with much older children and throughout the Finnish school system, aided by the rapid growth in the educational support and delivery capability of information and communications technology.

Perhaps what would be helpful to all learners, and those charged with providing that learning, is the adoption of a Learner's Charter outlining the rights of every learner living in a model liberal democracy. It would provide guidelines for every learning provider. Figure 3.2 suggests such a charter. Numbers 3 and 4 are particularly interesting in that they reinforce the concept of learner as customer with control over, and ownership of, learning. Other aspects of the charter are addressed in later chapters.

A Learner's Charter

Good food, good health and good learning are interdependent parts of the human bio-system

1. All citizens have the right to learn and to develop their own potential throughout life

2. The right to learning is irrespective of creed, ethnic background, age, nationality or gender

3. The learner is the customer whose needs take first priority

4. As far as possible, learners should have ownership of, and control over, their own learning

5. Learning should be actively promoted and encouraged for every age

6. Individual learning styles should be recognized and catered for

7. As far as possible, learning should be provided where, when and how the learner desires it

8. Learners should have access to modern resources for learning wherever they may be

9. Support and guidance systems, including access to learning counsellors, should be in place at all stages of learning

10. People with learning difficulties should have the right to expert help and support

Figure 3.2 A Learner's Charter

The new role of the educator

But, of course, such fundamental changes have implications far beyond anything dreamt of in an education and training world. If, in the words of the European Commission's Memorandum, 'systems of provision must shift from a supply-side to a demand-side approach, placing users' needs and demands at the centre of concern', there is now a transfer of power from provider to learner. And if, as we have suggested, learning is now more of a compact between teacher and learner encompassing many different forms of delivery and the tacit acceptance of the proposed curriculum, then the role of teachers and lecturers changes radically. It is true too at university level.

Weimer quotes the half-life problem, well known to engineers as far back as the 1960s, in which the university degree lasted in value no more than five years before the knowledge became outdated and had to be replenished. In the modern day the half-life of an engineer is less than one year and dropping. Furthermore, the 'half-life problem applies to all of us. Chemists, programmers, doctors, lawyers, teachers, building contractors, managers, secretaries, administrators, all must replenish their original education continuously.' For teachers, lifelong learning enforces a double whammy. It changes not only the content, but also the method-ology of their profession. They become transformed into organizers of all the considerable educational and human resources at their disposal in the interests of actively stimulating learning.

And far from diminishing the teacher's role, this actually enhances it. He/she is no longer a primary deliverer of information to be regurgitated back on exami-nation sheets — at best an activity with a dubious educational value — but the conductor of an increasingly competent learning orchestra, extending its reper-toire and improving its performance with each rehearsal.

This new role is recognized by most reports and observers of the 21st-century education scene. The OECD report on 'Learning for All', the UK and Finnish governments' Green and White Papers, the Fryer report, the European Commission's memorandum, the US National Strategy for Learning — they all describe a very different world of learning: new approaches, new curricula, new knowledge, new technology, all of them requiring a much wider range of skills, knowledge and competencies than presently exists. In this, teachers are mirroring changes in every other professional walk of life and cannot be exempted from those processes. They will have to acquire a range of new skills and knowledge, such as those suggested in Figure 3.3.

Teachers should have no fear of de-skilling. These are not trivial or easy skills to acquire. And they are crucially important for the development of a lifelong learning society. In the Finnish National Strategy for Lifelong Learning, the teacher's new role is the 'second pillar of lifelong learning'. It quotes many of the tasks listed above as the new domain of the teacher — and also supplements that role as managers of the experts, parents, grandparents, supervisors, coaches and mentors who would help them achieve their goals. These are also part of the physical, mental, emotional and intellectual learning and support infrastructure.

But words in reports compiled by educationists need to be translated into classroom practice, and here the picture is much more blurred. Reluctance to change is as strong in educational circles as it is in society at large, and is often tightly constrained by government and public attitudes. Equally, other learning systems, such as the huge standards and assessment edifices constructed around

Skills for learning counsellors – teachers of tomorrow

Leadership skills	**C**reate the habit of learning in people through a thorough knowledge of how people learn and their individual learning styles
Technology skills	**O**ptimize the use of open and distance learning technologies to make the best use of their power to create interactive feedback between the learner and the learning programme(s)
Classroom management skills	**U**nderstand how to organize classrooms into hives of active personal learning using all the human resources available from parents and the community
Networking skills	**N**etwork learners with other learners on a local, national and international basis and develop all the ways of using communications technology to stimulate innovative learning
Negotiating skills	**S**upport learning by developing and exploiting partnerships between industry, schools, higher and further education, local government and the informal education system
Counselling skills	**E**mpower each learner by helping to act and monitor personal goals through personal learning plans, mentoring techniques and individualized learning modules
Research skills	**L**ift the vision of students by involving them in audits, surveys and studies which enhance their appreciation of the world around them and the value of critical analysis
Resource discovery skills	**L**ink the results to learning opportunities locally, nationally and internationally and make use of all funding sources
Resource management skills	**O**rganize information programmes and schemes to mobilize the skills and talents of the whole community for education and learning
Self-improvement skills	**R**espond to the new lifelong learning world by continuously updating personal skills, knowledge and competencies
Inspirational skills	**S**timulate learning into an enjoyable and creative experience through a thorough knowledge of the psychology of learning motivation and how to overcome barriers to learning confidence

Equally at home in industry, schools, adult education, universities and all parts of education and social systems

Figure 3.3 New skills of the teacher (see initial letters)

19th- and 20th-century notions of the learner as failure-prone victim, will need to be modified, and this issue is taken up in Chapter 8. But there is evidence of movement in this direction, and one example comes from Essex. At Chafford

Hundred campus, primary and secondary schools share the same facilities, using joint headteachers, joint staffing and shared policies. The school's facilities are also for adult and community use. This has had an effect upon what it teaches and how it does so. The curriculum for Year 7, for example, is set out under six Unit headings – *Where's the evidence? Let's get organized, Changes, One to one, Fit and healthy, Communities* – and it identifies values, attitudes, and '21st-century competencies' that are intrinsic to the learning process.

The children are provided with planners listing key skills, and are asked to present evidence to support the development of particular competencies. The information is reviewed at the end of each term and recorded via the school's intranet. In addition, each child reviews weekly progress and targets, personally and in small groups. Such practices increase both the child's ownership of the process of learning and the teacher's competence in using a wide range of resources to support it. But they are rare. The need is for each learning provider to become a 'learning organization', constantly questioning its role, its curriculum and its methods of working, managing and teaching, bringing in expertise from outside to stimulate discussion, engender analysis and action, and generate change in practice with the consent of the teachers and lecturers – and the students. In those countries with a strong inspectorate of schools and colleges, it would be a refreshing new role for it, replacing fault-finding negativism with the positive task of fostering educational renewal. And/or it could be an additional function of the teacher training colleges. Difficult problems demand creative solutions.

Empowerment

Jim Botkin points to the private sector for further inspiration in this field. Total quality management principles lead to an entirely new empowerment of the workforce within a learning organization. Limits to learning don't exist here. For example, Mercedes-Benz opened a huge new factory in Alabama, the poorest state in the USA. Within a few years it had transformed agricultural labourers and people who had never worked at all into world-class car workers. In such learning organizations, individuals and teams are given the responsibility and the privilege of working out their own solutions to new processes, new procedures and the acquisition of new knowledge and skills.

Schools, colleges, universities, local authorities and governments can learn much from the critical success factors in industry – a focus on personal development, personal responsibility, personal empowerment and personal ownership of everything one undertakes. This theme is taken up in greater detail in Chapter 16.

Chapter 4

Learning to learn, learning to live – lifelong learning tools and techniques

Education and training C20th	Lifelong learning C21st	Action for change
Work-based – educates and trains for employment and short-term need	Life-based – educates both for employability and a full and fulfilled life in the long term	Provide and use the tools and techniques to empower whole person's learning needs. Career, job, leisure, family, community, interests, change – audits, personal learning plans etc

Figure 4.1 The need for tools and techniques

Article 26 of the Universal Declaration of Human Rights, written in 1948 when ideals were respectable and hope was strong, contains the following: 'Education shall be directed to the full development of the human personality and to the strengthening of respect for human rights and fundamental freedoms.' Although the sentiments are undoubtedly those which any liberal democracy would regard as unimpeachable, the history of the late 20th century has conspired to make us rather more materialistic and cynical, and it is only in the past ten years that such lifelong learning quality goals are now being revisited on a large scale.

But even among those countries which have accepted that lifelong learning is their educational future, there is often a reluctance to step out of the education and training paradigm. Partly it is a political consideration. Change, especially such a radical *volte face* from accepted wisdom, and even more especially when it concerns such a fundamental and emotional subject as education, is a difficult concept to sell to a population already battered by its effects in other spheres of activity. In the minds of much of the electorate, education is about fitting people to get jobs, about employment, about ensuring that children and adults are enveloped in a tried and tested system with tried and tested outputs, and that those who graduate from that system obtain the necessary pieces of paper to say so. Few elections are won on 'yes, but's – yes, but those jobs won't exist in ten years' time; yes, but the future of country needs creative people who can think outside the system; yes, but education is about the development of the whole person.

Short-termism is an unfortunate by-product of democracy and it is a brave politician who will initiate unpopular actions even though they may be in the long-term national interest. This is why, for many governments, lifelong learning priorities focus on economic advantage, adult education and getting people into work situations – in Clinton's well-known electoral dictum, 'It's the economy, stupid.' And this message is translated down the chain into the regions, cities, towns and organizations implementing the policy so that it becomes their policy too.

And yet there are many exceptions to this rule. In Finland, for example, the national policy on lifelong learning is one part of a national strategy to turn the country into a huge technological learning society in the longer term. 'The future of Finland and the Finns is strongly bound up with knowledge and expertise as well as the ability to utilize this know-how and expertise to create innovations', it says. According to the Finnish Member of Parliament Markku Markkula, the four pillars of lifelong learning are these:

- the child's learning skills and abilities;
- the new role of the teacher;
- the systematic development and appreciation of human capital;
- a fully open learning environment.

They are based on a much more holistic, whole-of-life-based set of values, with a longer-term vision, which, although still economic in its orientation, also includes the social, the environmental and the cultural. Indeed, the summary to the national strategy includes this statement: 'As a principle guiding the learning careers of individuals, Lifelong Learning means that people should possess a positive attitude towards intellectual, aesthetic, moral and social growth so that they gather the understanding they will need during their lives in different functioning environments.'

South Australia also has its own all-encompassing view that lifelong learning is both lifelong and learning. The South Australian strategy, articulated by Professor Denis Ralph, a former State Chief Education Officer, starts:

> South Australia will be a place where individuals are supported and encouraged to achieve personal growth, develop positive self-esteem, a real love for learning and to build a portfolio of knowledge, skills, values and capacities that ensure lifelong employability. It will be a place that promotes learning as a cradle-to-grave process, facilitates personal discovery and inquiry and assists individuals to fulfil their life's purpose.

And here we see two words – values and employability – that are now dominating lifelong learning thinking in the more perceptive regions, cities and organizations. Many UK cities, for example, have replaced their employment officers with employability officers, firstly acknowledging the crucial link between learning and the ability to get a job, and secondly accepting the notion that people will have several jobs during a lifetime. Put simply, to stay employable is to stay learning, and vice versa.

Tools for lifelong learning 1 – learning audits

And this is where the desperate need for techniques and tools to convince a larger number of people of the value of continuous learning becomes important. Susan Crichton and Ellen Kinsel put this neatly: 'schools do what they typically do, teach to the 10% who come able to cope with the academic, tolerating or turning off the rest. Increasingly, in Canada,' they say, 'we have reached the point where society is beginning to recognize that it needs the other 90%. We need a knowledgeable, capable workforce and we cannot afford to continuously support those whom the system has failed.'

The problem goes far beyond schools. The remit of the UK Learning and Skills Council, a body established by government to improve learning and skills in all people over 16 years old, is to pay particular attention to the learning deficit in large numbers of the country's citizens and to address problems of learning reluctance. Brian Sanderson, its chief executive acknowledges:

> We have a colossal task in front of us; to champion the power of learning to transform people's lives. This is the scale of the task:
>
> - There are almost 6 million adults in the UK with no qualifications.
> - 26% of adults in the UK have undertaken no learning in the last three years.
> - There are 7 million adults in the UK with serious basic skills needs in literacy, numeracy or basic IT.

And he is right. Changing the mindset of millions of people with an anti-learning attitude is indeed a Herculean task, and one which many past initiatives have tackled and failed to resolve, partly because the fundamental roots of the problem have not been addressed when they first manifested themselves. The second report of the NAGCELL committee on Lifelong Learning, chaired by Bob Fryer, proffers this opinion:

> Stimulating demand and developing learning cultures will require a multi-level, multi-stranded approach. Policy ought to be defined and implemented with the varying needs of different segments of the potential market for learning in mind. Some changes can be achieved in the short term, but the sort of cultural shift we commend will require prolonged and sustained effort.

Many of the solutions available to educators are designed to help in situations where learners are already moderately committed to learning, be they in schools, colleges, universities or the workplace. For people less convinced of the need to learn, or damaged by previous learning experiences, or who are coming back into learning with some trepidation after a long absence from it, there are some new tools to help. These are: Personal Learning Requirements Audits (PLRA), a series of stock-taking exercises to improve self-understanding and to generate the desire to get back into learning, and Personal Learning Action Plans, a series of similar exercises to remove barriers to learning and to initiate learning activity. Both are generically modified from those successfully used in some parts of industry for several years to encourage the habit of learning and improved performance at the workplace. However, the tools described below cover a much wider spectrum of personal activity, and can be used in more diverse environments.

A Personal Learning Requirements Audit, for example, is a tool to discover what, how, where, when and why people may want to learn. But it is also a tool to encourage that want, and, as such, it is carefully worded to appeal to a wide variety of potential learners. It asks questions about a wide range of topics concerning their own personal view of learning. It is not simply a questionnaire – it is a precisely and subtly worded document to encourage exchanges of opinion, exercises in self-reflection and participant comment. It tries to produce insights into an individual's voyage of exploration into a learning world. It normally requires the aid of a sympathetic learning counsellor or adviser with whom the voyager could seek clarification, make personal comments and discuss options.

Nor would it be normally completed in a single session. Potential learners who have been damaged by past experience, or who are part of a non-learning peer group, require time to come round to the idea of subjecting themselves to similar, in their minds, potential humiliation. But it also appeals to common sense and reason. We can take as an example the Long Learn route-map audit. It begins thus:

> Learning is the most natural human instinct. And in a rapidly changing world, each one of us needs to remain adaptable, flexible and versatile. Equally, each of us has a personal challenge to recognize our own greater potential and our ability to achieve it. This can only be done through motivating ourselves to learn continuously.
>
> There are new tools and new approaches to make learning more effective, more attractive and more pleasurable – throughout life, whether you are 5 or 95, whether you have found it difficult in the past or not, whether you are rich or poor. None of us is immune from the need, or the desire, to learn more. We may want to enrich ourselves in our personal lives by developing new skills or improving old ones; we may want to improve our performance, and our salary, at work; we may want to give ourselves and our families a better quality of life.
>
> Whatever your motive, we believe that lifelong learning is:
>
> - for everybody throughout life, from cradle to grave, from hatch to despatch, about making progress at work, about more enjoyable leisure and a better

quality of life – all those things which encourage you to live up to your own potential;
- about continuously acquiring new knowledge, skills and understanding;
- about learning in a variety of new ways and focused around your own needs, your own circumstances and your preferred ways of learning.

So this is not a strategy for imposing pre-defined ideas onto an unwilling mind in order to persuade it to conform to society's norms. Nor is it a document to seek out faults, real or imaginary, in past behaviours. Quite simply it is a tool, which one can choose to use with someone trained to tease out attitudes and values in order to improve inner understanding. Moreover, it is not only non-threatening, but actually allows the participant to influence what takes place during every session – and, incidentally, can be of benefit. This tool is not a training requirements survey with a narrow education and training work-based focus. Modern lifelong learning concepts demand a much wider focus than that. It is whole of life based, encouraging a wider perception and encapsulating every aspect of an individual's needs and activities. It works in three stages, dependent upon the level of sophistication of the learner.

Stage 1 looks at past participation in learning: an exploration into past learning experiences in school and after school in all aspects of an individual's life – personal development, leisure, family, employment and community. Having completed this, the participant should have gained some insights into his/her personal attitudes to learning and the reasons for it. The task now is to deepen that understanding and to address the participant's present participation in learning.

Stage 2 of the audit therefore explores a number of issues relating to current self-knowledge: personal self-view, ambition, dedication, leadership attributes, stickability, attitudes to career and the updating of skills, and learning styles and preferences. These are mixed with questions and exercises on present learning activities and the development of a more coherent view of personal attitudes to learning and what support might be needed.

But the process is not completed until the potential learner is confronted by the big lifelong learning questions of the moment. Questions requiring some thought about the impact of technology on employment, the link between learning and employability, flexible career structures, the need for adaptability and so on. Exercises like this, encouraging personal debate on issues affecting the value and desirability of learning, have an obvious purpose of also encouraging reflection on current personal levels in learning participation. Other questions explore future possibilities, personal mentors and guides, required skills and opportunities, family and peer group attitudes, and, to take the respondent out of his/her own concerns, the advice he/she would give to children and others. Finally the participant is invited to list those things he/she might find interesting to learn if the money, time and motivation were available.

The last stage of a learning audit explores how the respondent's own skills, talents and experience can be put to the service of others. Each of us has talents, skills, knowledge, values and experiences which could be valuable to others on their own learning voyages. They range from subject knowledge to interpersonal communication skills, to coaching and guiding talents for which one does not necessarily have to be a trained teacher. Further, in helping others, individuals can learn more about themselves and enhance their own learning experiences. So this last item in the stock-taking phase is to encourage the activation and sharing of such personal wealth. It might include, for example:

- delivering a course in some aspect of one's own knowledge;
- mentoring someone who is studying a subject area known to the respondent;
- being a 'shoulder to lean on' at the end of an e-mail line;
- actively encouraging someone who needs encouragement;
- regular 'learning' meeting with someone who lives or works close by;
- coaching a sport, a skill or a speciality;
- giving a one-off talk to a group of people;
- managing a learning project;
- joining or coordinating an electronic forum discussing a particular speciality;
- training to be a learning counsellor.

This process needs to be carefully handled by the learning counsellor, who should be prepared to take digressions from the text and explore the variety of side-issues which arise.

Not everyone, however, may be ready to participate to such an extent. In the Ismaili Learning Community project described in Chapter 10, for example, many respondents were grateful that their own talents and skills had been recognized, but preferred to leave their contribution until they had come to terms with their own potential learning difficulties. The learning counsellor would need to make a personal judgement on whether or not to administer this stage.

This would normally complete a Personal Learning Requirements Audit. At the end of it, the participant should know whether or not he/she wants to enter the action phase, which is the Personal Learning Action Plan.

Tools for lifelong learning 2 – Personal Learning Action Plans

Figure 4.2, a poster to encourage people to take up a personal learning plan, is reproduced by kind permission of Long Learn Limited.

The Personal Learning Action Plan is also a three-stage process normally carried out with the help of a learning counsellor. It can be used independently of the Audit or as a result of it. Again it is not advisable to hurry the process, especially with those learners who may be wondering whether or not they are doing the right thing. And it requires careful and sympathetic treatment, since it energizes a process of self-analysis with which not everyone is comfortable. Indeed in

Do you have a personal learning plan?

A personal learning plan can help you:

- Meet the future with confidence

- Understand your own learning needs

- Develop your own potential

- Give a focus to your life and your learning

- Strengthen your willpower

- Improve your creativity

- Enrich your self-respect

- Release your earning power

- Inspire your family

Why not start to develop one this week?

Contact XXX

A LIFELONG LEARNING COMPANY
(LONGLEARN1 @hotmail.com)
www.longlearn.org.uk

Figure 4.2 Personal Learning Action Plan poster

the same Ismaili project, this was frequently stated as a difficulty by both participant and learning counsellor.

Stage 1 gathers and gives information. It describes the processes the potential learner will go through and the reasons for them. It recognizes potential difficulties and tries to address them:

If you are not habitually an introspective person who examines inner motivations this can often be a quite difficult process. But the rewards of such understanding will make it more likely that you both set out a realistic plan and that you complete it successfully.

Again this is not a process to be hurried. How long it takes is up to you. You may decide to let the exercises you go through incubate in your mind or choose to deal with them straight away. You might want to rewrite what you have written several times. You may complete part 1 in a day or so, and you may want to take longer with the other parts so that you get it right. You can share your thoughts with other members of your family or use the help of someone who can stimulate you to keep up with your schedule (a mentor or learning adviser) – perhaps even several people. There are no prizes for finishing your plan quickly. But there are great prizes for making a commitment to carry it out, this year, next year, in the years to come.

Then follow questions and exercises to encourage the respondent to explore those aspects of learning he/she has enjoyed in the past and to recreate those positive feelings.

Stage 2 now gathers together all the information, about oneself, about the things one may want to learn, about the opportunities available, under one heading. It covers:

- working life – the skills that enable one to improve one's performance in an existing or new trade or profession and how these may need to be developed;
- family life – bringing up children, doing household jobs, encouraging family learning;
- sports, hobbies and leisure interests – the skills and knowledge needed to pursue and improve them;
- personal development – the new knowledge, experiences, attitudes and values which make an individual into a better person;
- contribution to the community – whether this be a religious organization, an interest group, a uniformed group such as scouts or guides, or the local community in the neighbourhood or town.

It examines future needs and desires, articulates realistic dreams and ambitions and envisions an improved quality of life. Respondents are encouraged to think freely and fully about things they know they can do and always wanted to prove, subjects they have always wanted to learn but could never find the time and skills they always wanted to acquire, lifewide.

Stage 3 stimulates the formulation of learning intentions into a written formal plan. This may be the development of new skills related to a hobby, sport or interest (improving tennis, taking up bird-watching, photography, building a cupboard, reading and writing etc), improving values and attitudes (meditation, self-reliance, personal communication skills etc) or gaining new knowledge (learning a language, learning to throw pots, local history etc). It can include an ambition, eg to join a club, to stop smoking, to slim, or a contribution (to committees, to a family, hospital or prison visiting). But this is the time to be real-istic — it should include the where, the what, the how, the time to be committed, the target dates, the people who will help, the end goals and the priority to be assigned. The plan can cover one year or two but will be continuously assessed and extended over time. Frequently there will be a qualification. Our society seems to demand them as evidence. But the process stresses that, in the end, the only indi-cator of success lies within the individual — better relations within the family, a more relaxed attitude to life, a renewed intellectual vigour, a more complete human being, a better golfer, a more creative person.

This is the learner's commitment, the contract with oneself, to a better future through learning, and the act of putting it on paper means that it is more likely, though not by any means certain, to be carried out. Finally, recognizing this, it remains to suggest ideas and tips on how to keep to the plan, such as:

- Using a learning adviser and/or mentor frequently.
- Reviewing progress regularly.
- Keeping the plan updated. It is not a rigid timetable to be adhered to come what may.
- Cooperating with one's inner self. There are no prizes for finishing first. There are enormous prizes for finishing.
- Setting short-term checkpoint goals.
- Incorporating faster learning techniques into the plan — for example, accel-erated learning.
- Never underestimating oneself or one's power to learn.

As examples of the types of tools and techniques which can be used to increase the incidence of learning in cities and towns, Personal Learning Requirements Audits and Personal Learning Action Plans can be important in the development of positive lifelong learning attitudes. They can be used and modified in many ways and for many purposes. They are, in various degrees of completeness, successfully used mainly in workplaces, though modified versions are now increasingly being used in educational institutions and communities, such as Blackburn with Darwen in the UK, reported by Wong.

They will be increasingly used by teachers, lecturers, administrators, learning counsellors and community advisers in schools, colleges, universities, workplaces, hospitals — anywhere where the stimulation of learning is recognized to be important — as the lifelong learning revolution takes hold. They will be used to activate the ownership of learning, to create learning communities and to overcome learning disabilities and reluctance. They will inform learning providers about the real learning needs and demands of those thousands of people who have never had the opportunity to express them, so that they can provide the courses people want, rather than those that the learning providers think they want, or want to provide.

Learning tools in action

The Scottish Power learning system adopts a similar approach to personal development. Companies in general have an economic interest in fostering the habit of learning in their workforce in order to remain competitive in the marketplace and Scottish Power is no exception. Its personal development plan starts thus: 'Taking charge of your own development is all about knowing who you are, where you want to go and how you're going to get there. It sounds simple but more often than not, people don't know where to start. As a result personal development is often left to chance and nothing much is achieved.'

The resultant plan is a mixture of audit and personal learning plan, following a similar progression from guided self-analysis, through self-realization to the elaboration of a plan for each individual. Like the process described above, it recognizes that learning covers many aspects of life, and the questions and exercises it recommends are wide-ranging. For example, under the heading of combining life inside and outside work, it asks the respondent to assess the importance of different values to him/herself, namely:

- geographic location;
- helping others;
- job security;
- being well paid;
- family life;
- achieving status;
- meeting challenges;
- learning new things;
- leisure and recreational pursuits;
- being seen as an expert;
- working in a team;
- improving efficiency;
- making a contribution to society;
- influencing people;
- being methodical;
- making things happen;
- wanting people to think your work is important;
- community activities;
- religious/spiritual activities;
- being creative and innovative;
- positive working environment;
- delivering quality and value to customers;
- freedom from stress;
- family happiness.

This is a full and eclectic list which challenges the individual to think hard about many aspects of his/her personal approach to life as well as career.

The development plan encourages a personal SWOT (strengths, weaknesses, opportunities, threats) analysis and continues by helping the respondent develop a personal action plan incorporating both career and personal objectives. Guidance is given on the many learning methods and opportunities available and how to monitor the plan once started. Learners are encouraged to use mentors and guides in order to help overcome the obstacles that may arise.

Although the results of this are geared more to a work and career situation, such a thorough and wide-ranging set of exercises can also have beneficial effects on the full range of personal development.

Summary

This chapter has described tools and processes in some detail because it is believed that they are important for the participation of a large number of people in a lifelong learning world. For this we need different attitudes to learning and different relationships between learners and learning providers. As William Ellis points out in *Creating Learning Communities*:

> Learning replaces the materialism and consumerism that is so much part of today's society with a deeper love. It is the love of learning for the sake of learning – of gaining a sense of being rather than of having – of valuing knowledge rather than knowing things. Nor is learning something a superior authority causes to happen to a lesser one… In the new paradigm, learning is an act of self-volition. It is a self-actuated process of creating skills, discovering knowledge, and satisfying ones' own curiosity.

It is this spirit that these tools try to rekindle. It is also why a full version of a Personal Learning Requirements Audit and a Personal Learning Action Plan needs to be thoroughly researched and modified to fit the organization. The tools and techniques described in this chapter are not just useful for developing lifelong learning values and attitudes, but can also be instrumental in helping many people to come to terms with the extent of their own enormous potential. They will be increasingly used in family and community environments as well as in business and industry.

These are not the only tools and techniques to be tried in a lifelong learning world. The use of the interactive technologies, the development of productive partnerships, the benefits to be gained from mentoring, guiding and coaching are all instruments for improving the quality of the educational product and are described in other chapters. But the net effect of using them is to increase the incidence of learning and understanding, and to reduce the incidence of antisocial activities which generate an even more expensive solution. The best learning providers in schools, colleges and universities will make increasing use of them.

Chapter 5

Everyone's right, everyone's responsibility – the community as a resource for learning

Education and training C20th	Lifelong learning C21st	Action for change
Teachers/lecturers as information and knowledge purveyors – sole distributors of resource	Teachers/lecturers as managers – of all the resources and expertise available in a community	Discover and use the talents, skills, expertise, finance and knowledge within the community from all sources. Each learning provider appoints a person to tap and distribute this resource

Figure 5.1 Tapping into the community

The changing role of the teacher from information provider to leader and manager of resource in a lifelong learning establishment has already been highlighted. Although there is obviously a need for some didactic component in the lifelong learning curriculum, the information explosion has rendered much of the teacher's present function as a purveyor of a small subset of that information irrelevant. The vastly increased range of skills which learners will have to employ in order to survive in the knowledge society dictates an equally increased range of skills in the teacher, many of them described in Chapter 3. Teachers and lecturers now have much more important tasks – to acquire and use the tools, techniques and resources that foster and maintain a love of learning in their students.

As shown in Figure 5.2, the first principle of learning in the Rover Motor Company's charter is 'Learning is the most natural human instinct', and the enormously complicated skills that the great majority of young children acquire during the early years bear out this truism. Walking, talking, laughing, manipulating, counting, writing, are incredibly sophisticated competencies, the majority of which are accomplished before formal schooling, and testify to the power and adaptability of the human brain. At no other time in our lives do we work it so hard and so creatively.

Paradoxically, for many people, formal schooling, an activity with the objective of building upon that creative potential, seems to turn off the tap of imaginative thought. After several years of conventional academic classroom life, learning no longer seems the natural thing to do, and indeed, in many it is firmly detested and strongly resisted, at least in its formal mode. It seems to bear out principle 6 in Figure 5.2 that creativity and ingenuity are vastly underrated. How to take steps to avoid this happening becomes a key challenge to the 21st-century teacher, and the answer to that challenge may be encapsulated in the educational equivalent of principle 7. The realization that management, that is, teachers and lecturers, do not have all the answers, that the goal is the empowerment of the learner and that they can effectively use the support of others, is a necessary acknowledgement of the impact and implications of the knowledge society.

Rover learning principles
1. Learning is the most natural human instinct
2. Creativity, involvement and contribution are fuelled by learning and development
3. Everyone has two jobs – the job and improving the job
4. People own what they have created
5. People need work and enjoy it if they are valued
6. Creativity and ingenuity are grossly underrated
7. Management does not have all the answers

Figure 5.2 Rover learning principles

Formal, informal and non-formal learning

The second acknowledgement is that not all learning is carried out in educational institutions. The European Commission's memorandum on lifelong learning highlights three basic categories of purposeful learning activity:

- Formal learning, which takes place in education and training institutions, leading to recognized diplomas and qualifications.
- Non-formal learning, which takes place alongside the mainstream systems of education and training and does not typically lead to formalized certificates. Non-formal learning may be provided in the workplace and through the activities of civil society organizations and groups (such as in youth organizations, trades unions and political parties). It can also be provided through organizations or services that have been set up to complement formal systems (such as arts, music and sports classes or private tutoring to prepare for examinations).
- Informal learning, which is a natural accompaniment to everyday life. Unlike formal and non-formal learning, informal learning is not necessarily intentional learning, and so may well not be recognized even by individuals themselves as contributing to their knowledge and skills.

We can quibble about the accuracy and usefulness of such categorizations, but it is evident that there *is* a distinction between the three and that all three play a part in the lives of individuals in and out of learning establishments.

Until now, formal learning has dominated policy thinking, shaping the ways in which education and training are provided, and colouring people's understandings of what counts as learning. The basic continuum of lifelong learning brings non-formal and informal learning much more fully into the picture. Non-formal learning, at first sight, appears to be outside the remit of schools, colleges, training centres and universities, though many adult education courses in the liberal arts would come under this heading. It is not usually seen as 'real' learning, and its outcomes have, until recently, little currency value on the labour market. Consequently non-formal learning is typically undervalued among learning providers, even though business and industry increasingly look for many of the attributes picked up as a result of non-formal learning activities, for example leadership, personal energy and participation in community projects.

Informal learning is likely to be missed out of the picture altogether, although it is the oldest form of learning and, as we have seen, the well-spring of early childhood learning. Informal contexts provide an enormous learning reservoir and could be an important source of innovation for improving teaching and learning insights, if only we could step outside the self-imposed mental prison which constrains our perception of the purpose of school, college and university.

There is also the increased use of the term 'lifewide learning' to be borne in mind. While 'lifelong' learning relates to the activity of learning throughout a lifetime, 'lifewide' learning relates to the spread of learning taking place across the full range of our lives at any moment in time. It includes formal, non-formal and informal learning, and it reminds us that useful and enjoyable learning can and does take place in the family, in leisure time, in community life and in daily work. Further, it indicates that teaching and learning are themselves roles and activities that can be changed and exchanged in different times and different places. Lastly, as the preface to this book shows, 'lifedeep' learning is a new term to describe the insights and discernments which increase our awareness and understanding of particular issues in the wider world beyond our immediate environment. In a globalized world this type of learning is essential for international harmony and peace.

Finding the resources

So how do all these different perceptions affect the way in which teachers and lecturers perform their tasks in a lifelong learning society? If, as we have suggested, the notion of learner motivation extends to the full range of lifelong, lifewide and lifedeep activities for each individual; and if it includes the formal, non-formal and informal resulting in a transformation into a skills-based approach to the curriculum as Chapter 9 recommends; and if the use of support tools such as learning audits, technology and mentoring is implemented; and if the focus is on the needs and demands of each individual learner, including values and attitudes as well as knowledge, then not even the most talented group of superhuman teachers can provide the knowledge and expertise to satisfy the new requirements. Nor can educational funding structures support vast quantities of new resource. To be sure, additional funding is always welcome to the hard-pressed school or college and there are a hundred worthy causes on which to spend it. It is a tempting prospect to think of more money as the only answer to all our problems.

But we also need to take a wider view of both the nature and distribution of existing resources and the assistance available in kind from within a learning community. For example, in every community there is a large group of people who are not teachers but who nevertheless pass on information, knowledge, understanding and, sometimes, wisdom. They include parents, friends, neighbours, doctors, lawyers, councillors, counsellors, scout and guide leaders, political and religious leaders, journalists, television presenters, comedians and actors, to name but a few.

If those of us over 30 years old think back and reflect on the people who have transformed our lives and made us into the people we are, doing the things we do for work, leisure and home, we can usually find that events have been influenced by a wide of variety of people in a wide variety of places. The formal lessons we received in school will not figure largely, though the part we played in the school play, or the trip to another country with a school group might do so. Museums, libraries and churches are not a part of the formal education system but they affect the knowledge, values and attitudes of many people. They are all part of our own personal community of learning. They have stimulated or they have destroyed our desire to learn.

The process of community support is under way in many places. According to Naisbitt, 'American business has begun to play an extra-ordinary dual role in Education today. In society at large, American corporations have become the nation's leading education activists. Furthermore, within themselves, corporations are... transforming themselves into universities in their own right, so vast, so competent, that they begin to rival the traditional education system.'

New resources to help in education can come from any part of the community, but partnerships are often the key to unlocking them. Longworth and Davies mention, in *Lifelong Learning – New visions, New implications, New roles*, the example of IBM and Woodberry Down School:

Woodberry Down, an inner city school, had a rich ethnic mix within its catchment area and a high proportion of one-parent families. It is situated in a difficult area of inner London with an unenviable local crime record, where only the suicidal policemen patrol alone at night and where there is very little background of learning, never mind lifelong learning. By contrast, the city location of the mighty IBM, 3 miles away, is situated in one of the richest areas in the world, employs 700 highly trained professional people – systems analysts, salesmen, managers, experts on all aspects of computing, many of them commuting in from their four-bedroomed houses with large garden in the more affluent suburbs of London.

These two apparently incompatible organizations began to explore how one could help the other. So meetings were held at both places and a social evening arranged. As a result of this a coordinator, actually the wife of one of the IBM managers, a former social worker, was employed to see what could be done. She talked at length with the staff of the school and with the managers in the IBM location and how the skills and knowledge of one could be used to improve the situation of the other. The results of this collaboration produced 30 different projects affecting individuals in both establishments.

For example, a trust fund for school visits was started, so that the handicapped children in the school could spend a week at a study centre in the countryside in mid-Wales. In return those same children created a huge collage from cuttings and computer pieces, which was installed in the foyer of the IBM location, and used as a talking point for visitors to the company. Example two concerned the unlikely subject of opera. IBM was sponsoring a new production at the Covent Garden Opera House, so it arranged with the company to run an opera workshop for children at the school. The children were bowled over. They committed suicide like *Tosca*, they fought with the soldiers in *Aida*, they swooned like Mimi in *La Bohème*, they ascended into heaven like Marguerita in *Faust* – and in that unlikely school an opera club was formed which lasted until the school was closed 10 years later.

The third example is the interviewing scheme. Teams of IBM people went in pairs to the school to run mock interviews with senior pupils to help make them more employable and to give them some hints on how to get a job. Again this was a fun event much appreciated by the students and much enjoyed by the participants from IBM, who also learned a great deal.

No one can expect a 100% response to such schemes. In total 10 percent of the 700 IBM people, that is 70 sets of additional skills, talents, knowledge and expertise, became involved in partnerships with teachers and staff on such items as curriculum reform, management and leadership, language and computer education. It is an example of what a productive partnership can do for a school and a company. This was a two-way communications exercise breaking down stereotypes, producing new insights into the needs of a 21st-century school and providing a huge new resource.

There are many examples of such programmes in the USA where, as Naisbitt reported above, industry is involved with schools in developing mentoring programmes, providing additional curriculum expertise, sponsoring recognition and award programmes, sharing management courses and supporting out-of-school events in 'adopt-a-school' programmes throughout the country.

But not all fruitful cooperation is industry related. Resource and expertise are available from the whole community. William N Ellis suggests that:

> Every aspect of the community is an integral part of the learning program. Libraries, museums, parks, health clubs, shops, banks, businesses, municipal offices, farms, factories, the streets and the environment provide learning opportunities, facilities and services for self-learners. At the same time, learning becomes a service to the community, as future citizens become involved in the local community.

It is therefore a two-way resource exchange in which the learning provider becomes an integral part of the community, contributing to it and drawing from it. The Adult Education project of Beijing, for example, describes itself as 'a full-scale tapping of potential Human resources across the city'. Neighbourhood committees in every part of the city are encouraged to use the human talent at their disposal in the service of learning. According to the UNESCO Institute of Education, such neighbourhood, or community-based, learning centres are to be found throughout Asia and the Pacific. Because they normally operate outside the formal education system they are useful in reaching learners who would not normally be in formal education. Similarly, in the West, the University of the Third Age encourages the formation of local groups to tap into the expertise and knowledge of each individual member, and to foster interaction between groups.

Resources and strategies in action

Such initiatives are especially encouraged in the city of Espoo in Finland. Its 'Learning City Project' highlights involvement and commitment to the city as a tool of development, a variant of the concept of 'Dia Viou Paediea' – the obligation of every citizen to contribute to the development of the city in Plato's time. Tommila suggests the following as a rationale for this:

- The whole city is a learning environment.

- Learning takes place in many domains of the city.
- Lifelong learning concerns everybody throughout life.
- Measures for social cohesion are mainly based on learning processes.
- The success of the city depends on partnerships in the community.
- Performance and innovation require a vivid collaboration between actors in the community.

Here we see the concept both of the city as a resource for the learner and the learner as a resource for the city written into the educational strategy of a municipality striving to move into the 21st century.

Summary

If we take the lessons to be learnt from these examples – namely:

- given goodwill on both sides, there are many, many more possibilities for positive and beneficial interaction in every situation than seems possible at first sight;
- good partnerships, creatively and sensitively applied, can achieve wonders when there is a good coordinator – someone to make it happen;
- new resources are physical, financial and human and can change not only the perceptions of people but also their attitudes and often even their lives;
- there are huge untapped resources in the community for schools, and other educational establishments, which are prepared to be flexible, creative and imaginative in finding and using them;

then it is possible to come to some general conclusions about how to increase the resource base of an educational institution. Schools and colleges can learn much from the practice in many universities of employing foundation departments to explore the contribution that industry and other funding bodies can make to the development of the organization. It should be the task of at least one person, and perhaps more – a teacher, a parent, a person of goodwill from the community – to explore the range of physical and human resource within the community for the benefit of the institution. He/she would be the community officer, using the growing number of volunteering opportunities described in Chapter 4, seeking out scope for sponsorship and donation (for example, of computers to the organization), innovating ideas and events, creating an image of competence and cooperation, and, most importantly, orchestrating the contribution of all of this to the more exciting delivery of the curriculum and the deeper understanding of students and staff.

Of course, one of the most powerful facilitators of community involvement is to create a community school or college, and indeed the number of such institutions is burgeoning in the developed world. They range from those cosmetic adjustments where only the label has changed, through institutions where children use the facilities by day and adults use them by night in resource sharing mode, to colleges with open access to children and adults of all ages at all times.

Mawson Lakes School, Adelaide, mentioned in Chapter 3, is an example of the latter. It goes the whole hog, inviting adults as students into school lessons, and unashamedly using the whole community around it as a resource in win–win partnerships. Such innovative ideas help to transform stereotypes, generation gaps, mistrust, frustration and the idea that educational institutions are cold, inaccessible prisons where disinterested students are force-fed with dull facts and drabber subjects, into vibrant cathedrals of fascinating knowledge and purposeful activity.

Chapter 6

Improving access – learning wherever, whenever and however people want it

Education and training C20th	Lifelong learning C21st	Action for change
Courses decided and provided by education organizations on their own premises	Learning influenced by learner and provided where, when, how and from whom he/she wants it	Encourage providers to provide learning where people are – homes, schools, workplaces, pubs, stadia, church halls etc Examine when ready, not when convenient

Figure 6.1 Improving access to learning

Those of us over a certain age will remember enrolment days at adult education colleges and universities. This was when we found out more about the courses the learning providers had chosen to deliver to us and decided whether or not we wanted to spend our time following them over the next few terms. At least some of us did. The vast majority of people did not, for a variety of reasons centred round motivation, past experience, accessibility, finance, time constraints and self-image.

The courses nearly always all started in a certain month – September in the UK – and if you were not ready or able at that time, perhaps abroad, perhaps in hospital, perhaps simply unable to make a decision, that was too bad. The opportunity had disappeared for a whole year. Moreover, the learning provider always set the end-of-year examination at around the same time, with little regard for the state of preparedness of the student, who might have been ready to prove familiarity with the subject matter several months previously, or wished to delay it to several weeks later. We danced to the tune of the learning provider, or we didn't dance at all.

And of course in many cities and regions it is still like that. The learning providers still decide the nature and content of the courses based on their own view of what they think people want, and deliver them from their own premises at the times they choose. It works well for those people well motivated to learn and willing to spend the time travelling to and from the place of learning. It also disenfranchises a great number of those people who might want to learn but don't have the means, the motivation or the support to fit into the system.

It also disengages those whose attachment to formal learning environments is suspect, perhaps because their past encounters there have not been happy ones, perhaps because of poor self-esteem. As a UK Campaign for Learning focus group member said, 'School was a major dislike. I didn't like anything about it. I left school with no GCSEs. I regret it now, but I wouldn't go back.' Clearly, some action is needed to offer a more flexible structure of opportunities for these people. In the words of the European memorandum on Lifelong Learning:

> Bringing learning closer to home will require reorganization and redeployment of resources to create appropriate kinds of learning centres in everyday locations where people gather – not only in schools themselves, but also, for example, in village halls and shopping malls, libraries and museums, places of worship, parks and public squares, train and bus stations, health centres and leisure complexes, and workplace canteens.

Improving access

As evidence that things are changing, perhaps we can make start at the Metro Shopping Centre in Gateshead, UK, where one can find 'Learning World'. Here a drop-in learning centre, fully equipped with computers and training staff, is available to shoppers as and when they feel they want to use it. Here, those who wish to do so can put down their groceries for an hour or two and enter into the world of learning through courses ranging from MBAs through Open University facilities to people who want to develop National Vocational Qualifications (NVQs) or simply learn a skill for no qualification at all. Access to the Internet allows people to obtain information about other courses in the region of Tyne and Wear and beyond. Learning World has been in existence for more than 10 years now, and its example has been copied by other British cities. Indeed, it is rare to find a large UK city without at least one 'Learning Shop' or drop-in centre.

Sunderland University, which pioneered the programme, is also leading the way in other initiatives. Its free telephone helpline, giving educational information to all who wish to know about where, when, how and sometimes why courses in all subjects exist, is now operated at national level by the vast Learn Direct programme established by the British government. Like many other universities and colleges, it uses local radio, television and the press to market 'learning' as an attractive activity, and extols the products it offers to prove it. More than that, the courses take place in 35 learning centres in the region – schools and libraries in the evening, community centres, pubs, factories, church halls.

Soccer to the rescue

The most popular with the youngsters are the courses offered in the football stadium. Here you will find children who wouldn't be seen dead in the standard educational environment – they have been so switched off by their experiences at school. But here they are excited by the novelty of learning in the place where they go to worship their footballing heroes every other Saturday. Learning becomes accessible, non-threatening, pleasurable and natural – all the things which, for many people, it isn't. Sunderland is not the only football club involving itself with learning in a city. Several other Premiership football clubs, Arsenal, Blackburn Rovers, Bolton Wanderers and Newcastle United among them, have responded to the Prime Minister's plea to get involved with education.

'Playing for Success' is a strategy, jointly funded by the club and the government, for engaging reluctant learners in learning in the areas in which they live. The magnetic appeal of following learning programmes at the football club they support week in and week out is proving irresistible to youngsters at risk of drop-out. They will willingly go there after school hours to take courses on ICT, numeracy and literacy skill development. The Blackburn Rovers club, for example, conducts two-hour sessions each evening for both primary and secondary school students, bringing the power of learning to truants and children who have little support at home. It is a masterpiece of subtle persuasion. Teachers are dressed in the football club track suits. The computer rooms are decorated with football memorabilia.

The curriculum has a football theme. The children even work with journalists on match days and develop new skills and self-confidence. The lessons they subsequently follow relate to these experiences. Their favourite footballers help out, dropping in on classes after training. Several thousand children are touched by this experience every year.

Making learning attractive

Such innovative projects demonstrate the effectiveness of making learning an acceptable, even a cool, activity by taking learning to the learner. While the local school or technical college does not quite have that seductive appeal, many similar initiatives can be taken to make learning more attractive. For example:

- the Yorkshire pub which responded to its customer needs by providing courses on 'computers and the Internet' and 'ordering drinks abroad' in association with the local technical college;

- the 'etälukio' project in Espoo, Finland which offers young and old adults a second-chance learning opportunity at their own pace, irrespective of time and place;
- the 'Learning at work' days organized by the UK Campaign for Learning which have energized more than 5,000 organizations to lay on a vast variety of learning experiences for their employees in the workplace, and generated huge media coverage through celebrity support;
- the Edinburgh Community Centres in each part of the city which don't offer courses – they invite people to participate in learning and plan the learning with that philosophy in mind;
- the drive at Lloyds to make learning more accessible to its 76,000 staff worldwide through learning cybercafés in all large locations, 30 regional training centres and learning Web sites for staff.

In China, local access to learning is being enhanced through the concept of Neighbourhood Learning Centres. These extend even to streets. In Beijing, for example, where adult education has received a huge boost in recent years through its 'learning city' project, Zhang Cuizhu tells us that there are 175 streets recognized as community education pilot areas. It is claimed that more than 1.6 million people have benefited from such centres, established by Neighbourhood committees. They are strong too in cities and regions in the UK.

These are the tip of a very deep iceberg in the new trend towards taking learning to where the people are. What can learning providers learn from this?

- Firstly, that if we can offer learning to people where, when, from whom and how they want to receive it – that is, we make it accessible – people will be much more likely to take it up.
- Secondly, there is now so much more flexibility in learning methods – we can e-learn from the Internet, through distance learning providers by satellite, TV, through the post, the Open University, through multimedia software; we can learn at home, at work, at a learning centre, on the bus, the train or plane and increasingly we are seeing that happen. The competition is hotting up. Multinational companies are establishing their own university faculties. The financial house, M&G, adopts the philosophy that learning is an integral part of the job rather than an optional extra. The management system establishes learning objectives for every employee and also supplies the learning in the workplace through 'I' personal learning sites. A host of universities from the USA and Australia are going global. Monash near Melbourne is no longer an Australian university – it describes itself as a global university with faculty in many countries. California Virtual University offers more than 300 courses. And they are flexible – they will teach wherever, whenever, whatever, however and from whomever; they will examine when the student is ready and not necessarily at the end of the academic year; and they will pose a huge threat to existing learning providers in cities – unless of course they show a similar flexibility and imagination.

- Thirdly, the way that education is presented to the potential learner is important: it needs to be marketed as fun, cool, valuable and important that he/she should have it – and it needs to compete with all the other 'products' available in the advertising marketplace.
- Fourthly, the support systems become almost as important as the learning – we have a lot of new learners here, many of them damaged by their experiences in education. They need tutors, counsellors, helpers, psychologists, mentors and coaches as much as they need teachers and lecturers, a concept taken up in Chapter 7.

Implications for adult education

Adult and further education will bear the brunt of all of these. It is already coping with the vast increase in learning demand stimulated by lifelong learning in towns and cities throughout the world. In future years it will change its policies, procedures and methodologies to extend it even wider. Figure 6.2, developed originally for the Australian National Training Agency, shows some of the changes which adult education institutions are already experiencing and can expect to increase in importance in the near future.

Such a vast range of changes and approaches presents enormous challenges to every adult education institution, and the pressure can only increase as lifelong learning concepts take hold, bringing more and more learners of all ages and abilities into focus. New strategies, perhaps using common interactive technology delivery platforms as in the Glasgow Colleges network, perhaps developing new tutoring and student empowerment techniques, perhaps involving experts from within the community, will need to be employed. Certainly learning will need to be brought to where the learners are, and a wide range of courses offered.

Bringing learning to the learner – a case study

The Monteney Community Workshop Trust, a community centre in Sheffield, UK, provides an excellent case study of the flexibility of approach needed to cope with this. Yule and Salmon describe the centre, which is to be found in a large housing estate the size of a small town, built to accommodate workers for the steel industry in the north-east of the city, as a 21st-century challenge. The demise of the industry has caused increased unemployment, poverty and associated economic and social problems. Over the years the centre has been funded from a variety of traditional education sources, but this has made it very vulnerable to changes in funding sources and it has increasingly looked to the internal strengths of its own community. It converted to an independent trust, with substantial local ownership, as a means of gaining some control over its destiny.

Bringing adult education into a lifelong learning world
1. APEL – Assessment of Prior Experiential Learning – Credit award strategies for life experience
2. New approaches to teaching for disadvantaged learners and those with learning difficulties – a full focus on needs and demands of the learner and learning support systems
3. A vastly increasing number of mature students from wider backgrounds, industry etc.
4. New access strategies in the community – taking learning to the learner wherever, whenever, however and from whoever he/she wants it
5. A more innovative approach to the use of education technology, networks and open/distance learning in teaching strategies
6. Professionalization of staff – continuous improvement programme in both content and teaching practice
7. More focus on the skills of learning and knowledge of the latest research into how people learn
8. Greater internationalization of courses and teaching practice through networks – global links
9. More partnerships within the community to increase resources and contribute to lifelong learning
10. More use of the talents, skills and knowledge in the community
11. Promotional, marketing and educational programmes reaching out into the community to teach and learn
12. More staff exchanges with industry, universities and schools
13. Strategies to provide leadership to the learning community in which the college resides
14. Strategies to turn adult education institutions into genuine learning organizations
15. New ideas on accreditation, qualifications and standards – examinations as non-failure-oriented learning opportunities to measure an individual's progress
16. Adult education as pre-higher education foundation learning – links with universities
17. Strategies to audit the learning requirements of people in the community and then satisfy them
18. The use of personal learning plans as tools for giving owernship of learning to the students
19. Mentoring programmes for staff and students to help increase motivation and application
20. Activities to celebrate learning frequently as a desirable, permanent and enjoyable habit
21. Posters to present learning as a natural and pleasurable human instinct
22. Enhancing self-esteem, confidence, creativity and the cultural vision of students through a wide range of non-curricular activities
23. More efficient internal administration and use of human resources

Figure 6.2 Adult education and imminent changes of focus

Challenging the barriers to learning participation and building up local ownership underpin the centre's entire outlook and strategy. Its view of ownership is crucial to its philosophy. Its principal role is to meet local needs, whatever they may be. And while it frequently consults all parts of the community, and takes into account the results of local surveys or forums, in this centre, the owners are the local community in a literal sense – the trustees live on the estate and are accountable to its residents. Ownership even extends to mobilizing the residents to lobby for funds in the various networks and political channels.

The centre believes that the community should define its own learning needs, which can then be delivered through workshops. The core programme includes ICT, multimedia and communication studies, and printing and publishing. A key output is the production of the local community newspaper, *The North East Sheffield Express*, which is delivered free to 19,600 local homes. This predominantly craft-based and media learning agenda aims to help individuals overcome their fear of formal learning. Accreditation is an option, but not compulsory, since it is often associated with expectations of failure and linked with previous bad experiences at school or with 'authority'. Most of the learning resources are offered on a supported, five days a week, open-access basis, as well as through structured and tutored courses.

No assumptions are made – or targets imposed – regarding the notion of progression. Indeed, progression is defined and valued in ways other than progress towards further and higher levels of learning. Ability and confidence to participate in community organization and activity, or to become more active and fulfilled citizens are just two socially inclusive examples of 'unaccreditable' but valued achievement. Many learners are happy to remain with the same group for several years, although others will wish to move on. Several groups are entirely self-run (eg painting and drawing group, spinning and weaving group, video production group, photography group). Here, the centre provides space and hospitality (tea/coffee) without charge, provided the group has an 'open access' policy. From time to time, group members might raise money in order to bring in a tutor or buy some equipment.

Although there is a list of courses provided by the Workers Educational Association, in practice most marketing is by word of mouth. For the centre, marketing is a two-way process. It canvasses views and listens, as well as promoting particular programmes. It uses 'bridge workers', a team of 20 local residents who knock on doors and raise awareness of local learning opportunities. Local residents will drop in on an informal basis with suggestions or queries. Similarly, many current learners in one group will opt in to a different programme as a result of themselves recognizing they have a learning need (eg basic skills or ICT), rather than as a response to an external marketing exercise.

Three factors are considered to be essential in encouraging residents, especially reluctant learners, to cross the threshold. These are a genuine welcome, a safe environment, and the encouragement and positive recognition of existing skills and abilities before any further learning is expected.

Learning providers may wish to take this on board. Certainly the European Commission has. Its memorandum points out that:

People will only plan for consistent learning activities throughout their lives if they want to learn. They will not want to continue to learn if their experiences of learning in early life have been unsuccessful and personally negative. They will not want to carry on if appropriate learning opportunities are not practically accessible as far as timing, pace, location and affordability are concerned.

Learning and the media

It may be stating the obvious, but so often the obvious is sacrificed in the name of convenience. But much of this depends upon the predominant culture of a nation and on the aims of its government. A dictatorship, for example, would find the process of opening up the minds of citizens a subversive action. And so it is, but then so is every act of learning. But here the use of the media would be as propaganda to enforce a governmental opinion. In a liberal democracy there is in theory more freedom and more openness, but even here everything is not always as it seems.

As Longworth and Davies say in *Lifelong Learning*, 'Those people with the mental scars of a divisive, and largely irrelevant, early educational experience will have doubts about their ability to learn, and will retreat into the escapist search for permanent media entertainment.' The huge popularity of tabloid newspapers and soap operas on television and a constant preoccupation with the trivia of life with the 'stars' are an eloquent testimony to this condition, and demonstrate how far the message of lifelong learning has to go, particularly with regard to the acquisition of discriminatory skills. Which is not to say that all such newspapers and programmes are poor in quality – on the contrary, in our present state of learning sophistication they often perform a valuable educational function, and one looks to them to improve their own quality as the quality of national education, and their contribution to it, improves.

A society confident with its own learning capacity, a broad range of horizons and a desire to create and contribute to the future will demand more from its media in the form of opportunity for greater personal fulfilment through learning. These are the places whose economic and social future is brighter. In a democratic society, television and the press know what their listeners, watchers and readers want to read and see, and exercise their right to feed it. It is a tricky issue, but rights involve responsibilities, and one of these is to also take into account the longer-term interest of a nation, a society, an individual.

In 1988, Canada's Northrop Frye wrote:

We are trying to marshal all the resources of culture and intellect we have in order to struggle with the problems that our civilization has created. We have outside us nations with different political philosophies, and we think of them as dangers, or even as enemies. But our more dangerous enemies, so far, are within. Our effective enemies are not the foreign propagandists, but the hucksters and hidden persuaders and segregators and censors and hysterical witch hunters and all the rest of the black guard who can only live as parasites on a gullible and misinformed mob.

What Frye is trying to say is that bad and unscrupulous newspapers tell their readers what to think, while good ones empower them to think by encouraging them to interpret the information they give. While incitement to violence is of course discouraged, some newspapers sail close to the wind when circulation matters predominate. However, incitement to mediocrity and limited vision, it seems, is not dissuaded, as a sample of any newsagent's shelves demonstrates daily.

But professional broadcasters and journalists, like teachers, have a responsibility to take into account the intellectual and economic interests of their audiences in the same way that professional doctors and nurses have to account for their long-term health interests. This means gently transforming what people want to listen to, watch or read from the trivialized, banal and often destructive to the informed, intelligent, positive and creative. Not an easy task, and not one with which many would agree, but in this way they can contribute positively to developing the sort of lifelong learning culture that each nation, each region and each person will have to nourish in order to survive.

Chapter 7

Supporting people, supporting learning throughout life

Education and training C20th	Lifelong learning C21st	Action for change
Sparse mass educational support and backup structures brought into service when problems arise	Sophisticated ongoing support structures available to all learners according to needs and demands	Provide a wide range of learning support people from scratch, including learning counsellors, community mentors, psychologists etc and make available to all learners of all ages. Forestall problems before they arise

Figure 7.1 Support systems for lifelong learning

It was suggested in Chapter 6 that, in a world in which learning is required throughout life by everyone, 'the support systems become almost as important as the learning'. It was also proposed in Chapter 4 that, in a self-guided educational world, teachers and lecturers will become learning counsellors, advising on learning pathways and creating and managing the resources that will allow learners to follow them. Further, in Chapter 1, the need for a step increase in learning achievement simply to allow future citizens to deal confidently and intelligently with the complexities of life in the future was regarded as key. In this chapter, those three imperatives come together.

Learning reluctance stems from many sources. Social problems within and around families at risk, educational problems around an inability to cope with the demands of curriculum, teacher or parent, relationship problems related to bullying and lack of self-esteem, health problems entailing long periods away from formal education in early life and psychological problems resulting from mental handicap, lack of care or physical disability, all play their part in switching young and old learners off learning activity. And of course motivational problems result from one or more of the above.

Experienced teachers in kindergarten will be able to detect such symptoms early. They can predict early which children will do well, which ones will paddle along benignly and which ones will be the cause of trouble in later life. And they will be able to detect the causes of the problem. Similarly, experienced lecturers in colleges and universities will be able to see the signs of learning turn-off and loss of motivation.

But detecting and seeing are not enough. The very roots of learning reluctance need to be addressed and the compensatory mechanisms to deal with it put in place with as much urgency as possible. There are economic benefits to be obtained from this course of action as well as social and cultural ones, in that the results of untreated learning reluctance are often paid for in increased crime in later years.

Unfortunately, this is where resources are often at their scarcest, especially at the level of the school. Teachers are rarely trained to identify the causes of cries for help coming from children with special emotional needs, often seeing disruptive behaviour as a challenge to their authority, which in many ways it is. The less mature look at it as a way of ridding themselves of difficult children from the classroom, and there is a tendency to seek to blame the parents, the families, the administration, the social services, the neighbourhood, gang systems, older children. And indeed most problems do come from one or other of these sources.

But blame is not a cure. The special tutors, counsellors, helpers, psychologists, mentors and coaches who could really help such children and their families are in short supply and often remote from the teaching situation. Where a local authority employs such people they tend to be housed in centralized offices far away from the source of the problem and beset by a huge overload of cases from all parts of the municipality.

In recent years there has been, in some countries, a massive increase in the numbers of bored secondary school children playing truant from schools. Often, since they are the ones who suffer from disciplinary problems in the classroom, the schools are content not to have them disrupting lessons for those children who want to learn. But the cost in terms of damage to municipal and private property, damage to the short- and long-term crime figures and, above all, damage to themselves and their future prospects is massive. In an effort to deal with this, some municipalities employ patrols of attendance officers who work with police forces to return large numbers back to the classroom, where they would rather not be.

It is a growing, expensive and extremely difficult dilemma to solve, one of the most complicated of our time, and asks serious questions about modern educational practice, and why children in such large numbers become alienated from it.

Similar problems exist at an older level with students who cannot complete their courses for a variety of personal, psychological and financial reasons, and with young, and old, unemployed adults with an anti-learning culture, often the result of their experiences as truants in school. It creates a cycle of crime, poverty and deprivation that becomes more difficult to break as people get older. Clearly the answer is to treat these problems at root before they have time to fester and grow.

What can be done

Of course governments, local authorities and educational institutions are acutely aware of it, and they employ a range of measures to combat it short of changing the system. So what would a lifelong learning system do about this? The European Commission's policy paper on lifelong learning suggests an answer: 'Guidance Services should promote equal opportunities by being accessible to all citizens, especially those at the risk of exclusion, and tailored to their needs through systems that are coherent, cohesive, transparent, impartial and of high quality', it says, and specifies the following as ways of implementing it:

- accessible guidance services for all;
- adaptable and flexible counselling systems;
- networks of guidance and counselling services across boundaries;
- European partnerships to exchange good practice;
- a European Internet portal on learning opportunities;
- an understanding of underlying guidance principles by teachers and lecturers.

In order to pay for all this, it recommends some of the strategies suggested in other chapters of this book:

1. 'an increase in public and private investment in lifelong learning' – it is interesting to note that private money is included, and that this would be regarded by the donor as an investment;

2. 'a re-channelling of existing resources' – into the places where they will help the most;

3. 'innovative approaches to developing new resources' – for example, from the community and, although not explicitly stated, this would include human resources as well as financial and physical ones;

4. 'integrated local lifelong learning strategies' – a combining of existing resources across departmental boundaries, and an increase in the sort of partnerships between institutions that could render the learning process more meaningful;

5. 'new tasks and roles for teachers and trainers' – teachers as learning counsellors and guides, managing the resources available from all sources;

6. 'fiscal incentives to learn' – vouchers, learning cards, grants, strategies that would take away the financial barriers to learning participation.

Recommendations, however wise, are one thing. Action to implement them is another. The standard way of dealing with children with severe behavioural difficulties is to take them from the system and institutionalize them into a referral unit or remedial school, often far away from their home environment in order to break the causal link. The *Observer* newspaper reports the case of the 14-year-old boy who was plucked from the South London ghetto in which he was a frequent truanting offender, and placed in a fee-paying private school in the rolling hills of Somerset to be transformed in one year into a model high-achieving pupil. The fees were paid for by a local computer company, which is so delighted with the results that it will continue to support the boy until university entrance. But, while such Pygmalion-like solutions may, or may not, indicate that motivation to learn is an environmental phenomenon, they are impractical with the large numbers of disaffected young people in the inner city areas of our urban sprawls. A more practicable, and equitable, solution must be found.

Second-chance schools

The so-called second-chance schools are another way to offer support. Thirteen European cities, including Marseilles, Malmo, Cologne, Leeds and Attika, have joined in a networked European project to widen the horizons of those who either dropped out of school or left it with no qualifications. They come from a variety of backgrounds with a variety of perceptions of the world. In the words of the head of the Cologne school, '80% of the students of the SCS don't have powers of concentration, punctuality, reliability and team ability. They know themselves how much basic skills are necessary to find a job or to go into further education. But they don't have that possibility because their milieus have the same deficits and accept and adopt them as a social norm.'

This is generally true of the students of all the European second-chance schools, and of many others in many other cities. The answer in many cases is to make the learning voluntary but at the same time to use every trick in the book to make it both desirable and attractive. In this way motivation comes from the students themselves. One would find a great deal of education technology as a learning medium in all the schools, in order to counteract the negative value judgements they are used to from human beings. One would also find small classes, more tutor groups, and a staff highly trained to deal with emotionally disturbed and behaviourally challenged youngsters.

They set up partnerships with local employers, and they have a full complement of guidance and counselling staff. They use innovative teaching methods, they interlink to expand horizons and they validate informal and personal skills and competencies. Edward Tersmette reports:

second-chance schools do indeed offer a second chance to young people who are left behind, helping them back towards learning and, with it, social and vocational integration. Almost 4,000 young people who tended to regard schools as places of discontent, adversity, frustration and failure, have persevered and only 6% have dropped out, a very low level of further school failure for a target group of pupils who have already suffered the traumatizing and debilitating experience of abandoning school.

Empowering the learner

Such observations demand the question as to why such methods and techniques are not used in the standard school environment, so that the need for expensive remedial education would be obviated – as indeed they are in the Ontario school system in Canada, where the objective is to involve learners in the development of their own learning programme. A combination of parents, guidance counsellors, teacher/adviser, school administrators and of course the students themselves are responsible for putting together the learning plan for the following term. In this way, each student knows what, why, when, where and how he/she will be studying for weeks in advance, a better motivator than ignorance.

Finland follows a similar path. The OK Learning Centre offers psychopedagogical learning and consulting services for the Olari-Kuitinmäki region of Espoo. Its starting point was an experiment with IT-supported learning launched in 1997 in the Päivänkehrän koulu school. But during 1998–9 a multi-professional cooperation project was initiated, comprising the tao method and learning by cooperating. It was extended into other schools in 1999–2000 in an interdisciplinary network using tools based on the philosophy, psychology and pedagogy inherent in lifelong learning principles.

Teachers work with logopedists, psychologists and others in multi-professional teams to provide the children with a learning environment of high quality, to offer the necessary support and a feeling of security, to support the development of metacognition, to help pupils acknowledge, recognize and choose among factors relevant for their own development. The children themselves are encouraged and given the tools to influence their own learning and their own lives. In addition, the project seeks to provide virtual environments that will increase learning and cooperation between themselves and with children from other localities, locally, nationally and internationally.

This sort of supportive environment requires transparent openness between all the participants, a great deal of energy and dynamism on the part of the teachers and staff, plenty of variety and cooperation, achievable targets and flexible work schedules that will support the pupil's development. Special educational needs are provided where they are required, either from within the schools themselves or from the regional cluster of educational services.

Two-way inter-generational links are made between the schools and other centres in the neighbourhood, including a family centre, a hospital, a regional social centre, the community centre and various day-care centres. Pupils play a full part in the processes. Psycho-pedagogical evaluation, planning and follow-up work are carried out together with research and evaluation of the methods used and their impact. Of course, information and communications technology also plays its part in both the curriculum and the methodology of learning, but it is supplemented by other educational methods, including teamwork, group dynamics and a range of social and cultural activities.

Currently, research is being done on teaching and learning styles in cooperation with a university centre in Jyväskylä with the help of expertise in Learning Style Analysis (LSA) and Teaching Style Analysis (TSA). The stated outcomes are learning children, learning parents, learning teachers, learning support staff and eventually, a learning community. Needless to say, there are very few drop-outs here, or indeed, since the knowledge gained is being used throughout the city, anywhere else in Espoo.

Community mentoring

In the UK, the city of Southampton's learning outreach project is another beacon of support, but at a different level. Its strategy is to develop and train a team of community mentors who will support the learning needs of all people in a neighbourhood. The aim is to raise levels of self-esteem and motivation amongst harder-to-reach learners in the city in order both to encourage them to return to learning and to provide ongoing mentoring support to help them fulfil their potential. Outreach workers come from learning institutions, from other agencies in the city which have day-to-day contact with local people and from volunteers who are keen to encourage and support people in their local community to return to learning.

They are trained and accredited to work at basic, intermediate or advanced level, and work through housing associations, further education colleges, community schools, careers services, the Workers Educational Service, parents associations, employment offices – any organization which can help them to make contact with people and spread the message of learning. They act as a support mechanism, assessing learning needs and opportunities and, most importantly, as mentors to those who most need encouragement to continue in learning. Other neighbourhood support facilities in Southampton are provided from the community centres, which run, for example, programmes for new mothers (the first babies group), parents of young schoolchildren (parents as teachers) and Voices (a project to give disadvantaged people the confidence to negotiate with city offices).

Mentoring, or its alliterative transatlantic equivalent 'study-buddy', is a growing aspect of a lifelong learning society, fed by the massive increase in volunteering and the enlarged participation of non-traditional learners in educational activity. As we saw in Chapter 4, mentoring can take many forms: as a shoulder to lean on in case of difficulty, as a guide through the minefield of educational provision, as a coach in particular subjects, as a counsellor expanding the horizons of what is possible. It doesn't need to be related to educational study. Longworth, in *Making Lifelong Learning Work*, reports on a scheme in Brixton to provide responsible and respected adult mentors for children with behavioural or learning difficulties, and the USA adopt-a-school programme contains many examples of managers and workers mentoring young people in schools in many different ways.

Indeed, North America is the spiritual home of mentoring, and especially tele-mentoring, in universities, research establishments, companies, churches, colleges and schools. Even film and sports stars get themselves involved in supporting single-parent families. *The Scotsman* newspaper reports that the 'big brother and sister' scheme, in which respected mentors spend two to four hours with children at risk, found that children with a mentor were 46 per cent less likely to abuse drugs, 57 per cent less likely to truant and 32 per cent less likely to be violent. The Scottish government is so impressed that it has set up its own national scheme.

Mentoring is not an easy task, nor is it one to be taken lightly. Each organization adopts its own rules and regulations, publishes guidelines and runs courses for potential mentors. And of course there must, unfortunately in today's world, always be safeguards against those who would abuse both the system and the person. But a properly run mentorship programme can mean the difference between success and failure for some thousands of at-risk children.

The US Government Guidelines on mentoring point out that:

> despite the importance of the course-taking decisions students make during the middle grades, in the United States it is common for guidance counsellors at the middle school level to be responsible for more than 500 students. For the most at-risk youth, the presence of an adult mentor can be essential for reinforcing the importance of school, fostering good work habits and study skills, and providing youth with the information they need to make the right choices.

Mentoring programmes should take into account the needs and goals of the mentees, students who will be mentored and their families, the mentors themselves, the schools, and the community in general. The following are some of the questions that should be asked in a school-based mentoring programme, but many are more generally applicable. For example:

- Why do you need mentors? What issues will they address? Is this a good solution for these issues?
- How can mentors best be used? Will they be acceptable to teachers, parents, and members of the community? Which age groups might benefit most from having an adult mentor? How will you assure the safety of the students?

- Who can serve as mentors? What special knowledge and skills should they have? Would they be appropriate for the children who will be in the programme?
- How many mentors are needed? What kind of time commitment can they make each week? Is there a need for a long-term commitment?
- What is the involvement and responsibility of the teachers and the school?
- What training will the mentors require? Who can provide this training? How much will this and the mentoring cost?
- When can mentoring take place? How often, and for how long, will mentors and students meet?
- How will the mentoring take place? Can it be telementoring, face to face or a combination of the two?
- What, if any, support or other materials will the mentors or students need? Will mentors or students need transport?

There is much more to mentoring than can be explained here and potential initiators of such programmes should refer to authoritative sources for examples of how to establish them. For example there is:

- *natural mentoring*, when a sustained relationship develops naturally between a coach, teacher, neighbour, or other adult and a student;
- *planned mentoring*, when a relationship is purposefully created to help a student who may need the wisdom and support of a caring adult;
- *team mentoring*, whereby students can be exposed to several mentors on a regular basis;
- *tripartite mentoring* in which, in addition to the usual adult–student relationship, the mentored student also serves as a mentor to a younger child.

Mentoring can be initiated by a school, a university, a community, a company, a voluntary organization or an adult education college. The Hewlett-Packard company's e-mail mentoring program is one example of the innovative ways in which new technology can be employed to provide help to needy students. Its aims are to improve mathematics and science achievement in secondary-level education, to increase particularly the number of women and minorities in mathematics and science, and to help motivation in children at school. The project creates a 'telementoring relationship' by e-mail. Students and Hewlett-Packard employee mentors collaborate on classroom activities such as science projects and mathematics lessons, under the direction of a supervising classroom teacher. Teachers are an integral part of the project. They submit a lesson plan for the student and mentor to work on together (and on which the student will receive a grade), and supervise the mentor–student interaction.

Mentors communicate with the student at least 2–3 times per week and agree to be a positive role model, using effective communication skills to encourage their students to excel in maths and science. Two thousand nine hundred mentors from 14 countries have helped operate the programme in the United States, Canada,

Australia, and France. Teachers have noted increases in student attendance, better use of technology, more motivation at school, and greater self-confidence.

There are hundreds of possibilities and opportunities for good mentoring programmes in all parts of the educational system. They have a proven track record and the coming years will see a large increase in their number as the lifelong learning philosophy becomes more accepted.

Family learning

Lastly, one of the most powerful support mechanisms is the family itself. A great deal of innovative work is being done to raise its profile as a generator of positive learning attitudes.

The UK Campaign for Learning, for example, is highly active in this field. 'The potential for family learning as a catalyst for changing attitudes to learning and increasing participation for all stages of life is firmly recognized, as is the significant impact it can have both on social inclusion and overcoming disadvantaged backgrounds', says 'Learning to Live', the Campaign's organ, and to follow this up with action it has encouraged the appointment of 'family learning coordinators' across the whole of the UK and stimulated them to use their imaginations to inspire learning in families.

'Family learning week' is supported by the effective use of the media. Newspapers, television and radio all broadcast the concept in special programmes, and celebrities well known to the public play a key part in marketing ideas and actions. Football clubs, museums, galleries and libraries also participate. In 2001 more than half a million people took part in activities ranging from helping garden birds and family singing and dancing to puppet-making and family story-telling and writing.

At the Arsenal football club, a much sought-after venue for many, children were given the chance to teach the skills of computing and the Internet to dads, mums, aunts and uncles, followed by a guided tour, five-a-side football and a picnic in the stands. By contrast, the Corinium Museum in Cirencester persuaded families to create a Roman newspaper. Such activities are not only educational, they provide the support that learners need and a means to celebrate it.

A final innovative example of learning support based upon the family comes from the UK. In 2001 the large electrical supplies company, Comet, offered its employee fathers one paid hour off work which they should spend in pursuing educational activities with their 11–14-year-old sons. This is in support of the Department of Education and Skills 'Dads and Sons – Give an hour' project, supported by a hints and tips booklet, providing advice and ideas for fathers on how they can get more involved with their sons' education, and suggesting joint learning activities and competitions to enter together. According to the Minister, Stephen Twigg, 'Dads often have a unique bond with their sons, and can make a real difference to what they achieve at school. Research shows that three-quarters of dads want to be more involved in their sons' learning, but almost two-thirds say that work commitments are a barrier to them spending time with them.' Although it is difficult to imagine how the scheme would work in practice, it is at least an acknowledgement by government that modern learning demands the support mechanisms which all parts of the community can provide.

Summary

What this chapter has suggested is that, while formal support, guidance and counselling mechanisms are in short supply in many places, there are many informal sources of support which can perform an equally valuable task in rescuing at-risk learners from the consequences of their actions. But it is not just at-risk learners who can benefit from these initiatives. Every learner needs support from time to time, and adult education, universities, and industry education establishments are now in the process of recognizing this.

The idea of coaches, guides and mentors, used for learning in such companies as Rover, Ford, Motorola and a plethora of companies that call themselves learning organizations, is now expanding into the community as a whole. It demonstrates the holistic nature of lifelong learning, extending beyond the boundaries of education organizations and departments and involving social services, police, the community, financial experts and down into the family. Learning support is no longer a matter of providing backup services for difficult children. It is a whole-community responsibility providing a network of interacting people for everyone in the community – social confrontation replaced by social interaction.

Chapter 8

Assessment in a lifelong learning world – taking failure out of the system

Education and training C20th	Lifelong learning C21st	Action for change
Examinations used to separate successes from failures irrespective of circumstance	Examinations as failure-free personal learning opportunities confirming progress and encouraging further learning	Influence development of innovative assessment tools embedded into personal learning curricula and examined when the student feels ready, not when convenient

Figure 8.1 Failure-free learning

Written on an obscure wall of an august university in the USA were the words 'Please don't give me any more information, I already know what I think!' It is a reflection of the information overload many of us suffer from and the difficulties of assimilating new inputs that would cause us to reflect on the assumptions we have made in the past. In another sense it is also a reflection of the conservative malaise which the assessment industry, the end process of the educational cycle, inculcates into our consciousness. It doesn't have to be like that. Good teachers and lecturers give encouragement – they inspire, they cajole, they stimulate, they lead, they offer enlightenment. That is their function in life and the objective of all this activity is to produce an expansion in the knowledge, capability and understanding of the learner within a particular subject or skill.

The student is required to prove that new knowledge and/or behaviour has been absorbed and, unfortunately, the way in which this is normally done is through the mechanism of an examination at the end of the course. Occasionally, more enlightened continuous assessment regimes dominate, in which the student proves capability in a more gradual manner during the period of education, but the higher the level in the system, the more it seems incumbent upon the student to swot up and remember vast tracts of information and knowledge in a very short period of time after the education has been delivered, including that which was taught some nine months previously.

The objective here is to weed out those without the necessary memory skills, and those who, for whatever reason – sickness on the day, inability to write legibly, emotional stress, laziness, under/overconfidence – cannot achieve the level required. In other words, failure is embedded into the system in order to celebrate success – it is one of education's paradoxes at work.

Few people would dispute the need to adopt and maintain standards. No one would want to be treated by a doctor who has failed to grasp the elementary principles of medicine, and few passengers would want to cross a railway bridge designed by an engineer who does not understand the principles of materials stress. Examinations are one of the few ways of obtaining the proof of competency. But there is also an uncomfortable feeling in many circles that mass examination systems of this kind are both ineffective and wasteful of talent, especially in the lower reaches of the education industry.

Bryce, from the Australian Council for Educational Research, identifies school certification as one of the major barriers militating against schools becoming lifelong learning communities. She says:

> The influence of year 11 and 12 certification is not entirely bad, but in many cases it encourages a competitive, more superficial approach to learning, What can I do well in?, How much do I have to know? rather than 'What do I need to learn? and Where do I go from here? … it moves the ownership of learning away from the individual and classifies some people as 'failures', which is one of the strongest deterrents to learning.

Lifelong learning concepts are changing the way we see assessment and accreditation. Perhaps surprisingly, the new thinking comes from industry. In 1996, the European Round Table of Industrialists published five essential ingredients of a learning society, shown in Figure 8.2.

The third and fourth of these are particularly interesting, coming, as they do, from such an august body of industrialists, representing the 42 largest companies in Europe. But it is not so extraordinary when one considers how few students fail in training courses conducted by industry. The volume of such courses is not insubstantial. In *The Corporate Classroom*, written in 1985, Nell Eurich pointed out that: 'USA industry spends 40 to 80 billion dollars per year on Continuing Education, comparable to all the funds available to public and private universities together'. That figure will have at least doubled in the intervening years, and it is unlikely that the possibility of failure will be deliberately built into such a heavy investment. On the contrary, there is a presumption of success for all.

Ten characteristics of a learning society
A Learning Society would be one in which ...
1. Learning is accepted as a continuing activity throughout life
2. Learners take responsibility for their own progress
3. Assessment confirms progress rather than brands failure
4. Capability, personal and shared values, and team working are recognized equally with the pursuit of knowledge
5. Learning is a partnership between students, parents, teachers, employers and the community, who all work together to improve performance

Figure 8.2 Five indicators of a learning society (Source: ERT/CRE)

New thinking on intelligence and how people learn

Much of this is based on new knowledge about how people learn. Brain-based research indicates that the ability to learn is significantly influenced by the way in which people cope with emotions, the nature of the learning environment and by teaching the skills of thinking. Hence industry classrooms are designed to take this into account. Equally, the research of Howard Gardner on multiple intelligences should have an influence both on the way we teach and the way we evaluate. His eight intelligences are:

- Verbal/linguistic – words, listening, speaking, dialogue;
- Visual/spatial – images, drawings, puzzles, visualization;
- Logical/mathematical – reasoning, facts, sequencing, ranking, patterning;
- Musical/rhythmic – melody, beat, classical, singing, playing;
- Bodily/kinaesthetic – activity, running, jumping, touching, feeling, performing;
- Interpersonal – interacting, communicating, charisma, socializing, empathizing;
- Intra-personal – environmental awareness, observing;
- Naturalist – flora and fauna recognition, the natural world.

He agonized long over a ninth – spiritual intelligence – but rejected it. However, most observers and researchers tend to include this in their own list of human intelligences, just as they also include Goleman's concepts of emotional intelligence, that is, one's ability to understand one's own emotions, to empathize with others and to behave appropriately.

Zohar and Marshall define Spiritual Intelligence as 'the capacity to make meaning – the soul's intelligence. It is linked to the capacity to see lives in wholes, not fragments, and to regenerate ourselves. It is connected to the ability to challenge whether we want to play by the rules of the situation in which we find ourselves. A person with a well-developed Spiritual Quotient may not make a business decision on financial grounds alone, preferring ethics.' SQ emphasizes the search for meaning, vision and value as the most important aspect of being human. It awakens the sleeping talent in students and workers and makes them much more productive. New techniques of learning, such as accelerated learning, owe much to the application of all these intelligences, which should be required knowledge for both teachers and examiners and indeed anyone in a profession which purports to concern itself with the business of learning. They provoke the need for a radical re-examination of what exactly it is that they should be measuring and the sort of education that should be provided.

Student-oriented evaluation

Public bodies, from schools to higher education, can learn much from the approaches adopted by industry. A first step would be the development of more flexible student-oriented examination strategies, having as their principal rationale an increase, rather than a decrease, in the confidence and performance of the learner. Inappropriately administered examinations are one of the prime causes of alienation at secondary level and more acceptable alternatives must be found which, at the same time, raise motivation and standards. Present systems switch huge populations off learning for the rest of their lives.

At this level, it is often governments and universities that have control over the development of the qualifications system and it is they who control the design of the examination hoops. If they value standards, they should, logically, do all they can to improve the standards they are trying to measure through more flexible assessment strategies. Much more research and development are needed into the design of non-threatening examination systems following a human development model, whose purpose is not to pass or fail, but to give information and stimulus to the student and the teacher. Lifelong learning demands a system in which everybody, or as many as possible, can win.

Taking failure out of the system

What needs to be taken out of the system is the possibility, and the fear, of personal failure. Late development, immaturity, handicap, inadequacy, lack of motivation, periodic sickness, preferred learning styles and social deprivation are all well-known facts of modern life affecting performance in examinations, and to transform such human failings into social failure is to negate the whole purpose of education. What people need is support and treatment to improve self-esteem and encouragement into the learning fold. The concept of failure has no place in a lifelong learning climate, where the objective is to switch people into, not off, continuous learning.

Again this flies in the face of accepted practice, though not accepted wisdom. In much of the developed world, the trend is towards more testing, more diagnosis. And no matter how much educational diagnosticians protest that this is not a threatening or stressful activity, but merely a tool in order to find a cure for the non-learning sickness, tradition and the reaction of examiners, the examined and the public at large say otherwise. Parents, teachers, governors, administrators, councils, local and national governments all focus their worry on the results of the tests, and of course this anxiety is passed on to the child in a hundred stressful ways.

The remedies for this are contained in many places in this book – the skills-based curriculum, curriculum-embedded testing within an educational technology framework, active involvement in school and community, personal learning plans, more support structures and, above all, an acknowledgement that each individual is travelling on his/her own personal learning journey at different speeds, from different starting points and with different destinations.

In such a world there could even be more testing than at present, but it would be delivered as a personal stock-taking exercise to explore how far up one of the many particular learning curves one is. David Hargreaves, former chief executive of the UK Qualifications and Curriculum Authority, comes part-way towards this view. In his eyes the transformation from formative assessment to what he calls 'assessment for learning' as an inherent component of the acquisition of knowledge is a key driver of the convergence between curriculum, assessment and pedagogy.

From such a powerful body this is a breakthrough, but it is still a teacher-knows-best position to take. Examinations and tests as continuous learning opportunities have great merit, but it is how the learner copes with the results of this process that is important. If he/she is given ownership of the assessment process and sees the result as a further opportunity to continue learning, where the only competitor is the learner him/herself, then we have the beginnings of a mature view of the true purpose of assessment.

Wider assessment

An idealistic nirvana maybe, and certainly one that would take many years to bring itself into the consciousness of a society conditioned to seek failure, competition and blame. But people change and cultures change. Until 20 years ago, the beating of children was allowed in British schools, and while a few backwoodsmen still lament its departure, most responsible citizens now recognize the link between such gratuitous violence and the continuing antisocial behaviour carried from childhood into adult life. Ontario schools at least widen the range of skills to be tested from the sterile memorization exercises utilized by many national examination boards. Their techniques put a little fun into the process through assignments, demonstrations, quizzes, performances and projects, as well as tests and examinations.

They use both formative and summative evaluation techniques. Each student has an achievement chart denoting four categories of knowledge and skills – knowledge/understanding, thinking/inquiry, communication, application/ making connections – so that at least the students know what is being aimed for and that their learning is related to the skills they will need to adopt in later life.

Certainly it would be a big step to take for governments in weaning people from a standards-dominated outlook, but there are some signs of activity, perhaps strangely from Japan, which has a reputation for giving accreditation an almost religious status. According to Okamoto, the national education authorities of Japan promoted lifelong learning nationally and locally in the 1980s with a view to 'overcoming the diploma-oriented society'. He suggests that the impetus for this comes from the employers who look beyond diplomas for the type of person they would employ, usually for life, and, in any case, had installed well-constructed schemes of in-house continuous education. And this is true in other countries where particularly the multinational industries look far more at personality traits and participation in non-academic activities when choosing their recruits.

The examination industry barrier

The idea that the learner should have some control over what is learnt is given some credibility by the European Commission in its memorandum on lifelong learning: 'Everyone should be able to follow open learning pathways of their own choice,' it says, 'rather than being obliged to follow predetermined routes to specific destinations. This means, quite simply, that education and training systems should adapt to individual needs and demands rather than the other way round.'

It is a challenging ideal with messages for the conduct of assessment, as well as education and training, systems. But here again, in many countries we are facing a huge examinations infrastructure – the bac, GCSE, abiturs, SATs – with a vested interest in maintaining the status quo, and education systems obsessed with intellectual standards and competitive endeavour – and of course inserting failure so that some may be said to succeed. They contribute very little to the overall competence, peace of mind or serenity of individuals in a learning society. Indeed, in many ways they work against its development in a world which needs it more than ever.

Even where the number of examination passes increases year on year, as it has in the UK (up to 93 per cent in 2002 ordinary-level examinations), governments, examination boards and schools are pilloried for 'dumbing down standards' by sections of the press obsessed with making sure that a goodly number of failures hit the unemployment registers. This in its turn puts stresses on the examination boards to re-grade success so that it is transformed into more failure, a bizarre action for a body concerned with improving standards of learning.

Such structures perpetuate the pretence that knowledge exists in separate compartments, as if there were no relationship between physics, chemistry, language and literature, art and biology, and in so doing, encourage a similar compartmentalization of the mind. Children, and adults, are frequently heard to say 'I don't like French, or geography, or history' because the system has taught them that these subjects exist in isolation from each other. It is tantamount to saying 'I don't like knowledge', which is an equally ridiculous statement to make, since if knowledge is power, the originator is relinquishing control over him/herself.

Back in 1959, towards the end of his prolific life, Aldous Huxley lamented this situation in 'the human condition'. 'What we need to do,' he said, 'is to arrange marriages, or rather to bring back into their originally married state, the different departments of knowledge and feeling which have been arbitrarily separated and made to live in their own monastic cells in isolation.'

Towards a new assessment system

The examinations industry has become so huge that it can no longer cope adequately and fairly with the sheer volume of papers it is being required to assess. This is true at all levels, whether it is in the schools, the adult education colleges or the universities. Year after year there are complaints and scandals because of this, and the tragedy of it all is that it is human lives and individual futures that are being affected. In the UK, disaffection with the results of public examinations is now at an all-time high. Despite their protestations, examination boards cannot cope, and a basic overhaul of the central tenets of the entire system is long overdue.

Surely it is not beyond the wit of governments and universities to devise an assessment system which is also an integral part of the teaching process – the encouragement process with which we started this chapter. A system which does not pass and fail, but whose whole purpose is simply to give information and stimulus to the student, and the teacher, that learning has or has not taken place. Or that it has only partly taken place and needs more attention, without pejorative value judgements and demeaning comparisons with others. This would be a human potential development model – as opposed to the 'look how clever I am and how thick you are' model which we have adopted over the centuries.

Community education in Southampton subscribes to these ideals. The Southampton City Lifelong Learning Strategy, agreed in March 2002, suggests the following approaches for its community outreach programmes:

- Learners take responsibility for their own learning, and engage on a voluntary basis.
- Learning is student-centred and the curriculum is negotiated between learners and providers/tutors.
- Learning is a group process and is participative. The experience of group members is valued within the curriculum.
- Learning occurs in places and under conditions which aim to maximize access/reduce barriers to learning. Particular attention is given to reducing barriers due to level of income, cultural difference, social class, language, previous educational experience, care/childcare responsibilities and inappropriate buildings.
- There is a concern for values and change. This includes the promotion of equality of opportunity and celebration of cultural difference.
- Community education challenges poverty and seeks to work with those with the greatest need, including learners with special educational needs.

Would that more academic systems understood the message that this gives.

Chapter 9

Skills, values, attitudes and knowledge in the curriculum

Education and training C20th	Lifelong learning C21st	Action for change
Knowledge and information based – *what* to think	Understanding, skills and values based – *how* to think	Develop personal skills- and values-based curricula that expand the capacity of people to enjoy and benefit from learning throughout life

Figure 9.1 The skills-based curriculum

An old educational graffitum says, 'If you learn one useless thing a day, in a whole year you could learn 365 useless things.' Much has been made in this book of the transition from information to skills in a lifelong learning society. We have said that, while the development of memory skills is important in educational development, the regurgitation of memorized information is no substitute for understanding, insight and knowledge – nor is it a reliable indicator of intelligence. The learning ladder, shown in Figure 0.1, demonstrates how information and knowledge *per se* are no longer sufficient to sustain the individual in a learning society, and how understanding and insight are levels at which learning systems should aim.

That is, 'what to think' is superseded by 'how to think'. If the focus is now on the needs and demands of the learner, then the old method of imposing large quantities of information onto people and hoping that some of it sticks becomes obsolete. Naisbitt and Aburdine are of the opinion that 'too many young people, brimming with creativity, are run through a system that recognizes and deals with only the linear, logical and rational side of human and social reality'. And they are right. Creativity, imagination, vision and insight have been too long absent from the curriculum of our education organizations, mainly because they are not easily examinable, and partly because they encourage a questioning of accepted wisdom and authority – in the more authoritarian cultures a difficult concept to cope with.

However, such attitudes cannot survive in a society dominated by change and knowledge explosion. The new emphasis is on the acquisition of a completely different set of skills and attributes – high-order skills of information handling, problem solving, thinking, teamwork, communicating and many others shown in Figure 9.2.

As we have seen, too, the 21st century will require people to make value judgements on a host of scientific, technological, environmental and financial topics, from bio-babies to single currencies. The curriculum of all educational organizations should therefore be focused upon developing insight and intuition, self-esteem and self-knowledge, and individuals who can judge critically what is acceptable and what is not, differentiate between what is quality and what is not, from the evidence put before them.

And all of this within a holistic framework and an unselfish system of values and ethics which treats all human beings equally, recognizes man's obligations as a steward of the planet and understands the rights and bases of other creeds, cultures, races and peoples. This is a tall order, and it won't be implemented under the present education and training paradigm.

Who should lead us into this brave new world? Undoubtedly, teachers and lecturers have a key role as guardians and deliverers of the message. That they do not in general do so at present can be attributed to a multitude of reasons, some of which have been enumerated in other chapters – government control of the curriculum, inadequate teacher training, resistance from society and parents, lack of leadership, a media which, in the words of Longworth and Davies, 'is being used, in ever more influential ways, to inform, distort, inspire, trivialize, challenge, deceive, stimulate, mislead, somnambulize, or make us ever more intelligent, bitter, complacent, enlivened, depressed, active, passive.'

But this is too pat an answer. Many educators are the front line in the struggle against the cynicism, ignorance and indifference they encounter in modern society. But the opposition is too strong for even the most heroic efforts of a profession long accustomed to dealing with failure. Teachers are but one change agent in the continuing development of human potential, albeit a crucial one. National and international governments, industry, communities, NGOs and visionary individuals will determine and implement the new pathways to effective learning in a learning society.

Core skills and competencies for personal survival in the Lifelong Learning Age	
Self-management skills	❖ Being determined to fulfil personal potential ❖ Continuously developing personal skills and confidence ❖ Setting and achieving realistic personal targets ❖ Purposeful introspection ❖ Maintaining perspective and a sense of humour
Handling and interpreting information	❑ Using information technology tools and techniques ❑ Collecting, storing, analyzing and combining information ❑ Recognizing patterns and links
Applying new knowledge into practice	• Seeing the connection between theory and practice • Transforming knowledge into action
Learning to learn	➢ Staying open to new knowledge and new learning techniques ➢ Identifying and using sources of knowledge ➢ Relating learning to personal objectives
Questioning, reasoning and critical judgement	✓ Knowing the difference between good, bad and indifferent ✓ Continually wanting to improve procedures, processes and situations ✓ Never being satisfied with the status quo
Management and communication skills	■ Expressing oneself clearly orally and verbally in formal and informal situations ■ Persuading others ■ Listening to others ■ Helping others to help themselves
Thinking skills and creativity	• Using creativity and imagination to solve problems • Thinking 'out of the box' • Anticipating situations and developing forward vision
Adaptability, flexibility and versatility	✓ Facing change with confidence ✓ Adapting to new situations and tasks ✓ Being ready to change personal direction
Teamwork	➢ Sharing information and knowledge ➢ Receiving information and knowledge ➢ Participating in goal-setting ➢ Achieving common goals
Lifelong learning	■ Continuously upgrading personal skills and competence ■ Cherishing the habit of learning ■ Contributing to the learning of others

Figure 9.2 Skills for a lifelong learning age

Skills and industry

We can learn from industry. In 1995, the European Round Table of industrialists (ERT) reasoned that European industry must embrace concepts of lifelong learning in order to adjust its workforce to the new realities of competitiveness in world markets. The thinking, high-order skills and flexibility of people at work, it argued, are exactly those attributes which should be developed from an early age in schools, and later at college and university. It proposed a seamless process of individual progress throughout life, from pre-school education to adult and leisure education in retirement. The issue, it contends, is not just about employment, or even employability – it is about effective socialization, creating thinking and contributing citizens, and developing life skills as well as technical capability. Five years later the European Commission's memorandum on lifelong learning proposed something similar: 'Most of what our education and training systems offer is still organized and taught as if the traditional ways of planning and organizing one's life had not changed for at least half a century. Learning systems must adapt to the changing ways in which people live and learn their lives today.'

And again: 'Learning how to learn, to adapt to change and to make sense of vast information flows are now generic skills that everyone should acquire. Employers are increasingly demanding the ability to learn and acquire new skills rapidly and to adapt to new challenges and situations.'

Note that the emphasis has subtly shifted from subject knowledge to skills, and not only to the skills of the teachers. As we have suggested, educational organizations are in business to prepare their students for the world of the future, not of the past, and to define the skills they will need in a very different world requires creativity and imagination, and the ability to think outside the box. Those listed in Figure 9.2 highlight how the old skills based on memory and manual competence are being replaced by knowledge and brain skills requiring mental dexterity and problem-solving capacity.

But we can all make lists of skills, values and attributes. One difficulty is how to instil them into the mind. And here again we can learn from industry. As Longworth and Davies point out:

> There are hundreds of examples of initiatives and techniques which have been used in industrial training courses to enhance learning capacity. Relaxation and learning techniques, T'ai Chi, visualization, meditation, brain-storming, creativity stimulation through music, right brain exercises, transactional analysis, imagineering – all of them proven techniques for stimulating the mind, increasing creativity, improving study skills and memory, enhancing performance.

All of them used successfully in industry and business and very few of them used in the educational mainstream, for wholly understandable reasons.

Persuading the stakeholders

The learning requirements of the 21st century have now changed. It is no longer enough to change the syllabus to a skills-based system and then implement it. A newly empowered constituency of parents and others in the community will demand to know the reason for such changes – how they work, how they are relevant to both the community and the world of work and why they have to be made. In most instances the current problem is confined to explaining the examination system, how the curriculum is designed to accommodate their peculiarities and how their students are being prepared to jump, or not to jump, over the hurdles set in front of them.

The task is to create a more discerning audience which will also demand relevance to future life, longer-term skills and competency development and an attractive learning, rather than teaching, environment. Having achieved that, the next task is to develop proactive strategies to involve children in understanding the information they receive and, as we have said, to give them some ownership of the process of turning it into knowledge and understanding.

Learning how to think

This is not just a matter of rewriting new curricula. The move to individualized, self-directed learning and the use of ICT will dictate the importance of the 'how to think' methodology. Giving students the responsibility for their own learning will require them to be much more analytical and creative at the same time. They have co-responsibility with teachers and others for their own learning. Although they may learn at different rates and use varying amounts of time to achieve learning outcomes, how to learn becomes the constant in all e-learning situations. The European Foundation for Management Development has great hopes for this: 'E-learning means new and better opportunities to learn with less space or time limitations. It means the possibility for people to be able to learn what they want in the way they feel most comfortable. It means more people having access to knowledge, more people being able to educate themselves.'

Would that it were so simple, but there is some light on the horizon. In the UK the Education Ministry is now called the Department for Education and Skills, presumably because the British government recognizes the importance of skills in the curriculum. It has encouraged the development of more than 100 Learning and Skills partnerships in the cities and regions. It promotes the development of 'core skills' in the curriculum of schools, though, sadly, these bear little resemblance to those shown in Figure 9.2.

There is even a Learning and Skills Council, doing excellent work in turning the curriculum gradually around in adult education. But little work is being done on the training of teachers to transform their methodologies from teaching 'what to think, remember and recall' to teaching 'how to think, remember and recall – and how to develop the many other skills and values required for a changing world'.

Other governments are aware of this need. 'The curriculum delivered in schools must cater for the diverse needs of schools and communities in the

Northern Territory. It should acknowledge and provide for local responses to the social, cultural and technological changes that challenge us daily. Schools need to provide conditions for learners to build resilience to assist them in adapting to the growing complexity of changing families, communities and cultures', says the Northern Territory's curriculum recommendation, recognizing the need for adaptability and flexibility in order to cope with change.

The European Commission's definition of lifelong learning is: 'All Learning Activity undertaken throughout life, with the aim of improving knowledge skills and competencies within a personal, civic, social and/or employment related perspective', putting skills and competencies on an equal footing with knowledge. Espoo good practices aver that 'Schools are open learning centres in which knowledge, innovation and learning by doing lead to skills and competencies. Projects and learning activities are carried out in cooperation with the different organizations of the city.'

Developing critical skills

The report from the UK Advisory Group on citizenship headed by Sir Bernard Crick emphasizes the point. It speaks of values and responsibilities as well as skills and competencies. Social and moral responsibility, community involvement and political literacy are, in its opinion, 'what every child should have more than a glimmer about' on leaving primary school. Further, it recommends that children should learn such things by being themselves active citizens, much in the same way that service education, described in Chapter 10, involves its students in solving community problems as part of their curriculum. All students, children and adults, should take part in the political processes, by experiencing democracy at work in the classroom and the school through class representatives and committees. 'Rights are balanced by responsibilities', it says. Children should be taught to become 'active citizens', and to play a full and energetic part in local democracy.

Of course, this is at the heart of lifelong learning. Indeed, in many countries it presents no surprises. Classroom democracy is a commonplace in Finland, and in many parts of Europe, Australia and Canada. Children exercise their democratic right to say what they think about their school, its teachers, the curriculum and the system within which they are being educated. In some countries it may be seen as a blueprint for anarchy. It is certainly subversive in the wholly positive way that education generally, and lifelong learning particularly, is subversive. Used responsibly, it encourages the sort of critical thinking and questioning of authority so important to the exercise of democracy in a world of change. It produces rounded human beings with a knowledge of who they are and a detached and mature sense of self-esteem, able to see through the rhetoric and the inventions, and to weigh values, possibilities, probabilities and desirabilities.

And this is not just a schools-based argument. The Standing Conference of Rectors, Vice-Chancellors and Principles of European Universities (CRE) wrote in 'Moving Towards a Learning Society': 'Tertiary Education seeks to awaken the critical multi-disciplinary minds, able to gain a thorough understanding not of a particular mass of knowledge, but rather the process of production of knowledge. Therefore it has to learn how to learn rather than how to teach.'

Of course, colleges and universities would suggest that this is what they already do. The development of a critical mind has always been the purpose of a higher education. Unfortunately, too few of the population ever get there, and for those who do, many of them receive, as at Dotheboys Hall in Dickens' *Hard Times*, a utilitarian education based on Mr Gradgrind's version of the facts. Perhaps it would help if we were able to define a model, let's call him/her the superlearner, as shown in Figure 9.3.

Superlearners – qualitative learning		
We all learn all of the time. But the quality of learning, and the way it is applied in the outside world, is what makes the difference between the learner and the **superlearner**		
L	Listen	They take heed of those who can extend their knowledge and skills and listen to their own inner voice which says 'develop your potential'
E	Evolve	They climb the learning ladder which leads from ignorance to knowledge and eventually to understanding and wisdom
A	Adapt	They modify their thinking, their behaviour and their mindset to cope easily with the changing world in which they live
R	Reciprocate	They recognize their own creative power to change their world through learning and participation in the community in which they live.
N	Network	They look outwards to the world and gather strength by sharing their learning and its results with others in the wider international community
E	Enjoy	They enliven their own learning and that of others through their enthusiasm and their determination to make learning fun
R	Reflect	They learn from the past, make sense of the present and contemplate the future through learning
S	Support	They stimulate others and act as empathetic mentors and guides in their voyage of self-discovery through learning

Figure 9.3 Superlearners

The skills required to be a superlearner might be likened to the characteristics of the learning organization shown in Figure 2.2. In this case the learner him/herself becomes the learning organization, flexible enough to adapt to the changing needs of society but also constantly adding to a core of personal skills which allow that transition to be smooth and non-stressful. But none of this will happen in the next days, weeks or months. A learning individual within a learning organization within a learning society is perhaps the ideal towards which we are aiming over the next 50 years. Chapter 18 expands the skills-based curriculum concept and describes how it would work in a school environment.

Chapter 10

Active citizenship – celebrating the learning condition

Education and training C20th	Lifelong learning C21st	Action for change
Learning as a difficult chore and as received wisdom	Learning as fun, participative and involving, and as perceived wisdom	Celebrate learning frequently and encourage active citizenship by individuals, families, organizations and communities

Figure 10.1 Encouraging active citizenship

Many years ago, the Spanish philosopher, Jose Ortega y Gasset, described the four stages of the human cycle. The first stage, he said, is the 'Age of God'. The important buildings are the churches, and the travellers on the road are pilgrims. Their purpose is to find out how we fit into the scheme of things. The second stage is the 'Age of Culture'. The important buildings are the art galleries, universities, museums, etc and the travellers on the road are artisans and troubadours. The purpose is to find out who and why we are. The third stage is the 'Age of Power'. The important buildings are the banks and commercial enterprises, and the travellers on the road are business barons and politicians. Their purpose is to control and build possessions. The fourth stage is the 'Age of Dissolution', the collapse of the structure leading to rebirth.

There is an argument to rename the fourth of these cycles as the 'Age of Lifelong Learning', since if Ortega is correct, it becomes a fundamental requirement of the rebirth process. But, rather than a circular story, the fourth might also be a way of reconciling all of the first three into a single all-embracing and holistic philosophy for the future. Whatever form this takes, the importance of community and of individuals is paramount. It envisages an active participation in the rebuilding of society much in the same way that, 2,000 years ago, Plato envisaged 'Dia Viou Paedaeia' as the obligation of every citizen to take up learning for the ultimate good of the city and community.

Learning and the city

Dr Riccardo Petrella, professor at the Catholic University of Louvain, Belgium, and President of the European University of the Environment, identified three 'urban realities' that prevent people moving from an adaptive culture (one that merely adapts to constraints such as new technologies, global financial markets, etc) to a sustainable culture (one which encourages contribution and participation). These were:

- They don't exist as full 'participant citizens'. They are excluded. At least, they feel excluded.
- They don't live together with the other components of the community. They do not believe that they belong to an urban community. They don't feel as if they share basic common goods and a common destiny. Social, economic, cultural fragmentations and separations within the city have increased in the past 20 years, despite the 'explosion' of information and transportation systems. Belonging is still to be constructed.
- They don't work together to define and implement common goals for the urban community. Each active group of citizens is fighting to achieve its own specific goal. Co-operation remains a difficult process.

In his report three solutions were offered:

1. An alliance with children. What children perceive of a city is primarily synonymous with violence, threat, danger. The alliance would be a compact between adult generations and all children to reconstruct the city over a period of 20–30 years.

2. Back to learning. There will not be any significant move toward effective co-construction of a sustainable city in the absence of a massive process of learning about cities, cities' issues, developments and prospects, and contributions that each citizen can make to the co-construction. Therefore in each city, special initiatives should be taken on a voluntary basis, with the support of mass media and local representative and participatory institutions.

3. Citizens are able to 'say good morning to the other': Citizens must be able to recognize and respect the existence of other citizens, in particular those who are different from us, and to be ready to promote the coexistence and the

cooperation of others. Learning to 'say good morning to the other' is the most important socio-political, cultural, and practical 'urban imperative'.

Dr Petrella is not immersed in the world of education. He is an environmentalist. Ortega was a philosopher. But their messages have the resonance of lifelong learning. Indeed, we could examine similar quotations from clear-minded industrialists, visionary politicians, enlightened financiers and others who are verifying the essential wholeness of lifelong learning and the importance of contribution.

Contributing to a learning community

Active contribution is undoubtedly a key indicator of lifelong learning. Otherwise all the measures and recommendations have no outward-looking purpose. 'Lifelong learning concerns everyone's future, in a uniquely individual way. The debate should take place as close as possible to citizens themselves', says the European Commission in its memorandum on lifelong learning. And again, as its second lifelong learning principle, 'to encourage and equip people to participate more actively in all spheres of modern public life, especially in social and political life at all levels of the community…'

The Commission is even prepared to put money where its mouth is by supporting projects under its R3L programme for 'Promoting active involvement in local governance, raising awareness of individual rights and duties as members of society, encouraging social solidarity and inter-generational learning in the local community, harnessing the experience of senior citizens for lifelong learning, protecting the local environment or cultural heritage as a dimension of lifelong learning, etc'. Such a powerful endorsement emphasizes the two-way nature of lifelong learning. It is both for the individual and by the individual.

The UK Secretary of State for Education and Employment, David Blunkett, wrote in 1998 that: 'Learning enables people to play a full part in their community and strengthens the family, the neighbourhood and consequently the nation. It helps us fulfil our potential and opens doors to a love of music, art, and literature. The Learning Age will be built on a renewed commitment to self-improvement and a recognition of the enormous contribution learning makes to our society.'

This of course became the foundation for the UK White Paper on Lifelong Learning, which, although hi-jacked by an adult and employment-focused agenda, was the most forward-looking document to come from a UK Ministry since the Newsom report of 1966. But there is little in this document to encourage the good burghers of Newcastle or Scunthorpe or Hull to take control, not only of their own learning, but of their active lives in the community. Instead, there are a whole host of initiatives taking place in every town, city and region to mobilize people as volunteers.

Volunteering in the community

Since 2001 was declared the international year of the volunteer, volunteering has grown apace in many nations, cities and towns. The Universal Declaration on Volunteering, proposed by the IAVE (The International Association for Volunteer Effort), begins thus:

> Volunteering is a fundamental building block of civil society. It brings to life the noblest aspirations of humankind – the pursuit of peace, freedom, opportunity, safety, and justice for all people. In this era of globalization and continuous change, the world is becoming smaller, more interdependent, and more complex. Volunteering – either through individual or group action – is a way in which:
>
> - human values of community, caring, and serving can be sustained and strengthened;
> - individuals can exercise their rights and responsibilities as members of communities, while learning and growing throughout their lives, realizing their full human potential; and
> - connections can be made across differences that push us apart so that we can live together in healthy, sustainable communities, working together to provide innovative solutions to our shared challenges and to shape our collective destinies.
>
> At the dawn of the new millennium, volunteering is an essential element of all societies. It turns into practical, effective action the declaration of the United Nations that 'We, the Peoples' have the power to change the world.

Noble sentiments indeed and fully in accord with the principles of active citizenship within a lifelong learning society. It supports the right of every woman, man and child to associate freely and to volunteer regardless of their cultural and ethnic origin, religion, age, gender, and physical, social or economic condition. All people in the world should have the right to freely offer their time, talent and energy to others and to their communities through individual and collective action, without expectation of financial reward.

Australia is fast becoming the volunteering capital of the world. Take the following description of the parade in Brisbane to celebrate the year of the volunteer. It was without doubt the biggest and most impressive showcase of volunteer effort this state has seen. Stretching over a six-kilometre route from Kurilpa Point to the City Botanic Gardens, it took the 6,000 participants in the parade one and half hours to pass through city streets. With everything from mounted police to fire trucks, belly dancers and performers on stilts, dogs and balloons along with bands of all kinds, it had all the colour and sound of one of the city's major public events. There were groups from a huge range of sectors: from the arts, heritage, sport, emergency services, aged care, child and youth care, environmental, health, disability, education, multicultural, social justice, advocacy and community welfare:

The primary goals for the Brisbane launch were met with amazing success. The Volunteers Parade & Festival allowed us to:

- showcase the strength and diversity of volunteering,
- recognize the huge contributions of volunteers across all sectors, and
- bring the community together to celebrate those involved in volunteering.

Media coverage was comprehensive with many radio stations running announcements and Channel 9 running a peak time community announcement in the lead up to the event. Channel 7, Channel 9, Channel 10, ABC and SBS covered the event in their main evening news bulletins.

The Brisbane launch of the International Year of Volunteers 2001 was a truly exciting occasion! Thanks to everyone who volunteered, organized, performed, marched, photographed, promoted, assembled and partied on Sunday 3 December.

Once started, such movements have the habit of continuing and growing, and many cities, towns and organizations are now able to offer greatly improved services to their citizens as a result of the thousands of hours of dedicated work offered free of charge. The following is an example of the role of individuals in the community from another part of Australia. Questacon, the National Science and Technology Centre in Canberra, recognizes the tremendous contributions of Volunteer Explainers. The following relates a story from one of their volunteers:

I retired from the Commonwealth Public Service in January 1996 and was enjoying a quiet life, with no thought of ever rejoining the workforce. Fortunately, in May 1999 my idyllic, or so I thought at the time, lifestyle changed. I read an advertisement calling for Volunteer Explainers at Questacon. Within a month, along with about 23 other people of all age groups, I found myself attending an information night at Questacon.

We were shown over the various exhibits by Questacon staff during a two-hour period and I remember thinking 'I will never remember all this… it's far too complicated for a bloke like me because I don't have teaching experience or a science degree'. My fears were to some extent laid to rest when it was pointed out that there was no point in being a brilliant scientist if you couldn't explain things to people, especially kids.

My application to join the Volunteer Explainers was duly accepted and I undertook a training course conducted by staff. This was the start of what has turned out to be a fascinating and enjoyable experience. The trainers had all worked at Questacon for a number of years and really knew what they were talking about. In addition, they were all extremely nice and very patient… not at all like the teachers I had at school! I was required to undertake at least 16 hours of training sessions and then be assessed on my knowledge and competence as an explainer. I was rather nervous at the prospect of being assessed and failing. I had read my notes over and over again at home and tried explaining various aspects of Questacon exhibits to my family. I was determined to master the complexities on one particular puzzle that had me initially stumped, but, would you believe, I wasn't asked to demonstrate that one.

Happily, I passed the test and became an Explainer. That was when the fun really started. I work a 4.5 hour shift, either morning or afternoon as many days as I desire each week. During school semester we have school groups visiting from all over Australia and sometimes from overseas. These children, of all ages, really keep us busy. Some just want to be entertained whereas others ask detailed questions. If we don't know the answers we can invariably refer them to someone who does.

These days one hears criticism of the younger generation along the lines of 'I don't know what's going to happen to the world and why can't they be like we were'. However, here at Questacon we get to see another aspect, the young inquiring people who will make the discoveries of tomorrow. I met a group of six teenaged boys who were dressed like a street gang but were engineering students asking all sorts of probing questions... you just can't pre-judge in this business.

One day a group of Japanese high school students came in. I was working in a Gallery featuring devices that demonstrated the principles of physical forces. They were interested in everything except a simulated earthquake... said they had real ones at home!

One of the great pluses of working at Questacon is the other people one works with. They are of all ages, from students to retirees, and from all walks of life. There are scientists, teachers, military personnel, former Antarctic expeditioners, police, public servants, housewives, tradespeople, to name a few. They all have one thing in common. That is, they are all interesting and have a story to tell. I have not met a more stimulating group of people in my life as I have here at Questacon. In addition, I have had a million laughs. As a bonus, my cholesterol level has declined, my waistline has receded but unfortunately my hair is still falling out. Seems one can't have everything.

Using volunteering to enhance learning

Many cities have established an office to mobilize contributions of this kind. In Southampton, UK, the 'Community Involvement Team' provides help, support and training to over 150 community action groups around the city. They describe it as an investment, which of course it is. Projects include the setting up and maintaining of children's play groups in the ethnic minorities, environmental regeneration, support in clinics, schools and voluntary organizations. In Southampton community action takes the action into every neighbourhood through purpose-built community centres staffed by a professional community worker whose task it is to act as a proactive interface between the need and the volunteering effort which will satisfy that need.

The city of Espoo goes one step further. It has established youth councils and elderly people's councils as an adjunct to city decision making. The latter, for example, serves as the interface between third-age people and municipal administration. It represents their point of view and influences decision making in the city. It also promotes opportunities for greater participation in the learning life of the city as well as the management of housing, social and health services, social security matters, culture and leisure activity for third-age citizens. Espoo City Youth Council operates in a similar way. It is an elected body under the city board with 30 members aged from 13 to 20 years. The objectives are to increase the influence of young people in city decision making, and to look for new ways of activating initiatives and ideas which allow them to play a fuller part in city life. In these ways, active citizenship becomes integrated into all parts of the learning life of the city.

Not everyone is happy with the concept of doing something for nothing, and sometimes even volunteers like to be rewarded in some way. In the USA, the 'Service Credit' scheme offers a kind of pay-back system for community contribution. The work done by volunteers earns a tax-free 'time dollar' for every hour spent helping someone else and this is recorded in a database at volunteering headquarters. Volunteers receive regular statements of their 'time dollar balance'. They can be used to 'pay' for health care, and in some participating companies exchanged for goods or as a form of old-age insurance. There is a sort of quid pro quo in that volunteers qualify for help and benefits if they become infirm. Time dollars qualify for such services as meals-on-wheels, house cleaning, nursing care, neighbourhood security patrols and computer training work.

In an innovative variant in Chicago, teenagers who agree to mentor younger pupils can 'cash in' their dollars on computer software. 'Community currency' programmes such as these could help to increase the rate of active participation in volunteering and are well worth exploring to improve the support for learning. Learning card credit systems already exist in several parts of the UK and Europe and it should not be too difficult to adapt these so that a 'learning credits account' in the 'learning bank', earned through a variety of voluntary activities, would give access to new learning opportunities.

Making learning fun

Learning Festivals are another manifestation of active citizenship and a way of celebrating the fun of learning. Stockton, an amalgamation of four municipalities on the River Tees near Middlesborough, established a learning towns structure in 1998 'by people and organizations who believe that "learning" is a major element in the future prosperity of Stockton on Tees', to quote the booklet it has provided for its citizens. Each summer, lasting several months, it organizes Learning and Skills Festivals giving the residents and workforce of the townships 'an opportunity to join in the fun'. Within the major themes of skills, health, music and numeracy, citizens are invited to participate in such events as family drumming sessions to encourage family reading, participation in live music on the streets, maths trails and number fairs in bowling alleys and community centres, and free skills tasters such as painting, sugarcraft, aromatherapy, and jewellery making.

The colleges run free taster courses on a wide range of subjects from computer skills to human biology to singing for beginners, with an entry to a prize draw as a reward for dropping in on them. As its support for national campaigns like Adult Learners week, Learning at work days and Family Learning days, it organizes outdoor activity sessions for health and fitness, bring a friend weeks to local adult colleges, school reunions, open bird-watching sessions and skills bazaars. The whole atmosphere is one of fun and relaxation in learning environments with the goal of 'driving up the demand for learning in the borough'.

Such events have the dual purpose of publicizing learning and of showing that it can be a pleasurable activity. We can learn much from these events, and indeed many cities have already done so. Learning Festivals are proliferating throughout the globe. They have taken place in cities as far apart as Glasgow, Marion (Adelaide), Southampton, Tampere, Sapporo (Japan) and Edmonton, and they are as much a part of the Learning City culture as is the Lifelong Learning committee. Some of these are mentioned elsewhere in this book. As a means of celebrating the joy of learning message to a wide range of people they have no equal.

There are variants on the theme. The city of Espoo runs an annual competition for the learning organization of the year from both public services and business and industry. It stimulates public and organizational interest and knowledge. Such annual competitions can be extended to communities, schools, individual learners, and teachers. To be really innovative the judging could be done by those who have been excluded from the system – the unemployed, the homeless, the under-educated – to provide a way of extending learning and motivation to the currently unmotivated. Indeed, the jury could be the public at large as a way of stimulating more participation.

The celebration of learning is an important function in a society in which mammon plays such a large part. It can be done in many ways. In Japanese families many people keep their own learning diary, including details of significant learning events and achievements during the year. It is celebrated annually in the learner's own family, usually on birthdays. The acceptability of that process in other cultures may be questionable, but the principle is one that can be adapted. Of course such celebration events already exist. Schools have fete and presentation days, and adult education organizations award certificates of achievement to those who have passed examinations.

But continuous reward and recognition programmes also have their part to play and here we are on stonier ground. Again we can learn from industry, where rewards such as dinner for two, complimentary theatre tickets, exceptional achievement awards and trips to conventions are regularly applied. While it could be difficult for a municipality or a public service organization to justify such strategies from the public purse, there are many ways of stimulating awards in kind through win–win partnerships with suppliers and local entertainment centres. Imagination and energy are all that is needed.

And of course all of these programmes could be driven by volunteer workers, who themselves would benefit from them. Active citizenship by individuals, families, organizations and communities is one of the most promising challenges and opportunities for the development of lifelong learning values and attitudes. It will expand considerably in the future.

Chapter 11

Creating learning environments – partnerships and processes

Education and training C20th	Lifelong learning C21st	Action for change
Education is compartmentalized according to age and ability	Learning is lifelong in concept and content, providing links vertically and horizontally between age groups	Provide whole-community-based facilities encouraging links between learning providers and people of all ages. Foster productive partnerships

Figure 11.1 Educational links

The 16th-century philosopher, John Donne, is perhaps most famous for his observation that 'no man is an island'. And despite all we have said about the important growth of individualism in lifelong learning, it is evident too that the community as a whole has a crucial part to play in providing the conditions within which a larger number of people can learn. Indeed, all sectors of society bear a responsibility for solving the formidable problems caused by the alienation of large sections of the population from learning.

Stakeholders in lifelong learning

Some stakeholders have a larger responsibility than others to promote and further the cause:

- *Local and regional government.* Since 90% of lifelong learning will take place in cities, towns and well-populated regions, local and regional government have a powerful and influential position at the heart of the communities under their

95

control. Their representatives therefore need to acquire a deep understanding of the challenges that lifelong learning concepts present to the educational organizations they manage, and the changes that are needed to implement them. Indeed, many towns, cities and regions are now well on the way to becoming communities of learning. Southampton, Derby and Birmingham in the UK, Espoo and Jyvaskala in Finland, Goteborg in Sweden and Adelaide, Ballarat and Bendigo in Australia come to mind as outstanding examples, and there are many others in China, Japan, the USA and Canada. Equally, there are also many cities and regions which have not yet seen the connection between learning, prosperity and social stability, and have no plan to exploit that knowledge.

- *Universities and higher education.* As keepers of the intellectual traditions of a nation, they need to apply their considerable intelligence to act on behalf of the whole community rather than that section of it which affects their own sectional interest. It is they who determine the contextual basis of the assessment and accreditation strategies which separate 16–18-year-old children into passing sheep or failing goats, with its knock-on effect on the nature and content of the curriculum. In many countries it is also they who train the teachers to administer this ageing and elitist system. But it is also they who have the intelligence and the knowledge to see that this does not fit into a lifelong learning philosophy and the power to change it to a friendlier, more personal, non-threatening, target-based system. In many places the higher education system is already highly active. The Catholic University of Leuven in Belgium, the Universities of Napier, Southampton, Stirling and Derby in the UK, Helsinki University of Technology and Tampere University in Finland, Auckland University in New Zealand and most of the Australian universities are already widening their roles and leading the way into a lifelong learning future.

- *National governments* themselves are principally responsible for creating a culture of learning within which everyone can feel comfortable, whatever their age, aptitude, ability and inclination. To do so they will need to use the media both to deliver the truth about the need for change and to promote the appropriate responses to it. Many local and national organizations are highly active in promoting a similar message, but it needs the governmental stamp of authority to drive it home. Great strides have been made in government thinking in most of the world's liberal democracies. Finland, Denmark, Australia, Spain and Holland are examples of countries where the full range of lifelong learning activities is addressed across the board in every sector, while the UK, Germany, Sweden, Japan, South Africa and Singapore are implementing highly active and sophisticated strategies within a narrower focus on lifelong learning for adults.

- *Schools*, often the whipping boys for society's ills, are perhaps the most isolated of the sectors in that they appear to work from within their own little world of education and training, operating within its own rules and regulations, and insulated from what happens in the rest of the community. If they are to carry out the foundation work for learning throughout life, they will need considerable help from everyone and every sector to help them do it. Here is where the most resources need to be put. In this book we have suggested many remedial actions, but the key to it all lies in sensitizing in-service teachers to the new tools and techniques of developing self-learning mindsets as a part of their ongoing continuous education. Perhaps even more drastically, evidence of lifelong learning knowledge could be linked to the pay and promotional structure of the profession. Again there are schools in the UK, Finland and Australia, many of them highlighted in this book, where lifelong learning is well understood and practised, but for the most part, as we have said elsewhere, this is the least developed sector of all. Part 2 of this book describes the crucial role that schools play in the development of a learning society.

- *Industry and business* have a less obvious, but no less important role. Successful companies turn learning into wealth creation in an increasingly knowledge-based marketplace, a task which becomes ever more difficult as they pick up the pieces of failure in other parts of the system. They too have a part to play in contributing to the development of positive mindsets both in their own workforces and in the communities in which they exist. Many of them have succeeded in doing this as they become learning organizations in their own right. There are many fine examples of companies exercising corporate social responsibility in the field of lifelong learning. Multinational companies such as IBM, BP, ICI, Hoechst, Microsoft and many others have been innovative in many aspects of lifelong learning, including the use of technology, active learning methods, skills education and encouraging their employees to engage in the community. In many ways, companies have pioneered creative lifelong learning ideas, while the public learning providers in the public sector have taken several years to catch up.

- Lastly, as we have seen, a true learning community is not defined only by its learning providers. The *informal education systems* are as much a part of the lifelong learning scene as the school, college and university. Voluntary organizations, NGOs, professional associations, special interest groups, sports clubs, quangos, hospitals, individuals and all the departments of the city from health to social services, from finance to law and order, each have something to contribute to the growth of a lifelong learning culture. In Japan, for example, every department of government has been required to produce its own lifelong learning action plan, while the European Commission sets a high priority on social inclusion as a part of the total lifelong learning effort.

Partnerships in learning

So every type of organization is a key element in the battle for lifelong learning hearts and minds, and each can mount an attack on ignorance and apathy. But while each can participate separately in the building of a learning community, jointly they can do so much more. Figure 11.2 demonstrates in pictorial form how sectors can work together to develop mutually beneficial partnerships and how lifelong learning ideas can take root in the exchange of knowledge, experience and skills.

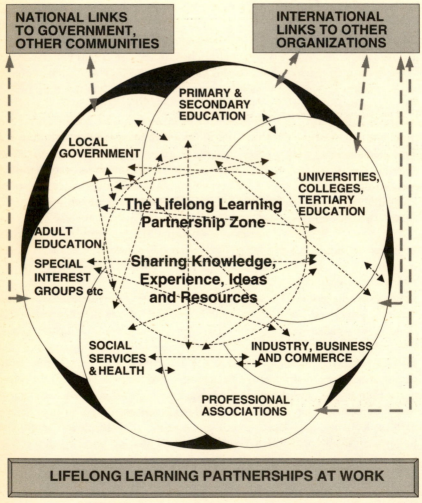

Figure 11.2 Lifelong learning partnerships

Effectively operated partnerships between the different sectors can create a win–win situation for all partners. They are an excellent way of sharing resources, of spreading ideas and experiences and of providing and acquiring skills and knowledge where they do not exist in certain organizations. The sending of teachers to company management courses in a schools–industry partnership, as described in Chapter 5, might be one example of the latter, and a joint research project between university and industry an example of the former.

Certainly the Action Agenda for Lifelong Learning prepared by Ball and Stewart from the First Global Conference on Lifelong Learning recognizes the value of partnerships. 'Each education institution should form at least three partnerships with business, industry and community organizations', it says, and conversely 'Within business and industry each company should form at least three partnerships with educational institutions and community organizations.' As long ago as 1989 Francis Musto, an Italian engineer, wrote in the *European Journal of Education*: 'One essential change in perception which will have to be made in industry is the shift from the notion that life is split into two parts to the idea that the learning process is continuous throughout life… This implies that industry and representatives of the world of work can, and should, contribute usefully to education during the years of schooling.'

In harmony with this, the UK Schools Curriculum Industry project package, initially produced in 1994, provides a wealth of ideas and examples of how fruitful interaction between industry and schools can enhance the learning of both. It describes how schoolchildren from years 4, 5, and 6 were invited to develop a special supplement on the local river for a local newspaper, writing the articles, supplying the photographs, finding the advertisers, and designing the pages. This provided active learning links between teachers, newspaper reporters and editors, and children, with the added bonus of education for the readership of the newspaper and new insights into the many aspects of the river in daily life. In mathematics, joint projects with local companies involved children in designing bedroom furniture, supermarket product control, land surveying, mail-order catalogue development and stained glass window design.

Such projects are the tip of a massive iceberg of existing schools/industry cooperation in the UK, the USA and elsewhere. They demonstrate that learning organizations do not exist in a self-contained educational vacuum. Companies draw their workforce from schools, universities and colleges which often espouse different cultures, values and objectives, both from the company workplace and between each other. Each worker brings along his/her own set of personal educational baggage and it is the task of the organization to create a set of positive and worthwhile company values from this human raw material and to encourage the habit of learning in each one. Universities and colleges likewise take in students from a wide range of backgrounds and cultures. Each has the task of widening the horizons of students beyond the narrow focus of individual institutional outlooks.

In a lifelong learning society, partnerships are a fertile part of that activity. They break down the stereotypes that exist when there is no contact between people and organizations, and they inject both reality and motivation into the learning process. As Longworth and Davies suggest in *Lifelong Learning*:

> In the new holistic, all-embracing world of the twenty-first century every organization, every nation, every individual become both depositors into, and withdrawers from, the bank of knowledge which comprises the learning society. They therefore need to understand and use its assets for their own development. To keep itself alive to the wider, real world, and often to remain economically viable as state funding diminishes, education needs partnerships.

The regional lifelong learning and skills partnerships in the UK are another example of fruitful, government-inspired interaction between different types of organization, though many have yet to translate friendly discussion into more urgent action, and many are very economy-focused.

The essence of partnerships is as a multi-way process of communication in which all partners articulate and debate their respective roles, and contribute to each others' thinking. In this way, genuine, non-threatening cooperation takes place. But there are other features to a successful marriage of ideas and experience. The new physical, financial and human resource that can be made available for each partner often exceeds the sum of its individual parts, as it did in the IBM–Woodberry Down example quoted in Chapter 5.

But partnerships don't produce useful resource unless they are fostered. They need commitment and creativity. Figure 11.3, for example, is taken from *Learning Cities for a Learning Century*. It shows some general guidelines for successful partnerships in learning cities, highlighting the need for management, two-way communication, regular meetings, celebration, and a set of clear objectives for each project. The more people participate the more successful it is likely to be.

Lifelong learning communities

But, in this world of change, nothing is static. In many parts of the world efforts are being made to integrate lifelong learning into the very structure of the community. Just south of Brisbane, for example, a public–private partnership between the local universities, a private contractor and three local authorities is constructing a 'learning corridor'. Here it is the intention of the forward-looking developer to build the lifelong learning ideas into the buildings and communications infrastructure of the new community at Forest Lake on the eastern end of the corridor and to link this into the older communities of Esk Shire to the west. Advisers from the University of Queensland and Queensland University of Technology are providing urban and social planning expertise. In some parts, every house will be linked by broadband cable into the community centre and to each other.

Partnerships – engines of organizational change
1. Partnerships should provide benefits for all partners. A one-way flow of information or service will lead to a loss of motivation
2. Partnerships should involve as many people as possible in the respective organizations in their activities
3. All people in the organizations should be informed about the partnership's objectives and progress
4. People in the organizations should be free to suggest improvements to the partnership and its activities
5. Each partnership should have clear objectives and goals, with time-scales and benchmarks for achieving them
6. At least one high-level person from each organization should be responsible for ensuring the success of the partnership
7. Regular meetings of the partnership should be held, at least once per term
8. The partnership should have a manager with secretarial support and ownership of making it happen
9. Partnership management should be proactive, encouraging people to contribute and participate
10. The partnership should be celebrated as frequently as appropriate to maintain interest and commitment

Figure 11.3 Features of a good lifelong learning partnership

But technology is only one part of the story. Community centres will also be linked to the school and to other educational providers. Small enterprises will also be integrated into the scene. The result is a corridor which stretches from a new development at Forest Lake in the east to Esk Shire and Ipswich to the west, taking in the existing master–planned community of Springfield in the middle. The ideas going into this project are still in the course of development, but they provide refreshing evidence of a cross–sectoral commitment to lifelong learning in the future. The development is also an interesting part of the Pallace project described in Appendix 1.

However, there are other initiatives. In many countries of the world lifelong learning thinking is creating a movement towards the concept of the community school and/or college. Models differ but, as was discussed in Chapter 5, the true essence of a community school is that it is open to the community at all times, rather than one which simply uses the plant, rooms and equipment at separate times.

We have seen the example of Mawson Lakes School, which opens it doors and its lessons to the community in the knowledge that this will enrich both the experiences of the children and the resources of the school. It is aiming to implement, as in the 'learning corridor', a new design for learning in the 21st century – a move from considering the 'school as a community' to developing the 'community as a school'. Communities of the 21st century will be learning communities fostering lifelong learning that is accessible at any time and in any place. Bruce Jilk lists the following as attributes of a 21st-century learning community:

- includes multiple settings [not limited to school buildings];
- dissolves borders among learning settings [connected to community];
- develops a coherent network of learning settings;
- adapts quickly to a variety of learning needs;
- provides a sense of place and learner identity;
- enhances social connectivity among learners;
- accommodates differences in learners;
- builds a learning community as something to do or practise;
- provides for both general and specialized study;
- enhances informal learning.

Learning across age groups

Such a list reinforces many of the points made in previous chapters. But even more radical is the idea of bringing down the age and access barriers in education. Traditionally we have been conditioned to believe that primary education is from 5 to 11, secondary from 11 to 18 and tertiary after that, and we have compartmentalized each into its separate box. And yet, in a world where the focus is on learning and the acquisition of skills and competencies, and where it is the individual who has ownership and decision-making power, there is no reason, other than administrative convenience, why this should be so. If mums, dads and grandmothers are allowed into the classroom, why should not a child of secondary school age attend an adult education college, or even a university? Why should not a parent attend a class in primary school? There are certainly a few examples where this is happening, but they are very few.

An example comes from Goteborg in Sweden. The island of Hisingen on the opposite side of the river to the main city is a former shipbuilding community. As with many other parts of the world, shipbuilding and its associated heavy industries experienced a massive decline in the 1960s and 70s. The island became an industrial wilderness. Warehouses were abandoned, plant lay idle and rusting, people moved out to where the new jobs were or stagnated on social security, waiting, like Mr Micawber, for something to turn up.

However, in this depressed and depressing environment something did turn up. New primary and secondary schools were built with a better range of equipment.

A vocational college followed down by the waterfront. But the *pièce de résistance* is the Lindholmen Knowledge Centre – a converted warehouse transformed into a modern high-tech learning centre. Computers, distance learning studios and classrooms, multimedia and self-study carrels were moved in – all the technology needed to provide both high-class learning and teaching, and develop world-class research. Chalmers University was persuaded to open an IT faculty using the centre as a focus.

Chambers of Commerce, and trade development associations, also helped to maximize the export and distribution potential and these attracted new small industries to exploit the learning infrastructure. Students from the upper secondary schools took IT and science lessons at Lindholmen, mixing with young entrepreneurs and research scientists in a fusion of ages, abilities and interests. In the evening it is used by the community – providing a vibrant, modern and constantly changing learning environment for more than 7,000 people and a true meeting place of industry, education and community.

There is a constant dialogue about the companies' learning needs and the content and methodology of education, and this results in courses tailored for particular companies, a workplace training and education aimed at increasing personal competence and technical skills, again attended by school students and the community. Smaller companies get help with product development and can test new products in a laboratory. Among the futuristic resources for better learning is a virtual reality facility, in which new technologies can be demonstrated and developed in cooperation between educators and companies.

From small beginnings the idea has grown. The Chalmers University involvement has increased from one floor of the knowledge centre to two large buildings adjacent to it, with yet more education and research equipment. The number of small industries has burgeoned and now the larger IT industries are moving in on the scene – Ericsson, Volvo IT, the regional telecommunications industries – contributing yet more expertise, buildings and money.

People are moving back in large numbers. Families move into tastefully designed new condominiums and houses, transforming what has now become an enterprise park into a living and breathing community once more, albeit one very different from the old Hisingen. Thus out of the debris of an industrial disaster has risen the phoenix of a high-tech community, fuelled by the motive power provided by learning. It is a modern morality story.

We can learn from this. A school, a college, a university might become a knowledge centre in its own right, feeding experiences, ideas and activities to and from the community in which it exists. And the technology is not necessarily central to it. Many of the huge lifelong learning centres set up in the Japanese prefectures, for example, provide a service to all parts of the community, including facilities for the arts, drama, and leisure facilities. They are modern lifelong learning cathedrals, attracting a congregation with diverse interests and diverse needs and demands to participate in a joint act of learning.

Chapter 12

Activating and revitalizing learning – involving the learner

Education and training C20th	Lifelong learning C21st	Action for change
Reactive – meets identified needs of organizations and some people	Proactive – encourages the habit of learning in all people	Encourage active learning methods – use technology wisely

Figure 12.1 Active learning

The Stamford experiment involved technology-based learning with disadvantaged learners in California in the 1960s. Professor Patrick Suppé's results showed that, in general, the young people who were confronted with screen-based learning for the first time preferred it 'because there ain't no one telling me what to do'. This is probably not the first intimation that the low expectations of teachers and lecturers can affect learning performance. Pejorative value judgements create poor results.

But it is also an early and powerful reminder that there are alternative ways of teaching to overcome such unarticulated cries for help. Suppé was testing computer-assisted-learning programmes on large IBM mainframes. Computer technology is rather more sophisticated now and, such has been the rate of miniaturization, one of today's laptop computers would have the power of several of those mainframes. Where we will be in another 40 years is open to the imagination. There could quite conceivably be microchip-based implants containing all known knowledge within a subject area for insertion into the human brain.

But, as we have seen, it is not the knowledge that is important – it is more the ways in which we deal with it, interpret it and use it as a basis for action. And even more than that, it is the strategies we adopt to cope with its rapid and massive proliferation. Information overload has afflicted all of us for many years and still we have not developed techniques for dealing with it. Multimedia education technology combining sound, vision, text, motion picture and graphics has also been with us for years without making a significant impact upon teaching methods.

Distance education studios using computers, satellites, cable, ISDN and telephone lines, video-conferencing, projectors, keypads, curriculum-embedded assessment and sophisticated software have also gained a foothold in the business education marketplace but not significantly in the public domain. The educational promise of combining the information, communication and broadcasting technologies has yet to be realized. Perhaps it is because many technical educators are still working in the old information-giving, open-the-lid-and-pour-it-in education and training paradigm, perhaps it is that real learning presents insuperable difficulties to education developers.

The educational promise of technology

For sure, technology will play a larger part in learning in the future, and not only because the massive increase in the number of learners makes that an imperative as the lifelong learning revolution takes hold. As Longworth and Davies have said:

> Networks can be used in creative ways. They can help break down cultural barriers between peoples and educational barriers to learning; they can build common databases, develop collaborative teaching strategies and deliver education and training; they can assist in language learning and networks to improve communication between people of all ages. Many such networks already exist, most of them based on the Internet. They offer access to worldwide webs of databases, forums on every subject, people of every creed, colour and age, maps and diagrams, information and knowledge, conferences and seminars and events, entertainment and education and obsession – all human life is there on the information superhighway. Perhaps less than ten percent of the world's people know about it, less than one percent is able to use it and less than .01 percent is used for educational purposes.

But these percentages are growing rapidly. They will have multiplied by at least five in another five years' time. Here is an opportunity for the taking. In a world which must increasingly become a cooperating global community in order to survive the future, networks can help us to promote an international outlook, cultural understanding and a global learning culture. Once we have developed more learner-friendly delivery mechanisms, there is little limit on the possibilities for better-educated populations through the use of information and communications technology.

This is one reason why e-learning groups are proliferating throughout the world, ready to take advantage of the Internet as a resource for learning. The

European Telematics, Esprit and Framework research programmes have spent hundreds of millions of euros in developing infrastructures, strategies and new knowledge for developing more new knowledge. Similar programmes in North America have dispensed billions of dollars. National governments have invested vast sums on educational programmes to set up learning networks such as Learn Direct in the UK, Learnnet in Canada and Learn in Australia. Smart cities and smart organizations have developed strategies for e-learning and the use of ICT through hundreds of individual projects.

Rotterdam is a case in point. In the 1990s it faced many problems. Unemployment was high, particularly among the 28 per cent of its population who were immigrants. As one of the world's busiest ports, Rotterdam became rapidly dependent on a workforce with well-developed information and communication technology skills to operate the increasingly digitalized harbour activities. The city became part of a national initiative to develop ICT skills in business, in local government, in the education sector and in its citizens.

It located 60 'e-centres' in neighbourhoods that were accessible and familiar to the 25 per cent of people who face barriers in accessing mainstream education. It developed computer training in the home for disadvantaged groups and focused this not just on the need to find work but also on the need to find enjoyment. The 'e-centres' are small open-access computer facilities for the general community financed by the city with in-kind and voluntary support, including guidance services. They can be found in schools, care homes for the aged, centres for the homeless, mosques and community centres. There are even portable e-centres.

The learning method is centred around the needs of each student – and this is one factor in its success. Not only are they successful in developing new skills through their active learning approach and their inspired location, they are also encouraging people who would not otherwise have taken up learning to further develop their potential. Shanti Wong, who made a study of this project, comments: 'The "e-centres" are breaking down the barriers to accessing education and demonstrate the City Council's commitment to encouraging people who are disadvantaged to access learning beyond formal programmes.'

E-learning and the schools

Schools are also involved in active learning through technology. Mawson Lakes School, near Adelaide, is an example. Its mission statement on technology says:

> At Mawson Lakes, technology will be an enabling tool to facilitate learning and to increase interaction between people. The Mawson Lakes School will demonstrate world-class practice in the use of information technologies and telecommunications products and services as innovative tools for the improvement of educational and organizational practices. This expertise will be offered as a service to other institutions, businesses and the community in ways that are commercially sustainable and provide productivity gains and benefits for users.

It intends to broaden the curriculum and enhance lifelong learning by establishing new learning environments for teachers and children. It will connect into the broadband fibre-optic networks linking homes, workplaces and educational organizations in the community, create innovative home–school links with all parents and join national and international projects through satellite. For a school this is certainly ambitious, but conditions and the assistance it intends to make available from the community augur a good chance of success. Its membership of the Pallace project described in Appendix 1 will further enhance its ambition.

One way of making technology available to schools, colleges and residents of the community is to establish a 'digital learning community' as exists in the Boroughs of Wandsworth, Merton and Kingston in London. Here, satellite centres of excellence are grouped around a community digital learning centre which provides the expertise for training, software and materials development and hardware selection. Digital learning partner schools complete the set. As in Rotterdam, it focuses on ethnic minorities but, unlike there, it takes the training into the schools as well as adult education centres. It thus has a number of objectives:

- to enhance teachers' and pupils' skills, knowledge and understanding of IT;
- to help schools integrate IT into their future planning;
- to extend the use of IT as a tool in the delivery of curricula;
- to design digital learning materials that encourage learning;
- to train members of the community in IT skills.

Wandsworth is an area of high deprivation in terms of both employment and the facilities available in its public buildings. At the beginning of the project in 1997, only 15 per cent of the schools had the capacity to connect to the Internet and only one-quarter were aware of the use of IT as an educational resource. Nevertheless, the 2002 target of 21,000 pupils was achieved by 1999 and it was estimated that more than 65,000 young people had benefited from personal and social development activities as a result of the project.

Such activities emphasize the potential of technology to enhance learning, but at the same time the enormous, and often costly, efforts that have to be made to persuade and train staff in the learning providers, and to implement solutions. Several schools, for example, refused to join the project because of security issues, another costly item on hard-pressed budgets.

Contrast this with the cities of Gothenburg, Espoo, Stockholm and many more in northern Europe where the local education authority has ensured that all learning providers are connected to the Internet, each other and learning providers internationally by broadband networks, and that every learner has a personal e-mail address. Or with the example of Maconaquah High described in Chapter 21.

Other uses of technology for learning

Of course, there are thousands of educational organizations for all ages making plans to mould the technology for improved delivery of their product – and, as usual, many more examples where this is not happening. The gap between the haves and have-nots is a reflection of society as a whole. What technology can provide, if effectively used, is the opportunity for choice and flexibility, and for a variety of programmes to suit individual learning styles.

Its usefulness operates at many levels – in business and industry for keeping scientists, engineers and managers updated, in universities for inter-student, inter-faculty and international links, in adult education colleges for the sharing of distance learning programmes and in schools in a variety of ways, and a hundred other uses. There will be many who prefer the traditional teacher–class environment and it is their right to have that. But equally there will be an ever-increasing number who prefer to adapt themselves to the discipline and the convenience of self-learning at home, at work or wherever they find themselves.

Other active learning methods

The considerable benefits of active learning through education technology are addressed in greater detail with examples in Chapter 21. But active learning is not just a case of the application of technology, though a trawl of the Web would have us believe it is so. The daily grind of accumulating information and knowledge in classrooms can be alleviated and improved upon in many other different activity-based ways.

Take the RSA Opening Minds project as an example. Its provenance is the recognition that education systems – curricula, content, assessment roles, teaching methodologies – cannot exist in a time warp within a rapidly changing world, in the pretence that it represents stability. They have to change with it in order to become relevant for the millions of young people whom society compels to spend 11 years at school. Valerie Bayliss, the project director, interviewed hundreds of teachers and social leaders in preparation for the project, and articulates the belief and concern among them that, in the UK at least, 'the education diet provided for young people is not the one we should be offering them. The people who pull the levers of power in education are looking backwards...'

In 1999 the RSA's first ideas on a competence-led curriculum were published, expressed from the point of view of what students should learn from their education, rather than what should be taught to them. There were competencies for learning, citizenship, relating to people, managing situations and managing information, a new diet of skills very similar to those outlined in Chapter 9. But going hand in hand with new curriculum content is the belief that learning methodologies should change from the passive to the active. Skills need to be practised, the acquisition of understanding needs personal immersion in the acquisition of knowledge, problem solving needs problems to solve.

This movement to active learning was the accompanying philosophy of the project testing phase until 2002. Twelve schools have taken the decision to participate, and each one of them quotes positive results. The city technology college in Birmingham, for example, combined a study of energy and religious festivals, recognizing that knowledge is, in reality, interconnected and interdependent rather than fragmented into subject labels. For the energy part of the module they didn't study wind-power – they designed and built windmills, with sail dimensions and shapes calculated in the maths lessons. For a better understanding of religions they cooked a Jewish meal, which led on to a discussion of the significance of food in religion, and then related it back to the energy involved in producing food. Throughout, the students used a self-evaluation grid to measure the progress of their own understanding.

Of course, active project work of this kind has been a feature of good education over many years, but those countries with a very full national curriculum, and a plethora of assessment tests for which extra in-school coaching is often given, have tended to focus the curriculum into a narrow, content-driven straitjacket, pipelining every child along pre-set pathways over which they have no ownership.

Inspiring participation

Active learning also takes place outside the school. The 'Odyssey of the Mind', for example, has a more competitive edge. Its world final is a huge international jamboree, taking place every year at a university campus in the USA, and attended by more than a thousand children from secondary schools in all states of America and the rest of the world. But these are just the finalists. Thousands more have participated in national and local heats to solve problems in physics and engineering, and to develop creativity in literature and the arts. One challenge might be to construct a balsa wood bridge to suggested dimensions and with materials not costing more than a few dollars. It is tested by having the team put weights very carefully and gently on top of it until it collapses. The bridge taking the most weight wins. Another would be to write and act a ten-minute play incorporating particular words and/or historical concepts to enable others to learn an aspect of history or geography or even physics.

Parents and teachers join in the act, becoming coaches and mentors to the teams of seven, and an enthusiastic panel of administrators from government, local government and universities perform the judging. Odyssey is not alone in this, of course. Similar events, such as the Science and Technology Fairs for children run by the Standing Conference on Science and Technology in the UK, take place in regions and communities throughout the nation. In all of these, the creative energy circulating round is almost tangible and the enthusiasm of the children for learning is palpable. In Business Education for Young People, the Young Enterprise scheme which encourages sixth-formers to set up their own companies, complete with their own chief executive, staff and production line, is an improvement on more didactic ways of teaching the subject.

Much of this is of course reciprocated in many good schools and colleges throughout the world. But its appeal tends to be to the already convinced and committed. The attempt to develop relevance for a wider audience might be found in a US initiative. 'Service Learning' is a teaching/learning method that connects meaningful community service with academic learning (the curriculum), personal growth, and civic responsibility. Students learn the knowledge, skills and values of responsible citizenship in the context of analysing and solving real school and community problems. According to the National Service Learning Cooperative:

> Most students are vaguely aware of their rights, but have no idea of the civic duty of active participation in interpersonal and community problem solving as a requirement for maintaining a democracy. They must learn the civic values of our nation and develop realistic goals and a vision of a future that meets the challenges of the 21st century. They must learn the social and problem-solving skills to achieve their goals and be empowered to practice these skills in school. This task should be done with a comprehensive plan that includes K-12 educators, students, parents, and community representatives.

So here we have the amalgamation of several lifelong learning principles into one desirable whole. The concept of active citizenship described in Chapter 10 links with the opportunity of involving the whole community in learning (Chapter 5), and with the insertion of meaning and personal skills into the curriculum (Chapter 9) within the concept of active learning recommended by this chapter. And students do learn.

A ninth-grade student from Yosemite High School in Oakhurst commented: 'Today many of us forget that liberty is the power to change things. People think liberty is doing what you want to do, but liberty is more than that; it's also power to choose things and change them.' Such insights are encouraging. They demonstrate critical judgement and make a nonsense of cynical governmental attitudes and posturing based on political manipulation, though the ease with which governments and media in both the developed and developing world can activate superficial, reactionary mob responses in vast numbers of people shows just how far we have to go before rational thinking becomes the norm.

The role of public education services

It is interesting, too, to note that the cultural services, museums, art galleries and libraries are reinventing themselves to meet the requirements of the lifelong learning age. Conferences on the subject will find enthusiastic librarians and museum curators eager to learn how they can add their expertise to the general learning effort. Museums are no longer the dry, dusty repositories of ancient artefacts lying in glass cases. They are educational organizations in their own right and contributors to the active learning scene. In a learning city they insert themselves into educational projects.

The museum of Espoo is not only part of the development team for a lifelong learning exhibition in the Pallace project, but another claim to fame is as the leader of the 'A Europe of Tales' project funded by the European Commission. Here folk stories from all parts of Europe are gathered together in one book and presented as an exhibition in the museum. Children help to relate them, just as they helped to collect them. Thus trolls from Iceland vie with pixies from Ireland and dwarves from Finland in a verbal, visual and written celebration of European folklore in the museums of the continent.

Providing materials for interactive learning

One last example brings us back to technology and its role in active learning. The European Commission's Learning Highway project was an attempt to put the principles of lifelong learning onto the Internet, based on the Longworth and Davies book, *Lifelong Learning – New Visions, New Implications, New Roles*. Billed as 'a course on the concepts , tools and techniques of Lifelong Learning and its implications for Universities, Schools, Business and Industry, Professional Associations, Teacher Training Organizations, Communities and Individuals', the materials are not presented didactically for people to read. Instead an approach was adopted to help course leaders communicate the concepts in a lifelong learning manner.

Thus materials are provided which 'lead the learner to understand the subject from the exercises he/she will do and the discussions he/she will participate in, and then to reinforce the learning through support materials'. The course leader becomes an enabler of learning, releasing the experience, ideas and creativity of the learners, rather than a transmitter of information/knowledge. The suggested exercises are intended to develop in the learner a feeling for the topic issues through his/her own experience and creativity. 'At all times the learners should sense that they have ownership of the learning they have to do and they are contributing their own experience and knowledge into the general pool', says the course introduction. To encourage this, the suggestions recommend a variety of techniques, including:

- small and large discussion groups with plenary report-back sessions;
- Web-surfing sessions;
- brainstorms and creative discussion sessions;

- visiting practitioners;
- questionnaires and audits;
- personal plan development exercises;
- computer conferencing;
- role-playing exercises;
- interpretation of pictures/diagrams/tables/charts etc;
- simulations.

In true lifelong learning manner, the course leader is expected to exercise creativity in the presentation of the modules, using a variety of techniques to stimulate the discussion sessions. For example, he/she may wish to use images like magic wands, desert island castaways, people stuck in a lift, explaining to visiting Martians etc to create an ambience for learning together. Of such stuff are the teaching methodologies of tomorrow made.

And of course there are barriers of time, money, expertise, uncertainty, laziness and opportunity to active learning of this kind. But this has been true for every change of approach since Socrates was marketing dialogue. Large class sizes, too, make active learning difficult. So they do, but only where teachers have not acquired the skills of classroom management for active learning, and where they are trying to implement them with no help. As Chapter 3 has pointed out, the teacher as a manager of all the resources at his/her disposal can overcome such problems.

Other objections would be that these are the methodologies recommended in the 1960s and 70s that have been discredited as 'trendy' or unworkable in practice. But the discredit, and the problems, are more on those countries using an 'all fits one' approach within a fully prescribed national curriculum, and ignoring the needs and demands of learners as individuals. They are now paying a heavy price in increased crime for turning many children off learning. They, no more than adults, will not be coerced into learning where they find it boring or irrelevant.

The European Commission recognizes the obvious: 'People will only plan for consistent learning activities throughout their lives if they want to learn. They will not want to continue to learn if their experiences of learning in early life have been unsuccessful and personally negative', it says in its memorandum. And it is right. Active learning methods are a form of learning marketing. They can inject relevance into the curriculum, and create the motivation which encourages people of all ages to get into the habit of learning once more, for life.

Chapter 13

From the age of education and training to a lifelong learning future – a summary

Education and training C20th	Lifelong learning C21st	Action for change
Addresses present personal learning needs and circumstances	Also prepares for future personal learning needs and circumstances	Change mindsets. Create a learning culture – market learning and communicate its value at all stages

Figure 13.1 Changing mindsets

Children entering primary school this year will leave secondary education in the year 2020 and the (hopefully) many who go on to further and higher education will graduate by about 2025. Hopefully too, few of them will consider that their learning is complete. In that period a great number of changes will have been made. The USA will have experienced the inexperience of at least three more presidents, the nations of Europe and Australasia several different prime ministers each, and even most of the dictators who bedevil our current world will be no longer be with us.

Advances in science and technology will have regaled us with ever more enticing products and prospects and there will be more than 100 times the amount of information in the world that there is now. The educational world may, by that time, have moved onwards towards the Greek notion of Paedeia – 'a society in which learning, fulfilment and becoming human are the primary goal of its institutions, and directed towards that end' – or it may not. The only thing we can know for certain about the world of 2020 is that we don't know for certain what it will be like.

It is with that knowledge, or lack of it, that the principles and ideas that have been suggested in the preceding chapters stand or fall. To paraphrase an old Polish saying, 'the man who believes himself to be more than 35 per cent right most of the time is a realist, the man who believes himself to be right more than 50 per cent of the time may be a genius or a charlatan, the man who believes himself to be right more than 70 per cent of the time is a deluded maniac and should be locked away in an asylum'. One assumes that this applies to women as well. So it is as well to be aware of that when pontificating about lifelong learning.

There can be few doubts, however, that present educational structures are far from perfect, and there can be more than a few suspicions that tinkering about with the present system is no more than a cosmetic exercise to hide the deficiencies. A system in which, according to Fryer, 'far too many people see learning as unnecessary, unappealing, uninteresting or unavailable' is failing its people. What is needed is a change of mindset that accepts and welcomes change as an inevitable consequence of being alive. Teaching for the year 2020 requires an education system that instils attributes of adaptability, flexibility and versatility into its victims. Easily said, but not so easily done. The culture of learning cannot be imposed. It has to be created from the natural raw materials of the human condition.

So who is arguing with this assessment? Certainly not governments. Their documents and Web sites are full of good intentions. The European Commission, for example, has put the creation of a culture of learning as one of its six main priorities. Its lifelong learning paper states that:

> Valuing learning is a key element in the creation of a culture of learning and for realizing a European area of lifelong learning a comprehensive new approach both to the mutual recognition of qualifications, and to the identification, assessment and recognition of non-formal and informal learning is needed in order to enable people to have individual learning pathways, suitable to their needs and interests.

It is a pity that qualifications recognition is equated with learning but that is the nature of the academic and political mindset, determined to insert failure somewhere into the system. The Eurydice group tells us that, in their White Papers on lifelong learning, Austria advocates 'the ability to learn to learn, personal development and social skills', Ireland suggests 'a critical spirit', Spain supports 'values and attitudes associated with citizenship', and Denmark advances 'sustainable development' as the major skills and competencies to develop in young people. More prosaic offerings were 'autonomous learning' from Germany, while the UK puts 'literacy and numeracy' at the head of its list of skills priorities.

All these countries, plus Australia, the USA and Canada, China, Singapore and many others, are heavily in favour of lifelong learning. The definition of its scope, and the means by which it will be implemented, sometimes reflect cultural outlooks as well as governmental mindsets influenced by the range of vision of its adviser organizations. Nevertheless, most of the recommendations made in the preceding chapters are expressed in government thinking right around the world.

Eurydice again: 'More guidance and counselling for children', says Austria, 'promotion of ITC as a teaching tool' repeats Sweden, and Denmark, Germany and the UK advocate 'increasing the inclination and motivation to learn in pupils'. Ireland wants 'more cooperation in family learning' while the democratic aspect is stressed in Germany (again), Greece and Holland in the form of 'greater pupil participation and choice'. Outside Europe, the South Australian Directions for 2001 proclaims that 'Young South Australians will be offered a range of adventurous, exciting and changing opportunities that promote self-reliance, self-confidence, voluntary work, leadership and community service.'

UNESCO gets closer to the point about flexibility in 'The Treasure Within': 'As the 21st century approaches education is so varied in its tasks and forms that it covers all the activities that enable people, from childhood to old age, to acquire a living knowledge of the world, of other people and themselves. It is an educational continuum, co-extensive with life and widened to take in the whole of society.' It bases its report on what it calls the four main pillars of lifelong learning – learning to know, learning to do, learning to be, learning to live together and with others. Although this report was published in 1996, it still contains a considerable treasure within.

OECD's interest in culture change is of course partly economic but, less predictably, very wide-ranging. In 'Lifelong Learning for all', it says:

> 'Lifelong Learning' embraces individual and social development of all kinds and in all settings – formally in schools, vocational, tertiary and adult education institutions, and non-formally, at home, at work and in the community. The approach is system-wide; it focuses on the standards of knowledge and skills needed by all, regardless of age. It emphasizes the need to prepare and motivate all children at an early age for learning over a lifetime, and directs efforts to ensure that all adults, employed and unemployed, who need to retrain or upgrade their skills, are provided with an opportunity to do so.

So we have agreement from the great and the good that systems need to change towards a lifelong learning approach. And it is happening, as any of the examples from preceding chapters and those to follow show. But there are also huge swathes of darkness where the lifelong learning light has yet to be lit. In the end it is mindset that determines behaviour. As Field says, 'It is not governments that will produce more learning among more people, but citizens.' He is right. It is the personal mindset that alienates so many people from learning; the organizational mindset that treats the future as if it were an unalterable continuation of the present; and the national mindset that seeks narrow nationalistic solutions to international problems.

If the mindset sees schools as places where children should sit politely in serried ranks obtaining information and carrying out instructions handed down to them from teachers with the full authority of the school hierarchy behind them, to be regurgitated back in examinations, it will not want to know about lifelong learning approaches.

If the adult mindset sees learning as a chore, a bore or a threat to expose its shortcomings it won't take its owner anywhere near an adult education college.

If the government and the media mindset sees an electorate and readership obsessed with examinations as the only arbiter of standards, and persists with success/failure-oriented systems of assessment to feed that perception, they will not want to lead, for the risk of offending the voters.

If the universities are overly obsessed with academic entry standards, they will not want to know about the personal skills and values of young people, or about systems that offer alternative ways of measurement, such as the Assessment of Prior Experiential Learning.

The truth is that all major change involves taking risks with other people's mindsets and the acceptance of a responsibility to do the right thing, even though it may be unpopular. But equally, in a democratic society dominated by the power of information, there are many opportunities to spread the message of the need for new approaches from all sources. Every stakeholder is a key marketer in the battle for lifelong learning hearts and minds, and each can mount an attack on ignorance and apathy. Mindset change is a long, large and complex process. Even where it is accepted, and even irrefutable arguments sometimes gain reluctant assent, a massive programme of initial and in-service staff training programmes will be needed in every learning provider. It will be an exciting world for the foreseeable future.

A summary

What we have tried to do in this section is to demonstrate the changes needed to take us from an educational world dominated by the education and training paradigm of education for those who require it, into the lifelong learning era of pleasurable learning for all. Figure 13.2 offers the full set.

All of these are holistic and interdependent. They may have been presented in linear fashion as 12 separate chapters, but the whole is undoubtedly a package. They should not be implemented piecemeal. There is no point in implementing the much-needed curriculum reform described in Chapter 9 unless there is an equal reform of teaching methods shown in Chapters 2 and 11, and assessment methods suggested in Chapter 8. Similarly, there is no profit in carrying out surveys and studies as suggested in Chapter 1 unless there is an intention to change the culture of learning into one which celebrates learning as described in Chapter 10 and gives additional support to learners as Chapter 7 proposes.

The wholesale adaptation of in-service teacher training to a continuous learning model, advocated in Chapter 3, needs the lifelong learning tools described in Chapter 4, and a willingness to engage the whole community in the learning process, outlined in Chapter 5. Nor, as Chapter 12 proposed, is there any educational logic in concentrating lifelong learning effort on improvements to

From the age of education and training to the era of lifelong learning		
	Education and training C20th	**Lifelong learning C21st**	**Action for change**
1.	Educational decision making rooted in a 20th-century mass education and training paradigm	Decisions are made on individual learning needs, demands and styles of all citizens of all ages, abilities and aptitudes	Find the barriers to learning and dismantle them. Develop and market a strategy based on lifelong and lifewide learning for all
2.	Ownership of the need to learn and its content is with the teacher	Learner, as customer, rules. As far as possible, ownership of the need to learn and its content is given to the learners	Involve in-service teachers in strategies to empower learners. Train a team to run lifelong learning courses in every learning provider
3.	Work-based – educates and trains for employment and short-term need	Life-based – educates both for employability and a full and fulfilled life in the long term	Provide the tools to empower whole person's learning needs. Career, job, leisure, family, community, interests, change – audits, personal learning plans etc
4.	Teachers regarded as information and knowledge purveyors – sole distributors of resource	Teachers as managers – of all the resources and expertise available in a community	Discover and use the talents, skills, expertise, finance and knowledge within the community. Each learning provider appoints a person to tap into and distribute this resource
5.	Courses decided and provided by education organizations on their own premises	Learning influenced by learner and provided where, when, how and from who he/she wants it	Encourage providers to provide learning where people are – home, schools, workplaces, pubs, stadia, church halls etc
6.	Sparse mass educational support and backup structures brought into service when problems arise	Sophisticated ongoing support structures available to all learners according to needs and demands. Early warning, early treatment	Provide a wide ange of learning support people from scratch, including learning counsellors, community mentors, psychologists etc, and make available to all learners of all ages. Forestall problems before they arise
7.	Examinations used to separate successes from failures irrespective of circumstance	Examinations as failure-free personal learning opportunities confirming progress and encouraging further learning	Influence development of innovative assessment tools embedded into personal learning curricula and examined when the student feels ready, not when convenient
8.	Knowledge and information based – *what* to think	Understanding, skills and values based – *how* to think	Develop personal skills- and values-based curricula that expand the capacity of people to enjoy and benefit from learning throughout life
9.	Learning as a difficult chore and as received wisdom	Learning as fun, participative and involving, and as perceived wisdom	Celebrate learning frequently and encourage active citizenship by individuals, families, organizations and communities
10.	Education is compartmentalized according to age	Learning is lifelong in concept and content, providing links vertically and horizontally between age groups	Provide whole-community-based facilities which encourage links between learning providers and people of all ages. Foster productive partnerships
11.	Reactive – meets identified needs of organizations and some people	Proactive – actively encourages the habit of learning in all people	Encourage active learning methods – use technology wisely
12.	Addresses present personal learning needs and circumstances	Also prepares for future personal learning needs and circumstances	Change mindsets. Create a lifelong learning culture – market learning an communicate its value at all stages

Figure 13.2 From education and training to lifelong learning

the adult education system without also tackling the underlying causes of reluctant learning at an earlier age in society as a whole and the school systems which feed it, as if they were two alien societies. Holistic systems are interdependent and interconnected.

Who pays? Who benefits?

Overriding all of this is the question of 'who pays?' for the introduction of lifelong learning. It is a fundamental question and one that has not yet been satisfactorily answered. Schools, adult education colleges, universities and other learning providers have enough demands on their stretched and very finite resources. In answer to this, Brennan suggests that the question should be asked in the same breath as 'Who benefits?' and here we have a much wider debate which has yet to be won.

Certainly society, the economy, individuals, industry, local government, national government, law and order come to mind when learning is regarded as an investment into personal, community and national futures. OECD's three lifelong learning rationales of economic prosperity, social stability and personal fulfilment resonate strongly in this context. But these are glib responses to a perennial problem. The battle for hearts and minds is still to be won and the debate continues. More flexibility in the form of shorter periods of study for those who can cope is one less commonly expressed ruse, and there are no doubt many others, including voucher systems, which the innovative organization can think up.

But all the time there is the economic imperative that education now operates in a competitive world. At higher and further education level, for example, new learning opportunities developed in the private sector could by-pass universities and colleges if there is a failure to address the issues that lifelong learning throws up. In the overall scheme of things, the issue for nations and communities might be connected to whether they can afford not to implement lifelong learning, and we come back once more to the enormous cost imposed by a culture of ignorance which is by no means confined to the developing world.

We have suggested that, unless a significant proportion of those children and adults who are presently disengaged from learning are brought back into the learning habit, the economic, social and cultural prospects of nations, regions, cities and individuals will suffer. This is well documented and accepted by most informed politicians and by community and business leaders. The most urgent task, therefore, is to break down the mindset of inaction, mobilize the people and broadcast the good news that learning is good, learning is enjoyable and learning is natural.

That message is one for which government should take primary responsibility, but it is also a whole society challenge. Actions should be supported by all those organizations in every city, town and region which have an interest in ensuring that that knowledge is driven home. These are the stakeholders investing in their, and our, future. The next section therefore looks at the changing roles, responsibilities and activities of schools, which together with tertiary education, local government, business and industry and the media, will play a large part in implementing lifelong learning imperatives.

Part 2

The impact of lifelong learning on schools in the 21st century

Why schools are important for creating a lifelong learning future. What they can do to help create personal fulfilment, social stability and economic prosperity. How they can move, and help others move, into a learning society.

Chapter 14

Where do the schools fit into lifelong learning? An introduction

The importance of schools in the creation of a lifelong learning society cannot be overstated. The European Commission's policy paper on lifelong learning is quite firm on the matter. 'Fundamentally transform learning systems, including initial education, with a view to making quality learning available to all', it recommends to its member states, recognizing the importance of schooling to a lifelong learning policy.

And it is right to do so. Here is where learners are at their most impressionable; here is where the values and attitudes that will serve them for life must be implanted; here is where the possibilities for dealing with social inequalities are at their most opportune; and here is where the early warning signs of learning reluctance, demotivation and emotional difficulty should lead to the application of remedial measures. It is where the love or indifference or hate for learning is engendered, affecting an individual's whole future course in life. What happens in the present has an inordinate influence on what happens in the future, as research study after research study shows. And so the 21st-century school will have a vision and a strategy for the development of values and attitudes extending well beyond the academic objectives and targets required of them by government diktat. This, as Figure 14.1 shows, will open the school mindset to the influence and ideas of organizations and people outside of itself, just as the child's mind profits from being opened up to a variety of experiences outside of him/herself.

Education and training C20th	Lifelong learning C21st	Action for change
Sets narrow academic objectives and targets and works to achieve these in the present	Works to achieve current targets and to develop positive future values and attitudes to learning	Develop more schools/life links and partnerships – industry, community etc – with the outside world

Figure 14.1 Targets, values and attitudes

Schools and society

Unfortunately, in some countries schools take a low priority in the lifelong learning hierarchy of needs. The lack of a holistic, seamless and integrated education system often leads to such rigid divisions between its components that schools appear to live in a different world from further, higher and adult education. Teachers in schools have different unions, attend different courses and operate under different rules than those in other parts of the system. Children in schools are often treated as vessels to be filled rather than candles to be lit, and because there are so many more of them, the per capita resources are much lower. At the dawn of the 21st century, what Longworth has called 'the learning century', few school-teachers are even aware of the existence of the lifelong learning movement, still less that it will affect the ways in which they will work in the future.

To be sure, the schools work under considerable difficulty. The minds of the young are attacked from every side by a confusing babble of urgent and conflicting voices each competing for attention. Vastly improved communication techniques exploiting basic human psychology increase the pressure. Neither the children, nor even the teachers and parents who nurture them, have been given the training or the skills on how to handle the sort of information overload which afflicts all of us. Television presents children every evening with most powerful visual and verbal stimuli, reflecting the sometimes exciting, often banal and occasionally distressing nature of life itself.

It is small wonder that schools experience an uphill fight to grasp the attention of a clientele already punch-drunk by information and more exciting vistas. Society expects them to be centres of learning excellence, models of social behaviour and examples of community achievement, almost as if the real world outside – of drugs, of explicit and pervasive sexual titillation, of deprivation and despair – does not exist within their perception. They have not been given the necessary resources and the authority to fulfil that role, either through the constant training and retraining of teachers, or through the increased funding which might enable them to compete with the professional media people.

Peer group pressures are also of paramount concern to the pubescent adolescent, struggling to reconcile the feel of adulthood with the taboos of home, school and the community at large. In this environment, learning is subject to group acceptance. If learning is cool within that group, learning takes place. If it is not, as in many of the sink estates of every large city, an anti-learning culture often results and the vast open world of information, communication and opportunity closes down for that section of the population.

Forward to basics

In such times of change and constant stress, there is a great temptation for society to withdraw backwards into the old certainties. The back to the basics movements, so popular with governments under fire, surface and re-surface each time society needs reassurance. No matter that the basics are themselves subject to changing times and that the traditional virtues become less relevant or inappropriate. Of course those old stalwarts of the diehard – reading, writing and arithmetic – are still important. Without them children and adults are disenfranchised from learning. But, as Naisbitt says, 'to stop there is to equip children only with the skills of their grandparents. It is like giving them a wrench to fix a computer. There is nothing wrong with a wrench, but it won't fix a computer.'

Schools are pressured, often by governments under pressure themselves to demonstrate their commitment to rising standards, to adopt ever more rigid structures, curricula and assessment processes in order to improve measurable literacy rates. Often these seem to work in the short term. But the in-built failure mechanisms in assessment systems, and increased parental, child and institutional anxiety to avoid them, often have, in the longer term, the opposite effect from what was intended. The objectives become to satisfy the objectives. Children become examination laboratory animals. Learning itself suffers. It becomes a less attractive proposition, no longer spontaneous and enjoyable, more of a chore to be endured than an experience to be enjoyed, and actively switches many youngsters off it for life. Bryce, a research fellow at the Australian Council for Educational Research, challenges this bleak prospect in the name of a new approach. She points out that 'many parents have an expectation that their children's school experiences will be very much like their own – with imposed discipline, mainly summative assessment and teachers who are remote figures of authority. A lifelong learning approach requires that these perceptions be changed.'

And yet, although the much longer term may bring a complete re-evaluation of mass schooling as an instrument of education – the home schooling movement is accelerating in every country – it is still the primary task of the traditional school to empower its pupils to respond to the modern realities of change, information technology, lifelong learning and the knowledge society. Its focus has to be on the future as well as the present. The means by which this transformation can be accomplished extends far beyond the schools/industry and schools/community real-life links suggested in previous and subsequent chapters.

Extremely valuable they may be, but they are only one technique among many. Certainly those children participating in the Woodberry Down project, described in Chapter 5, benefited immensely from their experiences with the people from IBM. They became more aware and more rounded as a result of their contact. Their attitudes visibly changed and their values expanded. But this in itself did not transform the school into a lifelong learning school. Many more actions are needed at all levels to do that.

Characteristics of a lifelong learning school

What is it that makes a good lifelong learning school? How can the human potential of all our children be developed without turning them off the process of learning, and without losing the goodwill and support of the community? How can children be transformed into confident, creative and contributing citizens as adults? How can the habit of learning be instilled so that it becomes an enjoyable and personally rewarding way of passing time throughout life? Such things take time both to prepare and to implement and the process should start as soon as possible. As Chapman and Aspin suggest, 'in this debate on lifelong learning there is presently emerging a discussion on the need for a new concept of obligatory or home schooling, which is more flexible than that which had had pride of place hitherto'.

In the spirit of this, what follows in subsequent chapters are 11 indicators by which a school can measure its performance as a lifelong learning school. But we must of course bear in mind that all schools are different, from region to region and from country to country. The needs of a rural school in Tanzania are very different from those of an urban school in the centre of Birmingham. In addition, many schools will have already implemented some of the lifelong learning strategies and actions suggested. But it is the ensemble of actions that is important. Lifelong learning is a holistic concept and actions taken in one domain will affect results in another.

There may also be a temptation to use this as a check-list for progress. But this is not a quantitative exercise to assess whether or not this or that action is being taken. Some suggestions may indeed be inappropriate for some schools. The indicators should be read in the spirit in which they are offered, as qualitative suggestions which would enhance the chances and the choices of those people passing through the school system to become lifelong learners, capable of adapting to a changing, and often hostile, world. They are not therefore about the school as an institution; they are more about its long-term effect on the people in it. Further, for reasons of space each topic is not expanded as much as it could be, but in Part 1 there are many additional examples from the schools sector to illustrate the points made in this chapter.

Chapter 15

Where's the connection? School strategies and business plans

Education and training C20th	Lifelong learning C21st	Action for change
Rudimentary short-term business plan usually around academic matters. Little effort to keep every stakeholder informed and on-side	A full written organizational strategy, available to all, for developing the school into a lifelong learning organization and covering all aspects of the school's activity	Develop longer-term school business plan and make it available to all – create information strategies to bring all stakeholders on-side

Figure 15.1 School plans and strategies

A local BBC television news item on 10 September 2002 described how a failing school in Bexley, in the suburbs of London, has revitalized itself by turning itself into a business. It continues to receive its normal funding from the local education authority, but also adds resources by selling its services to other members of the community on a commercial basis, and by tapping into the goodwill of local industry. The word 'teacher', it suggested, is 'old hat'. What used to be teachers are now 'learning managers', who discuss the content of what has to be learnt with each individual learner. The means of learning is principally through the copious banks of computers and screens shown in several classrooms and through the well-stocked library liberally fitted out with self-study carrels. Pupils themselves were non-paying shareholders in the company, the dividend being the amount of learning that they do, and, it was claimed, this new regime had turned the school round.

Such new approaches may or may not work in other environments. They would, in many societies, send a shudder of apprehension through the body corporate, either because they are seen as too extreme, or as a gimmick, or as an illustration that business and commerce have no part in academic life. However, whatever is thought of the philosophy by which pupils are brought to learning in this school, there are lessons to be learnt about motivation, technology and strategy. At the very least, this story illustrates that every school needs a sense of purpose and a firm plan for why, where, when and how it will develop in the future.

In industry a business plan would describe the organization's major goals and objectives; its marketplace and its products; how it intends to go about achieving the objectives, and the resources it will need to do so; how it relates to the world outside the organization; its management strategy for the empowerment of its workforce; and the methods it would use to satisfy its customers and shareholders. It would be a blueprint for action over a period of time, say three or five years, but modifiable according to economic or other circumstance, and containing check-points every six months or so when it would be re-examined in the light of the realities of change and business life. Further, as Figure 2.2 shows us, it would be communicated to all the people who have a stake in realizing the plan and, in a modern enterprise, they would be invited to discuss it and contribute to it.

This would seem, at first sight, to have little relevance to the *raison d'être* of a school. But if we consider that the school has its own wider constituency of stake-holders – parents, children, teachers, administrators, governors and members of the outside community – often with conflicting views and interests, the analogy is less remote. It will need to convince all this audience and involve them in the development of the strategy and its purpose. It will need tact and diplomacy, high-order management skills and the delivery of education in an appropriate way to each group. Modern schools now try to create the equivalent of a company culture, a sense of belonging to a worthwhile organization with worthwhile objectives and a common aim for everyone to aspire to. They do this by explaining their objectives and the strategy so that everyone – administrators, teachers, children, cleaners, governors, parents – has a sense of ownership and everyone a set of personal goals to help realize it.

There are of course some constraints. Much of what they do in terms of curriculum, assessment and governing statutes is determined by external factors; the burden on staff is already high and support systems are sparse; school administrators have had little training in executive management techniques. And there is also the fear factor faced by all organizations embracing change – fear of interference, fear of openness, fear of change itself. Meanwhile the world continues to change at an ever more rapid rate and to present ever more complex challenges, until further delay is no longer tolerable. Chapman and Aspin describe the three challenges in this way:

> To identify ways in which schooling can respond to national and international imperatives emanating from global pressures, at the same time as being expected by

governments on the domestic front to function with greater autonomy, and with much wider responsibility to generate funds to support their operation.

To provide an education for all young people that gives them access to a global society in regard to employment opportunities, cultural literacy and sensitivity and intercultural understanding, adaptability and flexibility.

To ensure that national and local cultures and traditions and a sense of community identity can be sustained and perpetuated, at the same time as countries are preparing their citizens to function in increasingly international and global settings.

One answer is of course to ignore all of that and teach the subjects in the curriculum to the required examination standard. But this does little service to the children beyond enabling them to demonstrate a piece of paper. It does not give them the skills and competencies to understand the issues that will face them in the longer term, nor does it contribute to greater harmony, understanding, tolerance, peace and the development of a better person. These too, as desirable outcomes, would be among the subjects of the school strategy.

The movement to lifelong learning presents an opportunity – indeed an imperative – to schools to learn in such a way that they can re-assess their *raison d'être* and their operational strategies. In working out its strategy, Mawson Lakes School near Adelaide, for example, describes the factors it will take into account:

- Whole-of-life education will be available to all at Mawson Lakes.
- Optimal use will be made of the new information and communication technologies.
- The principles of sharing, cooperation and collaboration will apply in the delivery of education at Mawson Lakes.
- Education will contribute to the economic sustainability of Mawson Lakes.
- New resource models will be required for education at Mawson Lakes.
- Mawson Lakes will be part of the global community connected internationally and a destination for learners from all over the world.
- There will be effective quality assurance procedures in relation to educational services at Mawson Lakes.
- There will be new partnerships needed in the context of education at Mawson Lakes.
- There will be special 'signatures' associated with education at Mawson Lakes.
- Educational services at Mawson Lakes must take account of the surrounding areas.
- The principle of transferability must apply to the design and operation of educational services at Mawson Lakes.
- Educational services at Mawson Lakes must be accessible to all and appropriate for all.
- Educational services at Mawson Lakes must be responsive to the inevitability of unforeseeable change.

This is an admirable set of basic principles incorporating local, national and international outlooks and giving rise to the development of a visionary plan to implement them of which we shall see more later. Each one of these aims is expanded into an action statement to say how it will be achieved. One can walk into this school, as the author did, and see, in one classroom, a grandmother learning with her grandchild, and next door a young eight-year-old child learning Indonesian through a television link to Djakarta provided by the neighbouring adult education college. Its vision is 'to create a lifelong learning community where learning is available for everyone, at any time, and in any place. Educational services will contribute to the economic sustainability of Mawson Lakes and become a catalyst and a conduit for the creation of a community that has a culture of continuous improvement.'

There are many other examples of schools now waking up to the need to develop organizational plans, to involve the community in doing so and to promote them in the whole community in which they exist. Malet Lambert School, a mixed comprehensive school in Hull, UK, started its journey into learning some years ago. It created a 'Learning Development Group' and initiated a survey of worldwide learning research literature. As a result it has completely transformed its teaching/learning strategy. According to 'Learning to Live' there are now weekly learning-to-learn sessions in Years 7–9, and, just as appropriately, it has started to bring external groups, especially from local families, into the learning process. It has produced a range of learning materials, including a 'learning-to-learn' video, which it uses to educate and involve parents and others in the community. The materials are designed to encourage families to learn together and are sold to help fund new development projects.

Such schools are becoming 'learning organizations', where the objective is to ensure that everyone within, and connected to, the institution is valued and valuable, and where the means of expressing this is through their love for learning and their behaviour. Such values should be proclaimed to the school, the parents, the governors and the community around the school. The poster shown as Figure 15.2 is reproduced with the kind permission of Long Learn Ltd. It encapsulates what a school might want to say to its stakeholders.

Such posters proclaim the value of learning and the mission of the school loudly and clearly to its stakeholders and bring them into the learning community around the school. Together with a variety of other communication strategies defined by the business plan, they engage teachers, children, parents, governors and people in the local community in the common task of making learning a positive experience.

This is a

Lifelong Learning School

We:

L   **L**ove all children with equal depth as individuals – for life

I   **E**mpower all children to develop their full potential – for life

F   **A**ssess all children without creating failure – for life

E   **R**esource all children with skills and values – for life

L   **N**ourish all children mentally, physically and spiritually – for life

O   **I**nvolve parents and the community – for life

N   **N**urture all children into full and fulfilled human beings – for life

G   **G**ive all children a respect for themselves and others – for life

A Lifelong Learning Company
(longlearn1 @hotmail.com)
www.longlearn.org.uk

Figure 15.2 A school charter

Chapter 16

Keeping everybody up to date – continuous improvement in schools

Education and training C20th	Lifelong learning C21st	Action for change
Some teachers go on educational courses according to need or desire. Occasional seminars in schools for teachers only	Every person in the school has a continuous improvement plan for academic and personal skill/knowledge development embedded into the management system, and part related to the school development plan	Develop written continuous improvement plans for academic and personal development of pupils, teachers and admin staff. Extend these to parents and community as desired

Figure 16.1 Continuous improvement

Rose and Nicholl, two of the progenitors of 'Accelerated learning', point out that 'even a well-educated, fully trained adult with a wealth of qualifications' can only expect to remain current with developments in a changing world for a maximum of three years. New knowledge, new procedures, new processes and new environments will enforce new thinking, new actions and new ideas. A professional person who does not understand and implement the need for continuous improvement in a lifelong learning world is not just standing still. He/she is falling behind. This imperative was argued in Chapter 2, as was the changing nature of the teaching function in Chapter 3. Schools in particular are probably the least prepared of all the education providers for this new environment, even though they will experience the greatest changes both in the things they do and the way they do it. Christopher Day, professor of education at Nottingham University, concentrates his research on the educational needs of teachers. He suggests that 'the maintenance of good teaching demands that teachers review regularly the ways in which they are applying principles of differentiation, coherence, progression and continuity. They also need to establish balance in the what and the how of their teaching and their core moral purposes. To be a professional means taking up a lifelong commitment to inquiring practice.'

Such thinking, emphasizing the need for school teaching methodologies and curricula to reflect the changes in society as a whole, is encapsulated into almost every report on education produced in the past ten years. The Finnish national strategy for lifelong learning, for example, points to 'new demands on educational institutions' to bring teachers up to date. 'The professionalism of teachers,' it said, 'is a key factor in determining whether it is possible to take the next step' (towards creating a lifelong learning society). It emphasizes the need for in-service training as the second pillar of its policy, and proposes a number of stratagems for cultivating this, including statutory local authority lifelong learning courses for all in-service teachers and the involvement of the Finnish Broadcasting Company to provide wide access to such courses.

A school is, at least potentially, an organization for learning. Everyone there – children, teachers and administrative staff – is a learner with a need to stay up to date and in touch with the demands of a world of change. For children, learning is the reason why they are there; for administrators and teachers it is a professional duty to stimulate that learning. Every person in the school would benefit, for example, from the development of a personal learning plan, which may, in these circumstances, be the full life version as described in Chapter 4 and Appendix 2, or a modified and cut-down version addressing issues of job and career. For teachers in particular the transformation of the school into a lifelong learning establishment will entail great changes. They will develop new skills and competencies. The psychology of how people learn, individual learning styles, open and distance learning technologies, how to motivate reluctant learners, using the Internet for collaborative teaching, creating fruitful learning partnerships, mentoring techniques, administering learning audits and personal learning plans are just a few of the skills and competencies they will need to update as a part of their continuous professional development, just as doctors and lawyers have to stay current with developments in medicine and the law.

And that is the easy list. To classroom management skills are added resource and person management skills, leadership and counselling skills and the competence to inspire and animate others. How to encourage creativity, how to identify barriers to confidence, how to use new learning relaxation techniques such as meditation and music, or transactional analysis and brainstorming, the psychology of learning stimulation, how to open up the mind to new learning and how to make learning fun are an even greater challenge to the teacher. All of this would be a part of a school management system aimed at transforming the school into a 'learning organization' (see Chapter 22) or a learning community, where every member of staff and every child has a personal learning target for the day, week and/or month and is actively engaged in continuous learning.

Of course, many conscientious teachers now work in this way. But it is not so simple as it seems. On top of the existing workload of book-marking, pastoral care, after-school classes, extra-curricular activities and all the additional tasks expected of the teacher, continuous improvement often takes a low priority. Rest periods which could be used for that purpose somehow disappear as staff have to fill in for absent colleagues. The constant rush and diversity of the school day is phrenetic and sometimes exhausting. In some countries the shortage of classroom teachers exacerbates the problem. In others, teachers are given a maximum class contact time and not expected to exceed that. Certainly there is a need on the part of governments, city councils and schools themselves to re-evaluate the ways in which schools are staffed, and to adopt flexible timetabling and small group/large group presentation strategies. Incorporated into this should be opportunities for teachers to update themselves on courses, in school and at home, and not to leave it only to the holiday break for this to happen. Further, this is not just an individual activity. In education, more than in most environments, there is a need for interaction, discussion and purposeful self-development.

Continuous improvement is nowhere more urgent than in socially deprived areas. There is often an atmosphere of resignation that the constant daily battle with poor motivation and antisocial behaviour cannot be won. Self-image in both teachers and students suffers. Youngsters assume they cannot succeed, receive little positive encouragement at home and develop behavioural attitudes leading to exclusion. In such circumstances, help from outside organizations can be useful to break into the mindset this creates. This is why the Speke Garston's *Investment in Excellence* programme can be instructive as a means to stimulate the continuous improvement and adaptation process of teachers. The Pacific Institute, a privately funded educational leadership organization, was funded by the European Social Fund and the UK single regeneration budget to develop appropriate new industry-based approaches to education in an area of South Liverpool with high levels of unemployment, social deprivation and teacher turnover. Seventy-five per cent of the staff volunteered to attend two full weekend seminars run by the Institute in which the motivational difficulties of the three key elements – pupils, teachers and parents – were confronted head-on, solutions identified and special training given. The programme concentrates specifically on the underlying negative self-perceptions of parents and pupils and ways of breaking down the 'us and them' syndrome which can be a major barrier to improvement. It is designed to help both staff and pupils face challenges, develop motivation and self-belief and to see their own development as a positive and continuous process.

Early results from the project show encouraging signs. Continual rein-forcement of good behaviour replaces negative reaction to poor behaviour and activity. Year 10 and 11 students who are in danger of underachieving are encouraged to stretch themselves at weekend residential courses. The school promotes a 'can-do' culture. Some teachers say that they have 'had their lives changed' by the process and feel much more confident in their relationships with pupils. Examination results have improved at the top of the school and those pupils who have been through the programme are seen as much more developed. But the major insight to be gained from this, assisted by the input from industry, is the need for continuous improvement for every person in the school.

A second example comes from Australia. Kormilda College is a low-fee-paying school in Darwin, in the Northern Territory of Australia. It has an interesting mix of pupils between those from the local community and those from indigenous, mainly aboriginal, backgrounds. Three hundred are boarders and 500 are day students.

Lambert, Willis and Sleep report that, within the first two years of working at the college, all staff – teachers, management, residential staff, administration and grounds and maintenance staff – are taken through a four-day self-management and leadership skills course in a resort away from the pressures of everyday school life. It is designed and delivered by college staff, in association with management consultants brought in from the outside, to develop both theoretical and practical skills and understandings about effective team leadership and team membership.

At the same time, a similar course emphasizing leadership and self-management has been developed for all students, so that every person connected with the school is pulling in the same direction. Following each stage, the students are required to participate in leadership activities in some aspect of academic, sporting, leisure or community life.

In addition to this, there is an ongoing teacher development programme to enable them to address the issues of 21st-century education with maturity and wisdom. Outcomes-focused education, what the college calls 'teaching for learning', ensures that learners are empowered to learn by the use of lifelong learning tools and skills. Teachers work constantly in teams, trialling and drafting their own ideas through circular and cyclical processes of review, development, implementation and transition. There are frequent workshops with outside experts to avoid the inward-looking approach that so often besets educational organizations. Key people are targeted to attend courses, and to run the workshops themselves for all staff on their return. Such dedication to the concept of excellence means that both staff and students are never satisfied with the status quo. They constantly seek to improve it through new ideas, new approaches and new projects, which is how any learning organization must operate in this world of constant change.

In industry learning organizations the word 'quality' is used as a generic to express this concept. Around it are placed reward schemes, special management policies, house styles, company identity and a whole range of strategies to inform, involve and continuously learn. How many schools have delivered quality management courses for all their teachers and administrative staff? And how many have thought to offer quality courses for the children? And are there any schools with a suggestion box, or a grievance procedure, or a strategy for the development of new teaching materials? Are posters, such as those shown in Figures 15.2 and

16.2, prominently displayed before the children and staff as permanent reminders of the school's purpose? A quality policy for a school, which involves also the children in its formulation, is not beyond the creative capacity of school administrators. Certainly, it is an essential step towards establishing the school as a learning organization, using the resources of the community, particularly those of the industrial or business sector, to help define, design and implement it.

Lifelong Learning
LETS YOU

L ead a fuller and more fulfilled life

E arn more in a better job

A ctivate your creativity and imagination

R elease the power of your own mind

N ourish your own inner strengths

I nspire yourself and others to greater things

N urture and make possible your dreams

G enerate more knowledge and self-respect

LEARNING IS <u>THE</u> MOST NATURAL HUMAN ACTIVITY

A LIFELONG LEARNING COMPANY
(Longlearn1@hotmail.com)
www.longlearn.org.uk

Figure 16.2 A learning poster

Chapter 17

New resources for old everywhere – using the community

Education and training C20th	Lifelong learning C21st	Action for change
Teachers only human resource for curriculum delivery supplemented by helpers. Other resources supplied from local government and school events	School adds human resource by tapping into skills, talents and knowledge of governors, parents and everyone in the community and other resource by exploring funding and other sources in the community	Appoint someone to identify and use ALL the human and other resources in the community and beyond. Use innovative strategies to involve the community in school development

Figure 17.1 New resources from the community

For a long time in the early 20th century the school gates were a formidable barrier to any person other than teachers, children and administrators. Parents and members of the community passed them at their peril and usually with trepidation. What went on inside the school was the preserve of the headteacher and (usually) his staff. Academic values and disciplines ruled. The curriculum was determined by the school, taught by the teachers and absorbed, with various degrees of efficiency, by the children. Where this absorption process was less than perfect, more physical means were used as an aid to memory. Indeed, memory was all. The ability to recite long lists and poems by heart was the only proof of understanding and appreciation required. This somewhat idealized and uncritical view of the way things were in education of course hides many exceptions, but, in general, respect for authority was a strong feature of that period. It is a condition which recalls fond memories in many older people, and indeed, in many countries where education is in short supply, it is still the norm.

However, schools now operate in a complex world becoming ever more complex and diverse. Respect has to be earned and the democratic concerns of a wider constituency of people and organizations met. Knowledge has proliferated, a greater number of skills and competencies are needed to survive in an often hostile world and values and attitudes have changed. The sources of information have burgeoned and become ever more urgent. The job of the teacher has changed with all of this. No longer is he/she God, the fount of all knowledge, the ticket to prosperity. Teachers need help. John Abbott recognizes this:

> For adolescents to develop skills and attitudes needed for a knowledge economy, learning must be viewed as a total community responsibility. It is not just teachers who must teach nor students who must continually learn, nor is it the classroom that is the major access point to a range of information and expertise on which knowledge is built. Good schools alone will never be good enough. Successful 21st-century societies will have learning communities in line with the needs of continuously changing economic and social environments.

Despite a hard-fought rearguard action by professional teacher associations intent on preserving the image of an all-knowing and all-powerful teacher, the idea that one person can fulfil the hopes, ambitions and demands of more than 30 young individuals in the same space over the same time now looks as ridiculous as the notion that Canute could hold back the waves.

Many schools still display a fortress mentality which sees non-professional help as an intrusion and a confession of failure on the part of teachers and the school. Indeed, the first is true – it *is* an intrusion, but a wholly positive one in that the introduction of new knowledge, new faces, new wisdom, new outlooks widens the horizons of both children and teachers. In many junior schools in Europe and North America, teacher aides, parents and experienced helpers from the community are now invading the sanctuary of the classroom. In schools like Mawson Lakes in Adelaide and Espoo in Finland, everyone who wants to help or to learn is welcomed, be they mothers, grandads, subject experts from the university or people from industry. Each offers an extra resource and the teachers become managers of that resource.

In the long run, schools operate within a community and are responsible to it. At the same time the community makes ever more stringent academic, social, environmental, compartmental, managerial, political, cultural, spiritual, and economic demands upon them which, from their current resource base, they cannot possibly meet. They are, for the most part, mid-20th-century organizations with a 21st-century burden of expectation. As Longworth and Davies say:

> They are variously asked to become more open to the community and more restrictive and closed in their objectives, more flexible and more rigid, more adventurous and more timid, more gentle and more brutal, more visionary and more dogmatic. They are asked both to take on board new educational discoveries and to reject them. Small wonder that the reputation of schools has been falling. They have been given an unenviable task.

However, if the community demands improvement, the community should also be expected to play its part in supplying the means of that improvement. This is not only a matter of more financial resource, though that of course would always be welcomed. It is a willingness to provide the knowledge, skills, talent and personal assistance usable by schools. And, as the growing army of volunteers described in Chapter 10 shows, this is available in abundance from parents, grandparents, third-agers and individuals of goodwill in every community. No young child in a class of 30 should be left to wait for the seven precious minutes of available one-to-one teacher time in the school day, when there are so many who are able and willing to help stretch minds, develop potential and/or simply listen to reading under the leadership of the professional teacher. Such a classroom should be a hive of inter-action between children and adults, children and children, children and teacher, all orchestrated under the leadership of a teacher trained to manage every resource available to him/her. This is the true leadership of the 21st-century schoolroom, promoting the excitement and versatility of learning instead of the boredom of waiting and inaction. To re-quote a Markkula and Suurla metaphor, the sage on the stage has been replaced by the guide at the side. Of course, such aid has to be managed properly against the possibility of racist or political propagandists, or indeed sick people who might be harmful to children. But the traditional sources of expertise from policemen, nurses and parents are now being supplemented by engineers and technologists, craftsmen and third-agers. Indeed, the only barrier to the deployment of the vast resources available in every community is the use of creative imagination, and the time to organize it all.

Nor is this only useful in the junior schools. Secondary school pupils would benefit hugely through contact with expertise from the real world they expect to inhabit. In a world where, according to Naisbitt in 1984, '7,000 scientific papers are published every day. The amount of information is 4 to 7 times what it was in 1980, and since this is a self-generating process, the amount of information is doubling every 4–7 years', few people expect teachers to have a complete knowledge of his/her own subject, in addition to the skills demanded in doing the job. Teachers are more and more conductors of the orchestra of learning, introducing the instruments which facilitate the learning in a wide range of symphonic variations and only the exceptionally talented are both conductor and soloist in the concerto of wisdom.

There are many stories of schools using community resources on the lifelong learning journey. Chapter 5 contains some excellent examples. Kormilda College, quoted in Chapter 16, has a ten-year plan with the Rio Tinto company which has not only helped with the development of staff and students as described above, but also in capital works programmes such as the provision of computers, health facilities and support for the performing arts. The IBM–Woodberry Down School project, described in Chapter 5, made a huge amount of expert human resource available to the school in addition to its support for the language and field study trips. In several versions of the US adopt-a-school programme, business acts as a benign contributor to school-life and funds. For example, *Learning Cities for a Learning Century* quotes:

> the Walt Disney corporation operates a challenge programme in Florida, in which high school students at risk of drop-out are offered a way to stay at school, and merit awards are offered to innovative teachers. The Georgia Pacific lumber company funds teachers to teach computer modelling and simulation as a new way of thinking developed at MIT. Sara Lee supports arts programmes on the grounds that creativity in the arts can lead to creativity in the development of new products. Apple and IBM have donated thousands of computers to schools and paid for research into computer-based learning techniques.

Such programmes also exist in the UK. The large groceries company, Tesco, tells its customers that a proportion of their purchases will provide computers for schools. It is a prize example of enlightened self-interest. For similar reasons, the Nike company operates a football coaching scheme for schools, IBM supports the development of young tennis players and the Royal Bank of Scotland provides free finance courses for teachers and children. The UK government supports these actions, particularly in the poorer parts of the country, where the concept of Education Action Zones gives local authorities a right to raise private sector money with matching funding supplied from government.

Of course there are those who deplore such interference with the academic process, and others who find a sinister purpose in the participation of big business in the affairs of schools. And these are well founded where the donor requires a quid pro quo in the form of undue influence, as happened in 2002 in a Gateshead school, where it was a requirement to insert 'creationism' into the curriculum in order to receive the beneficence of a company. But few companies see it this way. Industry gains little benefit from operating in a socially divisive, high-crime environment, and would see its contribution to the school sector as at best corporate social responsibility – that is, its responsibility to support the society in which it operates – or, more realistically, enlightened self-interest.

No government or city education budget can afford the resources needed to implement the transition to a fully inclusive lifelong learning society, and it is that inclusiveness which legitimizes and adds value to community involvement in education. Such opportunities are more abundant in some communities than in others but there are also national and civic opportunities. The Bolton School in the UK, for example, has a contact point working on a semi-professional basis to tap into the resources available nationally and locally. It looks to its former pupils, the Old Boltonians, to donate the wherewithal to construct new classrooms and provide new facilities and bursaries, and seeks out financial and other support to implement its drive into the 21st century. Many other schools work in this way using volunteers under the direction of an administrator. The financial resources to help create a lifelong learning school will come from such imaginative activities.

Chapter 18

Success for all – the skills-based curriculum

Education and training C20th	Lifelong learning C21st	Action for change
Curriculum based on discrete subjects, and assessed on memorization of facts with pass–fail philosophy	Curriculum based on skills and knowledge, the enhancement of self-esteem and the acceptance of lifelong values. Examinations as stock-taking part of the personal learning process	Incorporate personal skills development into the curriculum. Take the notion of failure out of the system and replace it with strategies for improving personal self-esteem

Figure 18.1 The skills-based curriculum

Administrations of any kind often become locked into systems of delivery simply because to change them would involve a high financial cost, political and management upheaval and a mindset change of Herculean proportions. Such is the state of the present-day school curriculum. A subject-based timetable teaching a subset of information in discrete topics at pre-set times during the school day ignores the realities of the information explosion in a fast-changing world and is surely irrelevant. A didactic communication methodology ignoring modern-day knowledge of retention patterns and learning psychology has to accept that some of the imparted knowledge will fall by the wayside and is surely inefficient and ineffective. An examination process designed to fail a good proportion of its students is surely wasteful. A value system setting greater store on academic and intellectual performance over personal attributes such as self-esteem, self-knowledge and tolerance for others is surely misguided. An assessment procedure testing only the skill of the memory to regurgitate facts and information, and ignoring the importance of other high–order skills such as information handling, decision making, communicating, thinking and others enumerated in Figure 18.2, is surely inappropriate for the 21st century. They are all legacies of a mediaeval education system adapted in the 19th century to divide sheep from goats and provide undergraduate material for the universities.

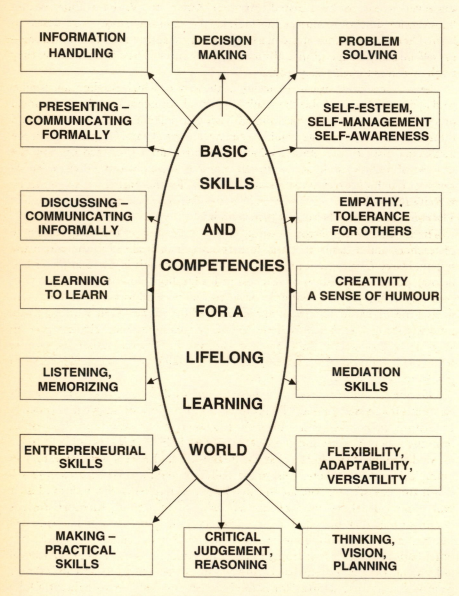

Figure 18.2 Skills and competencies

There is no shortage of educational commentators who recognize this. The well-known American educationist John Holt pointed out as long ago as the 1960s that: 'Since we cannot know what knowledge may be most needed in the future it is senseless to try to teach it in advance. Instead we should try to turn out people who love learning so much and learn so well that they will be able to learn whatever needs to be learned.' Another American, William Ellis, wrote, 'Conventional schools restrict the individual's natural curiosity and desire to learn. They exemplify our authoritarian, hierarchical and patriarchal culture based on self-interest, competition and survival of the fittest. They teach by how they teach as well as by what they teach.'

Nevertheless, since that is the reality of the way in which teachers are taught, paid and promoted, and also the result of political domination of the educational process, schools are in the position of having to adhere to the system, stupid though it may be. To change would be an enormous upheaval. We may lament the intellectual paucity of a content-dominated curriculum inspected only by the exercise of memory skills at a particular moment in time and the divisive irrelevance of much of it to the real needs of children for the future, but we are stuck with it until such time as it is seen to be harmful to social cohesion and economic advance – which may be sooner than we think.

There are also other factors at work, related to the limits of the energy and time of teachers, and a desire to avoid further stress than is already inherent in the system. Harry Cruse, the founder of the 'Du Kan' schools in Sweden (described below), posed the question to teachers in his locality: 'How do you work with your pupils? Do you use textbooks or do you allow them to work on their own, freely I mean?' More often than not he received the answer 'Well, working freely is not my thing, I don't believe in it. One of my colleagues once tried but gave up after a couple of weeks. She thought it was so messy. I would rather keep to the textbook. It is calmer that way. Everyone is at the same place then and it easier to give homework and to give fair marks.'

Of course these teachers are right. It *is* much calmer and makes for a much easier life. It also switches off half our future. It takes a leap of imagination, energy, conviction and courage, and, it has to be said, sometimes political suicide, to break from the way things are into the way things should be. But it is possible to move forward through stealth, if the right techniques are applied. The issue of skills is an example. Figure 18.2 shows a list of the skills required for survival in tomorrow's world. But few of these skills are independent of each other. As any industry leader will point out, there are well-known ways of improving memory, today's dominant accreditation requirement, and these could quite easily be incorporated into the curriculum with quite dramatic effect within the current system. So can other high-order skills of learning to learn, thinking, problem solving and critical judgement. Even a content-based curriculum can benefit from developing new generic skills in its victims. Nor is the issue one of skills versus content. Quite evidently, information and knowledge are useful things to have. It is more the way in which it is presented. Consider this quotation from *Lifelong Learning – New Visions, New Implications, New Roles*:

> At the age of sixteen or so we tend to release them from a kind of bondage system in our schools into the open-endedness of an increasingly complex world. They have indeed acquired a great deal of data about many things – literature, science, geography, language (sometimes) and history, and most of them have also acquired the facility to memorize it and rewrite it onto an examination paper. However, they seem to have little understanding of what it all means, where it all fits together and how to use it effectively. It all seems to be a little irrelevant, a product of a system whose only objective is to achieve its only objective. Having acquired information in a compartmentalized way, children (and adults) have difficulty turning the data into information, the information into knowledge, let alone into the understanding which comes from putting it together into a conceptual whole. Nor do they have any love for the knowledge they have so painfully acquired. Having started in this way, the resentment and sense of failure lasts well into adult life, inhibiting the further growth and development of the enormous potential resident in all human beings.

The admixture of content and skills into the curriculum would undoubtedly improve it, but, as was suggested in the previous chapter, there also is another missing factor – that of values. The world is a large and complex place. The essential learning and navigational skills to enable students to take at least an informed view of new employment patterns, sustainable development, minority rights, sex roles, sexuality, personal responsibility, global politics, different cultures and creeds and the need to invest in a lifetime of learning would be an essential component of any 21st-century curriculum.

And of course there are many programmes where schools have adopted this much more open approach. As long ago as 1993 the European Secondary Heads Association, supported by grants from business and industry, developed a 'Personal Effectiveness Programme Initiative' (PEPI) encouraging groups of teachers to introduce competencies to pupils, and then to continue to develop these during their normal classroom studies. They included communication, presentation, teamwork, time management, problem solving and decision making. Teachers selected one competence and emphasized this in their teaching for half a term. Business employees were involved in demonstrating the relevance of these competencies for working life. At the end of a school year students receive a certificate which identifies the skills which they have gained. The results showed clear evidence of increased self-esteem and confidence, as well as improved academic achievements, especially in young people from deprived areas. But, as is often true of large international projects, it finished after two years and only those participating schools benefited at the time.

The 'Du Kan' schools in Sweden put their teachers in a position of leadership. Cruse comments: 'There is no best leadership. An effective leader is interested in both the tasks and the individuals he leads. When pupils come to school they have different readiness. Some of them have high ability and high willingness. Some have low ability and low willingness. The teacher must then know how to lead.' The four different styles of situational leadership – Telling, Selling, Participating and Delegating – hand over responsibility for decisions and implementation to the learner. Working like this is a process where each individual's learning and development depends on his/her ambition, teamwork skill, and attitude. A good social climate in the class and a corporate character such that every learner dares to hang out his/her assumptions will generate fruitful dialogues and new knowledge, generating new knowledge and so on. Border guards, that is, pupils who understand the network of knowledge, will help pupils who do not yet understand to grasp the principles. In Du Kan the skills mirror those in PEPI and other programmes – communication, interpersonal, time management, self-management, research skills, problem solving and team working.

The intellectual roots of the skills-based curriculum go back many years. 'Information Skills in Secondary Schools', a student-centred course written and tested by Longworth in the early 1970s, contains a hundred hours of course materials encouraging children to understand how information is all around us, how it can be analysed, acted upon, distorted, expanded and proliferated in a variety of environments. When they are properly used, such discovery-based methods of teaching, often under threat from cash- and brain-strapped administrators, develop curiosity, flexibility and understanding in children. It is true that life and social skills, as shown in Figure 18.2, are difficult, perhaps impossible, to examine. They are also, as it happens, the most important skills for lifelong learning, best developed by the school in conjunction with parents, governors, professional organizations, interest groups and industry.

This is what has happened at St John's School and Community College in Marlborough, UK, which has a different approach to the curriculum. Its head, Patrick Hazlewood, recognizes the challenge. 'At a time when ICT holds the promise of unlimited horizons,' he says, 'the National Curriculum and other initiatives continue to force schools into a straitjacket of conformity. The opportunities for learners to develop a love of learning, an understanding of preferred learning styles and "to think outside the box" have at best not been encouraged and at worst, have been squashed.' He deplores the head-down, nose-to-the-grindstone philosophy which turns the natural creativity of so many youngsters off.

The school's response has been to experiment with a thematic curriculum based on the Royal Society of Arts competency framework (learning, citizenship, relating to people, managing situations and managing information). Twelve teachers were involved in devising joined-up themes such as 'making the news' – the story of communication, travelling through time from early days to the present, examining methods and how they work, and incorporating history, geography, physics, technology and information studies into one thematic whole over a period of five weeks. The emphasis throughout is on the learner learning how to learn, think and take personal responsibility for the processes. Because they have been involved, the enthusiasm of governors, teachers, parents and students is high.

Other schools are exploring new curriculum approaches. In the Adur region of West Sussex in the UK, an area with a declining manufacturing base, schools are building bridges to local industry to give children skills and insights into the world of work through active participation. The project has three main elements. Teachers from participating primary schools are placed in a local manufacturing company for a short period of time. During this period they devise with company people a practical student activity linked to the curriculum, for example electrical buggy design, and then carry it out as a joint exercise. The industrial awareness element focuses on young people as citizens. Lower-secondary pupils carry out real-life studies of facets of local industry to develop an awareness of the inter-action between the public and the private sector in economic life. Teachers again develop materials while on secondment to local industries. For older pupils there is work experience for all, each pupil being given a specific task to do in the company to give them a taste of the workplace. The result of this is the development of new skills and knowledge in a practical way, working with local experts. But there are also valuable spin-offs in the science and technology, history, geography and drama departments of the schools, in the increased motivation which spills over into other aspects of schoolwork, in the number of people from the community able and willing to help out in the schools and in the employability of young people in the whole region.

Unfortunately, for every pioneering activity there are hundreds of schools where the system rules, and the reluctance to change without being required or authorized to do so is strong, even though the intellect dictates its need.

But of course curriculum cannot be separated from other aspects of pedagogy. The question of assessment and how it links into curriculum delivery is raised in Chapter 8. The recurrent UK scandals of top-heavy A-level examination manipulation betrays just how entrenched is the culture of 'must-fail', and this is repeated in many countries around the globe. Curriculum-embedded testing and assessment for learning would be an improvement on the current conception of examinations as something that follows teaching and learning in order to test the memory. But, as we have said in that chapter, there is still some way to go in the development of the maturer concept of lifelong learning before ownership of the learning becomes also ownership of the testing, with the notion of failure replaced by the concept of personal knowledge stock-taking. Similarly, the transformation of teaching from passive to active methodologies, described in fuller detail in Chapter 10, can have an enlivening effect upon the way the curriculum affects the learning process by engaging the learner, as it has in St John's school. Given the need to convince sceptical teachers, parents and others in the community of the wisdom of these new approaches, these are change processes that will not happen overnight. But the incorporation of personal skills development into the curriculum and a greater concentration on building self-esteem in the learner would be a giant step towards creating a lifelong learning culture. Schools should start with the pilot testing of new curriculum ideas and approaches before launching into a full-scale curriculum refurbishment, and they should share the reasons for the necessity of such change with teachers, parents and the students themselves. The one thing they cannot afford to do is nothing.

Chapter 19

Creating an environment for learning – guidance, support and counselling

Education and training C20th	Lifelong learning C21st	Action for change
In-school pastoral care systems staffed by overworked teachers. Sparse support services to identify and solve individual learning and social problems early	Guidance, support and counselling systems available for all learners and their families using all available resources. Rapid identification and solution of learning and social problems	Introduce individual learning guidance systems for all pupils and update frequently. Use resources in school and community – mentors etc. Involve the family. Initiate rapid response system

Figure 19.1 Supporting learning

Although the curriculum at teacher training colleges is a full one, much of it focuses upon the theory and practice of classroom management and is rarely oriented towards alleviating the mental and emotional difficulties of children. Such tasks are left at a later date to the health and social workers who receive special training in the complex mixture of physical, social, mental, emotional and psychological processes involved when something goes wrong. But equally, in most areas of the world there is little cooperation between the various agencies providing such support, and a huge shortage of trained counsellors who can step into a situation where a child needs extra help. As we have seen in Chapter 1, the high drop-out rate in schools in the poorer housing estates of major cities is an eloquent testimony to the inability of schools to provide an education which can compete with the lure of the street, the helplessness, and sometimes fecklessness, of parents, and the shortage of professional assistance to catch and cure antisocial behaviour early. Clearly it is a situation needing special attention.

Schools find themselves in an invidious position. They are variously asked to become more open to the community and more restrictive and closed in their objectives, more flexible and more rigid, more adventurous and more timid, more gentle and more brutal, more visionary and more dogmatic. They are asked both to take on board new educational discoveries and to reject them. Small wonder that the reputation of schools has been falling. They have been given an unenviable task by a society that is not prepared to grant them the means to achieve it.

Of course, there are effective pastoral care systems in many schools to attend to the non-academic needs of children and many of them are excellently managed. The example of Espoo in Chapter 7 is one example of this and Mawson Lakes School has its own set of principles to address the situation through community involvement. 'Our achievements,' it says in its strategy document, 'will be supported by:

- Families who are engaged in both their own and their children's learning.
- The quality of the partnerships between parents, staff from all settings and the community at Mawson Lakes, that support the learning of all children in the service.'

It goes on to enumerate the ways by which it will engage that support, including:

- ensuring that the principles of early childhood development and a focus on children in the context of their families and the local community are sustained from birth through the early years of schooling;
- building a service that anticipates and adapts quickly and effectively to the changing needs of families and children, including a changing workforce;
- tailoring service responses and resources to the needs of individual children and families;
- delivering consistent quality across all settings within the service and a common approach to continuous improvement;
- valuing and celebrating the contribution of all partners (families, staff and community) in the early years' service;
- establishing and maintaining clear accountability for performance to their families and the wider community and using evidence as the basis for change;
- showing a willingness to acknowledge that each child has a right to his/her own learning pathway.

Clearly the school puts its faith in parents and anyone else in the community to help it achieve its goals, and recognizes the value of excellence and accountability.

A second example comes from Durham in the UK. The 'Partnership scheme for young people' addresses the vicious circle of children not being cared for properly, leading to disinterest at school, leading to poor achievement and eventually a life of crime. The County's behaviour support service devised a scheme to provide the support that children in care need in order to lift their levels of attainment, using people from a variety of agencies such as, among others, educational psychologists, special educational needs workers, police, careers advisers, social workers, soldiers, family support and 'Save the Children' workers. Every children's home in the county has a computer room and an educational coordinator, and every school a 'looked after children' contact. A 24-hour curriculum is offered, including working with the army on such activities as command tasks, assault courses and abseiling. Visits to museums, companies, mines, theatres and libraries are organized to raise awareness and self-esteem. One young girl who had been difficult to work with found her métier at a poetry reading and is now publishing her own poems. More than 50 external agencies are involved in this effort, but the early rewards are seen in improved school attendance and examination success figures, fewer school exclusions, better coordination between education and other local authority agencies and departments and, although little research has been done on this, less crime.

Such innovative and resource-intensive programmes are often expensive in the short term, but the alternatives are a greater long-term drain on the public purse. And nor should they be confined to children at risk. In many developed countries education takes little account of late development, multiple mentalities, brilliance damaged by dyslexia, new methods of identifying dysfunction and preferred styles of learning. All of these can lead to loss of self-esteem and need support and attention to ameliorate their effects. Such actions can not only vastly raise educational standards, but also promote a new appreciation of the multiple intelligences which human beings need to develop in order to grow into mature adults.

Lifelong learning precepts require teachers to act as counsellors in order to identify, and then develop, flexible and more individual methods of learning in a school as a place of excitement, opportunity and enjoyment. Such fundamental changes in practice will need time and major cultural surgery through lifelong learning research and development. The non-formal education sector – all those educational influences on children and adults, parents, governors, libraries, museums, professional societies, uniformed associations and religious organizations – can, and does, play a supportive part in opening the doors of perception for all. It has a breadth of vision for all which exists in very few places and which will take a long time to create. It makes the school a central focus for learning for everyone in the community, and enlarges its function. This more holistic and interdependent new educational approach can develop the skills and the knowledge which enable today's children, tomorrow's adults, to play a genuinely participative part in the society of the future.

Involving the family

Education and training C20th	Lifelong learning C21st	Action for change
Parents invited to school to discuss child's progress once a term. Occasional public information meetings	Involves the family in the life of the school through increased home–school cooperation and active participation in school events	Write a family participation guide outlining all the things parents etc can do for the school. Open an e-mail line. Establish a contact point

Figure 19.2 Involving the family

The family is one of the most important units in a young person's life. For most children, it is a secure environment within which life can continue when everything else fails. But not all families are such secure havens. Perversely, the generation gap tends to be wider in societies that proclaim liberty of conscience and freedom of thought, and alienated children tend to bring family discord with them into the school building and demonstrate it in their behaviour. Most schools will have their stories of the parents who won't cooperate, who abuse their children, who are the ones they should see and who never turn up at the evenings set aside for meetings with teachers. In many cases this is a result of their own bad school-day experiences. Thus anything that can improve this situation is a welcome advance.

One recourse is mentoring, also described in Chapter 7. Chapman and Aspin quote the example of St Bede's school in Blackburn, where mentoring is seen as a way of improving learning achievement. Each fortnight pupils are taken out of the classroom for 10–15 minutes for individual mentoring. This approach has been very effective and successful, especially for pupils with learning reluctance problems. Indeed, several schools in the UK use mentoring as a way of improving both behaviour and learning. In Wigan pupils are responsible for setting their own learning objectives and putting them into action plans, receiving help and guidance from teachers in the early years but needing less and less as they mature. These action plans are discussed with parents in line with the school's policy on home–school partnership and assessed frequently with the teacher/mentor. This has been so successful that the older pupils write their own performance report, which has to be endorsed by the tutor.

School and home

Such written home–school contracts are becoming increasingly common. But many schools have not always communicated effectively with the home. A lifelong learning school will try to think of strategies to make learning a family concern. In this scenario, a list of strategies for improving home–school cooperation might include:

- Devising courses for parents, running parents clubs and societies, encouraging sporting links between schools and parents and ultimately opening the doors to parental participation in classes, either as assistants or as learners.
- Marketing the school better to the home. School newsletters with a parents' page, brochures and informative handbooks and magazines with chatty chapters by the teachers and contributions from the children.
- Tripartite partnership arrangements between industry, school and home. Meeting the parents in the work situation and using their expertise in school.
- Carrying out learning audits (see Chapter 4) with parents and governors. Assessing the learning needs of parents and understanding how they might be satisfied. Questionnaires might be devised by the school and personal interviews carried out by the children.
- Appointing teachers and governors as a primary link to the school. Communicating school objectives and changes to the parents through these. Offering a parental advice service in whichever form the parent wants to receive it. A telephone hot-line. Inviting a parental suggestion box.
- Running a brainstorming session with members of staff on ideas of how to improve home–school cooperation. Use an industry or local government friend to do this.
- Establishing an e-mail link between school and home – setting homework tasks to be done on the home computer.
- Involve parents in extra-curricular activities – trips and journeys, school plays, sports teams, choirs, clubs and societies.
- Devise explicit signed home–school contracts outlining the responsibility of each for the education of children.
- Use friends of the school – parents, governors, members of the community who wish to make a contribution – to make friends with the school and run these programmes. They tend to be closer to the problem – and the solution.

Creative ideas are not difficult to produce and improved home–school cooperation is a prize worth seeking. But the last of these might provide the key to making it happen. Bournazel talks of 'reparenting' the system. '*Il faut reaparentalizer le système scolaire en recherchant une plus grande implication des parents. Ce qui peut necessiter parfois des mesures d'accompagnement pour les parents en difficultés.*' [We must reparent the school system in order to seek a larger role for parents. This could sometimes mean taking accompanying measures for parents with difficulties.]

Here is a new dimension for those parents who themselves have learning difficulties or who have insufficient knowledge of the school system to help their children. In France, there is a long tradition of parental responsibility for the cultural development of their own children. They tend to respect the traditions and disciplines of the school as a quid pro quo for their own involvement at home, and rarely do they question the authority of the head and staff. This situation is gradually breaking down under the pressures of modern living, the increasing irrelevance of a rigidly applied and measured school curriculum and family breakdown. Hence Bournazel's approach to make schools more accountable to the family. It echoes what is happening in the rest of the developed world.

Home–school agreements

But such accountability should not flow all in one direction. If parents are increasingly to be given the right to have a say in the education of their children, they have an equal responsibility to keep themselves up to date with educational trends and to discuss with the school how they may cooperate in implementing them. Home–school agreements have been a responsibility in British schools since 1999. There are some dangers in having too formal a contract, however, as Barrie Wyse indicates. 'The achievement of genuine dialogue between school and home can lead to greater understanding and insight on both sides,' he says, 'but it is not necessarily achieved by simply fulfilling the legal requirements for a school's link with parents. Nor will it automatically be achieved by the introduction of a home–school agreement.' He recommends a focus on the process, believing that a joint discussion with parents on the contents of such a document would be a far better means of passing over the philosophy and objectives of the school and the ways in which parents can help further the interests of the child, than a legally binding document setting out rules and regulations. In this way both parents and school have ownership of the process.

The fundamental needs, resources and purposes of a modern educational institution whose pupils will enter a world demanding flexibility of outlook, adaptability of mind and versatility of knowledge will be very different from the environment in which they themselves were brought up. In order to exercise their new influence on learning, people must learn themselves, becoming seriously informed and aware of how children really do learn, of curriculum matters, and of new techniques of learning. And, in a world of change they must continue to keep themselves informed about those things: thinking, thinking about and thinking through. The practice of educational democracy is one of the key challenges facing schools in the lifelong learning age.

Chapter 20

Bringing the school to the world and the world to the school – the social curriculum

Education and training C20th	Lifelong learning C21st	Action for change
Focus on curriculum and examination success within the school. Social curriculum dealt with on an ad hoc basis. Some social and community programmes	Looks outward to the world, learning by contributing to the community in which it exists. Strong social curriculum to promote a sense of tolerance and understanding of different races, creeds and cultures	Introduce an active social curriculum in and out of school to enhance tolerance and understanding. Use Internet networks in projects to link pupils to other pupils throughout the world

Figure 20.1 Looking out to the world

In 1990, the conference of the International Federation for Information Processing, the world's leading information technology organization, was enlivened by a group of schoolchildren from Paramatta, a town near Sydney. They described the results of a project they had carried out with 30 other schools in 20 countries to measure the incidence of acid rain in their own locality, using kits specially developed for the purpose. From the data they obtained, they had traced its origins by studying wind currents and put together a pollution index for the various participating countries. One school in Norway sent a video of the rain dance they performed in order to provide enough rain to give a measurement. It was all great fun and both the students and the audience not only enjoyed the presentation, but also learnt a great deal from the exercise.

The Pallace project, described in Appendix 1, is another example of the fostering of creative international links between both teachers and children in schools in order to produce desirable insights and outcomes, in this case into the active participation of schools in the development of a learning city. The fostering of such collaborative links is one of the essential skills of the 21st-century teacher. They will proliferate as the technology becomes more accessible and powerful. And not only do they allow children to learn academically in a novel and interesting way, they also provide them with a more outward-looking understanding of other creeds, cultures and races.

The need for understanding

And this is not just a feel-good exercise. Both children and adults have need of the mental apparatus to learn and to understand their learning. Otherwise they become easily manipulable. The extremes of our systems in both developed and developing world have never felt the need to insert balance or provided the right to weigh arguments. This is true whichever extreme is waging the propaganda war, and the advent of far more sophisticated instruments of information technology makes the means of manipulation so much more accessible, plausible, powerful and insidious. Both political and religious fanatics flourish when the mental tools for considered judgement are absent, as we discovered on 11 September 2001 and after. The ability of teachers to confront these issues with their pupils in such a way that maturity, moderation, tolerance and the need for problem solving, rather than revenge, prevails, is a complex and particular skill. So is the instilling of such critical judgement skills as a part of the curriculum. It contributes as much to ensuring the survival of a free society as it does to the development of a liberated individual.

Schools serving the community

The school's involvement in the outside community can take many forms. Ontario High School in Canada even makes it a curriculum requirement. Its credit programme emphasizes the acquisition of knowledge, skills and values, the first two through the standard curriculum and the latter through the social curriculum in the form of community service. In grades 9 and 10 there are 30 credits, 18 of them compulsory and 12 of them optional, so that the student can take some ownership over the learning he/she does. Additionally, each student completes a minimum of 40 hours of community service to improve awareness of civic responsibility. Chapman and Aspin approve. 'Programmes of community and "service" learning and student leadership programmes in schools can provide the opportunity for students to develop a sense of commitment to others and of service to further the interests of all groups in society', they say, and follow it up with the notion that while schools may no longer be places to acquire knowledge, they are becoming much more important in the socialization process and development of 'moral awareness' in young people.

Such involvement in the community is rapidly growing all over the world as lifelong learning ideas take root. Many German schools offer children the chance to work with partners in community-based activities such as assisting in child care and support, assisting refugees, visiting in hospitals and day-care centres and working with old people on family histories The village of Eus in Southern France devised a scheme whereby children would interview the older people in the village in order to preserve their memories while they are still alive. Such activities are becoming more and more prevalent and creative in many countries. Sponsored walks, sponsored swims, sponsored balloon flights, sponsored talks for the Red Cross, the homeless and other organizations for the disadvantaged are all burgeoning, and often these activities carry on into adult life through the volunteering programmes described in Chapter 10. In China too community service is valued. Zhang Cuizhu proclaims 'the importance of the relationship between the classroom as a learning community and other, wider contexts in which the classroom finds itself and with which it interacts – the school, the community, families, other classes and communities'.

Citizenship and the schools

Such outward-looking ideals may be a feature of schools in many countries, but they have only recently been formally introduced into the curriculum of UK schools, following a period in the 1980s in which the prime minister of the time initiated legislation against such a focus, believing that it opened the door to political indoctrination by left-leaning teachers. However, times and perceptions change, and citizenship lessons and activities are now increasingly seen as important. A former Minister of Education described it as the equivalent of the new three 'R's – that is, learning about rights, wrongs and responsibilities. The *Independent* newspaper, in a special supplement to launch the new citizenship curriculum, reports, for example, that children at North Walsham school, near Norwich, use resource packs which encourage debate and discussion on topics ranging from the legal rights of children, through democracy and governance at all levels from the school to civil society, to issues connected with the social and moral responsibility of people and organizations. It is this latter topic that causes some misgivings in countries where morality is seen to be the responsibility of the family and the church. The Crick committee, which established the guidelines, was partly motivated by the lack of interest shown by young people in politics and by the disturbing effects of increasingly visible violence in UK inner cities. But it also considered that a return to the dry 'civics' lessons, often taught as an unpopular extra in earlier days, would be unproductive. It advocated a more robust and hands-on approach with interactive materials, frequent visits to council chambers, school parliaments and active involvement with those less fortunate in the community, such as the aged, the handicapped and the dysfunctional.

Industry, schools and citizenship

Business and industry are also contributing to the new social awareness. The Barclays Bank New Futures programme, for example, described in the same newspaper supplement, puts more than a million pounds into the hands of schools and their community partners for fostering community involvement. With the aid of such a grant, Furness School, a residential school for boys with emotional and behavioural difficulties, created a playground for disabled children and converted a redundant farm building into an activities centre. In the process, of course, they also learnt some very useful construction skills. In another example, school students in High Wycombe carried out in-depth research on the causes of shoplifting, meeting with shopkeepers, police and community leaders, and visiting prisons and restorative units to deepen the experience. The result was a performance and workshops which the older children took round the primary schools. Such activities and schemes not only bring students face to face with many of the great issues of the day, but also encourage the development of critical thinking skills to encourage a more mature and informed approach.

Schools and international commitment

Community activities can also be carried out at an international level. The international baccalaureate, an examination becoming increasingly popular with schools throughout the world, requires 50 hours of community service. The UNESCO Co-action programme also encourages such a global focus. The Belfast School for Girls first became involved as long ago as 1976 and supported ten separate projects in the developing world, including support for a school for the deaf and blind in Malaysia, a training scheme in Tonga, a fund-raising scheme for school fees in the Philippines, a school for the mentally handicapped in Madagascar and a special education centre in Peru. Pupils became convenors, keeping in touch with the target projects, relaying information in the form of letters, photographs and materials back to the school and parents. Pupils and staff also attend ceremonies held by UNESCO where they meet people from the projects for first-hand experience. The Philippines project is particularly interesting. Each child there is given an animal to rear, for which it is responsible until sold at market. The money is then used for school fees. Different strategies are used for fund-raising in Belfast, from sponsored discos to walks, car-washing, bob-a-job, 'spell-ins' for junior school children and 'starve-ins' simulating the deprivation experienced in the project countries. Replicated among the thousands of schools in the developed world, such philanthropic programmes could go a long way towards alleviating the suffering experienced in the developing world as well as providing valuable insights for children in the more comfortable zones.

Of course, many schools run schemes for helping the less advantaged in other parts of the world and use them to instil ideas of tolerance and understanding, but few have an outward-looking philosophy on this scale, despite the opportunities afforded by modern technology. At the heart of it is the attitude of the head and the teachers. Without their sanction community action will not take place. Without their active encouragement it will not get started. As Day puts it, 'Teachers are potentially the most important asset in the achievement of the vision of a Learning Society... They are at the cutting edge. It is they who hold the key to students' growing or diminishing self-esteem, achievement, and visions of present and future possibilities for learning through their own commitment.'

Schools and the value of extra-curricular activities

Education and training C20th	Lifelong learning C21st	Action for change
In some schools a play or a show once a year. Out-of-school activities led by enthusiastic teachers. Annual School Fair and Presentation Days	Enhances confidence, creativity and the cultural vision of staff, parents, children and the community through a wide range of extra-curricular activities	Establish an impressive programme of school societies, out-of-school activities, cultural events etc and involve the community where appropriate

Figure 20.2 The value of extra-curricular activities

The social curriculum is also enhanced by the way in which the school encourages a wider outlook on the world through extra-curricular activities. The school with a vibrant and thriving orchestra and/or band will enhance the musical potential of its children for life. The school with a solid sports and gymnastic agenda will produce fewer couch potatoes than the one without. The school that organizes a play, a musical or a drama event and involves as many children as possible will provide a lifetime access to, and love for, theatre and music culture. The school that offers pupils a variety of lunchtime and after-school clubs and societies will expand horizons and open up a lifetime of interesting hobbies and passions. The school that provides the opportunity to travel – to another country, another environment or a study centre – will widen the horizons of its children for life. It also tends to be the sort of school that gains the long-term affections of its staff and children. As mentioned in Chapter 11, lessons and examination slogs are not the memorable highlights of a school career. These other events and experiences are what stick out as important in the mind after long years of absence. As Longworth and Davies suggest:

Certainly the successful school has a thriving set of extra-curricular activities associated with it. Such activities are also the opportunity for children and staff to know and respect each other better through shared experiences. Participation is also learning – it is one of the most effective ways of understanding and instilling respect for any cultural field, whether it be the theatre, music, literature or sport. It goes without saying that a Lifelong Learning school will be one of the liveliest, most stimulating and inspiring organizations in town.

Confident learning organizations will hold learning events, learning festivals, learning courses and learning parties. They will promote and publicize it in every way. They will want to share it with everyone. They will want to celebrate the state of learning. The school that can take that on board is well on the way to success as a lifelong learning institution. Many schools have always provided such facilities, though they present some difficulties for rural schools where the children are bussed in. However, what used to be regarded as side-issues and add-ons to a good education are now appearing as a part of the modern curriculum of a lifelong learning school. They are no longer extra-curricular, but a vital component in the process of producing well-rounded and motivated children with a wider vision of the world and a determination to do their bit to make it better. In order to make it happen, they are using a range of professional expertises from the community to help – teachers, assistants, producers and directors, leaders of clubs, societies and sports, musicians, poets and authors, scientists and stage managers.

Chapter 21

Making it work for learning – teachers, technology and tools

Education and training C20th	Lifelong learning C21st	Action for change
Teacher as a passer of information through didactic teaching methods using chalk, talk and paper exercises	Teacher as enabler of learning through individualized active learning programmes using motivational power of ICT and other tools, new knowledge of how people learn and management of all available resources	Train all teachers in the management of learning, use of ICT and other learning tools. Increase resources through innovative programmes with industry etc

Figure 21.1 Use technology wisely

Awareness of the value of the use of computers in schools has risen dramatically, together with the rise in ownership of desktop and portable computers in society as a whole. It is an argument which still meets pockets of resistance, but one which has been won by the power of the technology itself. E-learning is an accepted fact of life at adult level and is becoming more and more acceptable in the schools. The questions now being asked are how they can be used to the best advantage and how schools can obtain more of them. As Longworth and Davies suggested in *Lifelong Learning* back in 1996:

> the potential impact of the personal computer on learning styles is akin to that of the discovery of the wheel or of fire on social habits. Personal computers, in their role of extenders of the human intellect, can act as tools to enhance the natural creativity of children, not least because their use will become pervasive as the technology becomes cheaper, more miniaturized, and increasingly accessible. The task then becomes one of harnessing and applying that creativity in a structured and disciplined way.

Eight years have passed since that was written and there have indeed been great advances in the use of computers in schools, though these have not always been associated with creative application. More often than not, the creativity comes from the children rather than the teacher. In its early days the perception of the computer was as a tool for delivering some aspects of the curriculum. Thankfully, the initial experiments using the machine as a sophisticated page-turner to deliver drill and practise factual information much in the same way as a book have died a partial death, though many programmes for the revision of basic knowledge for examination purposes have now hit the marketplace. Indeed these, and other educational software products, are the computer manufacturers' major marketing point to families desperate to help their children succeed in the examinations rat-race.

Using computers for learning

But there are also other advances. Word-processors and even spreadsheets are coming into everyday educational use, not only by administrative staff and teachers for lesson planning, but also by the children themselves to improve their story-writing, presentation and mathematical skills. Discussion still rages over whether the use of spell-checkers by children is cheating, much in the same way that the use of calculators used to be regarded as harmful to basic mathematical skills (and nor has that debate gone completely away!). The educational software itself, particularly that designed for very young children, is a deal more sophisticated than it used to be. Programs featuring children's television favourites will subtly introduce number theory or literacy concepts into play activities. Such 'edutainment' – though there is sometimes more 'tainment' than 'edu' – exercises seem to have caught the imagination of the young and had a beneficial effect on formal school lessons, in that they are now more active and interactive. There is still scope for making much greater use of the power of multimedia to combine text, sound, graphics and motion picture into genuinely interactive educational experiences, though this would entail much more equipment than is common in the ordinary school, and teachers trained to use them effectively.

As we have seen in Chapter 7, there are several strategies for increasing the amount of computer equipment in schools. The Tesco 'computers-in-schools' project could be replicated at a local level and some computer manufacturers have established donation programmes for such activities. Partnerships with local industry can also be a source of new hardware, as well as other resource, and parents are always seen as a soft touch where the education of their children is concerned. Indeed, planned effectively, the computer in the home is an auxiliary piece of equipment for the school. Some schools offer home purchase advice for parents, so that they can standardize on similar systems, and laptop computers can, of course, be used in both places. Those schools which are also community or adult education centres have other opportunities.

But, as is normal with power of any kind, the secret of success lies in the way it is used or administered. In addition to the use of word-processors and spreadsheets, databases, time management programs, logic games, simulations of real or imaginary events, 'what-if' software and skills development software are revolutionizing the way in which industry works, and can be of equal benefit to schools. The advent of lifelong learning tools and techniques gives a new impetus to the use of the technology. It is now more possible to give children much more control over the content and nature of their learning and to monitor that that learning is actually taking place. School–home interaction is potentially easier, the tools for managing community contribution more available and the organization of continuous learning programmes more interesting.

The proper and effective use of educational technology is therefore a step on the way to creating a lifelong learning community in the school. Figure 21.2 shows some of the ways in which it can be used to help motivate and galvanize both children and teachers into better learning.

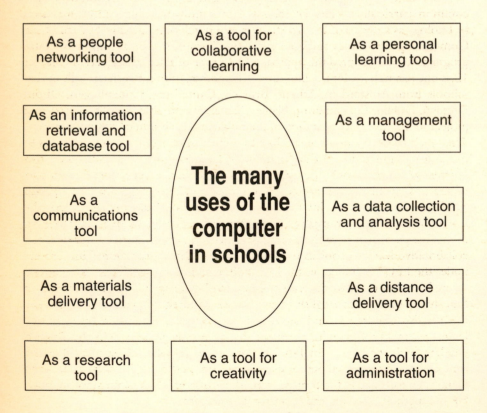

Figure 21.2 The many uses of the computer

The computer as a people networking tool

Putting children in touch with other children, experts, mentors and others who can help them achieve their goals, fulfil their potential and add to their maturity and happiness; putting teachers in touch with other teachers, experts, partners and others who can give new insights, increase resources and provide added value – the Pallace project described in Appendix 1 is a prime example of this. It involves both teachers and children in schools in five countries in a monitored interaction to explore how schools can contribute to the development of a learning city. In another project, scientists at the National Aeronautics and Space Administration in the USA have made themselves available as contacts for schoolchildren worldwide. 'Telementoring' is now well established in the USA as a means of helping young people both academically and socially.

The computer as a collaborative learning tool

In this, teachers develop new courses jointly and teach them collaboratively in a common curriculum between schools internationally, using communications technology as a means of teacher–teacher and pupil–pupil linking. Several of the Comenius programmes initiated from the European Commission's Socrates programme have adopted this approach. 'A Europe of Tales', described in Chapter 12, is one example. 'Adopt-a-monument' is another. In this, Beernaert tells us that schools from Amsterdam, Athens, Brussels, Canterbury, Copenhagen, Dijon, Dresden, Dublin, Luxembourg, Naples, Santarem and Toledo collaborated in a project to improve understanding of their own and each others' cultural heritage. They each adopted a monument close to them, researched its history, related it to the cultural and political development of their country and exchanged this knowledge between each other. Some even made themselves responsible for part of the upkeep of the monument. The increase in learning motivation among children in these types of interaction is significant. And this emphasizes that the main task is not the learning itself. It is persuading children that they want to learn in the first place. And here the computer as firstly a networking tool and then as a collaborative learning tool can help. For example, in a groundbreaking project under the PLUTO project in the late 1980s children in Manchester were linked through computer networks with children in Copenhagen. The objective was to find strategies to teach English to the Danish children using strategies whereby the English children would set and mark exercises, supervised by a trainee language teacher. It would, as an incidental advantage, also help the English children with their own English. This proved to be relatively successful at the time, and one unexpected outcome was the desire of the English children to learn Danish. Unfortunately the project expired because of a lack of financial support, but the methodology, and the opportunity, still exists.

The computer as a personal learning tool

The use of the new generation of computer software as a learning tool has been mentioned above. But there are other ways in which it can be used directly as a personal learning tool. One of them is in language teaching. Language learning has been a problem area in most English-speaking countries for many years. It is caused partly by a shortage of language teachers, who can find more lucrative, and less stressful, employment in the world of international trade, but mostly by the 'let them speak English' attitude so prevalent in most of anglophone society. Nor have expensive language laboratories usually been within the purchasing power of most school budgets, and so the methodologies of language teaching have focused in on the easier and more measurable aspects of correct grammar and memorized vocabulary. To be sure, there have been innovative projects such as the laserdisk produced under an IBM grant which inserted the learner into conversations in French and Japanese, but these were not specifically aimed at schoolchildren, and the technology became obsolete. One two-way language programme that does still exist is the 'Translate a Poem' project described on the armadillo Web site (see References). Here students from different countries exchange poems written in their own languages and write what they think the poem is saying in a foreign language. Where used, it has been successful not only in raising awareness of languages but also in increasing sensitivity to poetry.

Of course, it is not only in languages that the computer is valuable as a personal learning tool. And it can start to be useful at a very young age. In Victoria, Australia, Whitefriar's Year 1 class has been researching the topic of animals – wild and domestic and endangered species. Children were encouraged to access, retrieve and present information they had discovered using as a primary source the CD-ROM *Dangerous Creatures*, a disc with excellent multimedia capabilities (graphics, video and sound productions). This was important, as the children are only beginner readers. In the first activity, the children were asked to choose one animal and to carry out research using the disc. In so doing they became familiar with the mapping, the buttons and hot spots and researched the relevant areas of interest. For example, if the chosen creature was a snake, the disc asks 'What good are they?' The child then plays the video and listens carefully for the answer. This approach enhanced the students' skills in successfully accessing and retrieving relevant information. To follow this up, a picture of their animal was printed and the children were asked if it was an endangered species. The software provided clear illustrations of where the endangered species are located and this helped the children visualize the issue from a global perspective. A third activity involved the children printing in their own words at least one fact about their animal. They chose the graphic to go with their information. The lesson provided very young children with the knowledge and skills to retrieve information from the computer and turn this into knowledge and understanding.

The computer as an information retrieval and database tool

Here is where the greatest challenge lies, and where the advantage of the Internet makes itself apparent. Indeed, it is where the inadequacy of the standard curriculum becomes glaringly obvious. The massive amount of information on the Net grows exponentially year on year and, given that the usual safeguards against accessing doubtful and abusive material are applied, much of it is useful for producing insights, understanding and knowledge. Both children and teachers can use it effectively, the latter for identifying information and materials sources, the former for homework assignments, personal projects and interest. The environment might be typical of the many database examples possible. Offerings range from the Global Monitoring Systems at UNEP-GRID, through national weather and environment databases such as CORINE and NASA, to an enormous range of local environmental databases available from local government. One example of this comes from Japan where school students went on a field trip in order to find rocks and fossils. Using a local computer database, they identified the items and wrote up their findings and results. This led to further study on the sources and history of the rocks, the superimposition of strata, the distribution of volcanoes and riverbeds in the region and eventually land-use patterns and the human geography that had been superimposed onto the physical geography. For the latter they used the computer to access data from national and local sources. They even contributed valuable data not already on the database. In so doing, students learnt the techniques of basic research and discovered the convenience of computer use. As resources to underpin strategic teaching and learning, and as developers of the mental tools and techniques which enable people to cope with the explosion of information, they are invaluable.

The computer as a data collection and analysis tool

Chapter 20 described the experiences of children from around the world collecting data on rainwater quality. And of course there are hundreds of variations on the same theme in the local environment. Trees, birds, gardens, rivers, plants, flowers, streets, houses – all are potential objects for personal or class databases in the vicinity of the school giving rise to environmental, biological and botanical insights. But there are other focuses for the collection of data. De La Salle College, Cronulla, Sydney, is a senior coeducational college of approximately 500 students. History students there are often required to make oral presentations based on the results of their investigations. One example of this is a unit on the First World War, where Year 11 students are investigating the effect of the First World War on the lives of young Australians, both at the front line and in Australia. Students used photographs, documents and various memorabilia as well as interviews, letters and diaries as raw material. In some cases, the grandparents of group members also proved a valuable resource. In others the computer itself was the resource. The outcome would be a reconstruction of the impact of the war on the lives of individuals, and, through this, insight into its broader context. This is a valuable exercise in data collection and analysis. However, there is a further dimension to this project, in that the computer was also used as a presentation medium. By linking the video camera and a computer to produce digital images, it was found that the students were given greater control over what they were doing and were able to produce semi–professional presentations that could be used by their fellow students to further their own learning. The school also gained a permanent record. The use of technology in two ways – for the storage and analysis of the data, and for the preparation of video presentations – has provided another effective strategy to the teaching of history in the school. There are many examples of such projects building up geographical, historical or family databases both locally and across country and regional boundaries. They not only demonstrate the power of the computer to stimulate more meaningful and relevant work in the context of real–world examples, they also change the pupil–teacher relationship. Peter Smith puts this more succinctly:

> Taking advantage of this new capability will require profound changes in the roles of teachers, students, and school. Instead of being the repository of knowledge, teachers will be guides who help students navigate through electronically accessible information. They will use the new technologies to build networks with each other, with parents and students, with academic and industrial experts, and with other professionals. Schools will look less like the factories they were set up to emulate and more like the workplaces of a post-industrial age. The distinction between learning inside of school and outside will blur.

The computer as a communications tool

The world is shrinking and Schumacher's global village is fast becoming a reality. It takes the press of a button to send e-mail speeding around the seven continents of the world in trillionths of a second. According to Rose and Nicholl, a single hair-thin optical fibre can transmit all 29 volumes of the *Encyclopaedia Britannica* in less than one second. Satellites encircle the globe and enable visual, as well as verbal, communication and link into the several million computers now used in offices, studios, universities, homes and, if they believe themselves to exist in the modern world, schools. There are now forums, Internet groups, discussion marketplaces and chat lines on every conceivable subject in every place where human beings interact. The communications revolution has enriched, in different ways, both the Internet service providers and their rapidly expanding customer bases. Schools cannot but be a part of that scenario if they are to enable their charges to come to terms with the real world.

As we saw in Chapter 1, this eruption of information and communication has the effect of disenfranchising those who are unable to cope with it. Teachers and children find themselves in exactly the same dilemma – too much information, too few strategies to cope with it. And of course there is also disinformation – the opportunity for broadcasters, dictators, unscrupulous communicators from every walk of life, to manipulate thoughts, feelings and actions in ways that inhibit the growth of a mature society, replacing one sort of tyranny with another. It is a situation of great urgency for schools. One way to deal with it is to use the communications capability of the computer to communicate with others. Heatherwood School in Victoria, Australia, services students from 12 to 21 with mild intellectual disabilities. Its philosophy is based on the belief that every student has the ability to learn and succeed and it aims to develop self-motivated individuals who have the necessary attitudes and skills to lead independent, socially productive and personally fulfilling lifestyles. To this end it publishes every week the *Heatherwood Star*, a newspaper for parents and the community. All classes in the school are involved and teamwork in writing the stories is encouraged. Planning and discussing ideas often takes place in the classroom and students may prepare drafts to bring to computer sessions. On the technical front, word-processors, digital cameras and publishing software such as PageMaker are used. But the real benefits come from the activity itself. It promotes many of the skills identified in Chapter 9 as essential for a lifelong learning world – teamwork, critical judgement, communicating, information handling, decision making and others. Teachers use the results for further reading and discussion work. Entrepreneurial skills are added since the students also sell the newspaper, and communications between school and home and school and community are enhanced. They own both the process and the outcomes. This is an excellent exemplar replicated in many schools today, and it opens the door to other communications–oriented exercises based on the increasing capability of the computer, such as the making of videos, CD-ROMs and professional standard publications.

The computer as a creativity tool

Computers are machines. They do only what they are programmed to do, even if, to the untutored mind, much of it seems to be astonishing. They also do it very fast. Any creativity surrounding the computer must therefore emanate from the people using it. And in today's and tomorrow's world creativity is a key attribute for every human being. Rose and Nicholl lament: 'Children are leaving school ill-equipped for the jobs of the future – the jobs that will require very high standards of analytical ability, creativity and flexibility. In fact we don't even know what those jobs will be. They have yet to be invented.' The second part of the quotation is most certainly true, as is the first. But there are now a large number of schools where creative applications around the use of the computer abound. Many thousands of children are adept at making their own home pages on the Web and this is one of the reasons why the Internet is growing so rapidly. At Rosny College in Hobart, an establishment for Years 11 and 12, students are making heavy use of computer graphics and design programs. No longer do traditional design methods using 2D paper space and primitive drawing tools to illustrate a concept apply. Students' creative thinking skills and conceptual ideas are developed in a three-dimensional, computer-generated, virtual environment. They are put into a problem-solving situation to produce an initial model and use further computer simulations and prototyping steps through the various stages in the design process. If the design is to be produced or manufactured, final working drawings are printed and collated at the end of the design exercise. The course they take progresses through an ever more complex series of tasks leading at the end to a solution which only the computer can generate. These design exercises extend the students' ability in the various software tools available and enable them to experience the many and varied methods of developing a design from the initial concept to a final three-dimensional solution. They were enabled to proudly present their work and ideas in a range of formats to future employers and tertiary institutions.

The computer as a research tool

Computers are also used as tools for research in many environments, usually associated with universities, laboratories or advanced manufacturing industry. But schools too can use the ability of the computer to store, analyse and present data in order to develop the critical thinking skills needed by citizens of the future. One example of computer work stimulating cooperation between schools comes from the Hobart region of Tasmania in a partnership between the Department of Education, the local newspaper, *The Mercury*, a primary school and several secondary schools. All participating schools have varying degrees of access to the Internet, ranging from single line up to multiple computer lab access. *The Mercury*'s 'News in Education' programme identifies key issues in the news and current affairs and produces special materials for schools. The targeted areas have been written specifically for publication on the World Wide Web. Schools can then gain immediate access to material that is being constantly updated. For example, themes have included: 'Celebrate Tasmania', an historical feature on Tasmania's past, 'Antarctica' and the Opinion page of *The Mercury*, looking at the editorial, daily cartoon and letters. Each of the published themes has a combination of text and graphics, as well as teacher's notes, suggested activities and ways of utilizing the source material. *The Mercury* provides students with access to the initial copy as received from journalists, the first edit with comment and the final edit that appeared in the newspaper. This gives students a special insight into how a newspaper operates. Prior to the publication of the newspaper, the students were able to pull this material off the Web site and assume the roles of writer and editor to create a page of the newspaper. When the paper was published, the students were able to compare their page with the real page published in *The Mercury*. Fast reliable access to the Internet is an absolute necessity as many of the activities and the source material rely on the use of pictures, cartoons and significant amounts of text. Such projects promote interactivity between schools and industry, between schools and schools and of course between schools and computers – all in the context of a real and relevant learning experience.

Such illustrations demonstrate the ability of the computer to enlarge the vision and horizons of today's school students. Smith agrees:

> Because of their immersion in a computerized world, children absorb information differently than their parents do. Instead of following information passively from beginning to end – as people tend to do with television shows, newspapers, and books – children interact with the new technologies. Watching them use a computer is more like witnessing a conversation than a monologue. They skip from place to place and draw connections. They construct their own realities by experimenting with what already exists.

The computer as a materials delivery or development tool

New resources for lifelong learning are unlikely to come from local taxes or national handouts. Strategies for increasing the resource available to the school have been discussed in several chapters in both parts of the book. However, the computer itself is an enormous source of new resource available to schools, and much of it entirely free of charge. In the UK, the English and Scottish National Grids for Learning are setting an example by developing a library of films, case studies, sample lessons, videos, graphics material etc suitable for use by schools and other educational organizations. But there are other sources emanating from all over the World Wide Web. Longworth pointed out in *Learning Cities for a Learning Century* that:

> A vast library of downloadable materials highly relevant to many curricula, including video clips, graphics, text, sound, motion picture, is now available there, much of it free of charge. Want to know about Kangaroos? Look up the Kanga company's Web site for educational materials suitable for geography, history, natural history and home economics. Want information and materials on oil and petroleum? Look at any of the oil companies' Web sites for graphics, learning materials, clips and sample lessons for teachers. This new richness of resource, while often industry based, is not always an advertising gimmick and much of it is professionally prepared by active educators.

And nor is this simply available to teachers. It is there to be used by the students as they construct their projects and develop their presentations in order to make yet more materials available.

Bannockburn Primary School in Victoria, Australia, takes a whole-school integrated approach to curriculum delivery and uses the learners themselves in Years 3 and 4 to help develop it. Children work in groups of three or four to create a mini television programme to demonstrate special effects, using software developed principally for creating learning materials. The emphasis is on whole-brain learning with a mix of dynamic, imaginative, analytical and commonsense tasks.

Firstly, they are taught how to draw pictures, add text, record music and students' voices, and use the slideshow component of a computer program titled *Kid Pix Companion*. Secondly, the children survey their peers to find out their favourite television programmes and advertisements and to ask their opinion on:

- what makes a TV show popular;
- what special features make one advertisement more successful than another;
- what audience is targeted for particular advertisements and TV shows.

They then list key words from the information collected and presented, and classify advertisements and television programmes into different types.

The next stage is, in groups, to produce their own slideshow, generate their own special effects and link pictures to create an animated sequence. They use a combination of word-processing, drawing, sound recording and special effects to input into the software. Only if groups are unable to solve a problem can they request assistance from their peers (peer tutoring) or teachers. Off-computer tasks include script-writing, and the research, design and construction of a radio or television system (from microphone or TV camera to receiving the signal in our homes). The outcomes are new multimedia productions, but in addition children have also used other software to produce 'living books', school magazines and newspapers. The quality from such young people is high. This is a good example of the usefulness of the computer to raise the standard of achievement and learning in children, and to act as a focus for innovative and creative activities.

The computer as a distance delivery tool

No discussion on the use of technology can ignore the advances being made in distance delivery tools and techniques. However, not only are the studios expensive, but the pedagogic techniques used are often ill-suited for use in schools, except at the older levels. But no such constraints exist at the Maconoquah School in Indiana, USA. Here a sophisticated interactive network of video technology, state of the art computers and voice services link the 2,000 students and teachers with anyone and anywhere in the world. The school is completely cabled through fibre-optic technology, every room and every desk linked to each other and to the outside world. In-school recording technology allows teachers and students making a trip, for example, to the Indiana State Museum to record a VCR tape of the visit, and indeed students are encouraged to make their own video learning materials, with background music, edited footage, subtitles and narration for others to learn from. Teachers from any classroom can call up videotapes, still videos, laser discs, CD-ROM and CDI discs, motion pictures, computer software slides or satellite images onto the classroom desktop monitors and large screen facilities. Every classroom and administrator desk is equipped with a data port giving access to central file-servers, multimedia software, e-mail, word-processors, presentation systems and desktop publishing. Voice mail is linked to homes and other buildings in the locality. Students use the technology to develop newspapers, do homework, access language programmes in Spain, Italy and France, download books and video materials, learn at their own pace and test themselves on the knowledge gained. Every teacher has been trained to use the technology in the optimum way.

For some, such technological *richesse* would be the ultimate nirvana, a foretaste of learning efficiency for the future. For others it is a horror story in which the machine has taken over the function of the teachers and is transforming children into non-creative techno-junkies. But of course, even in the most technologically oriented school, there have to be multiple opportunities to interact without the technology. And it will not diminish in the coming years. Because of its extensive use of ICT, Maconoquah claims that it can deliver a continual skills-based curriculum with accompanying self-assessments. Students with special needs, whether deficient or gifted, can be catered for individually. A wide curriculum can be provided, bringing in expertise from all over the district and even internationally. The school goals encourage creativity and innovation, and a strong partnership with the local community and parents.

Summary

This section is longer than the others simply because it is evident that the use of information and communications technology is one of the keys to opening up the lifelong learning society in the modern era. But it is not the only one. Technology used indiscriminately and for the sake of itself will not solve the problems of the schooling system. It is only a part of the complete package. As Roy Romer, Governor of Colorado has said: 'When we bring technology into a school, we must make it a total part of the mission of education, not just a peripheral item. Technology alone is not enough. If we leave the system as it is we will not accomplish the changes that we need. To be successful we need technology and restructuring together.' And, coming from a senior politician, that is an insightful statement to make.

Chapter 22

Putting it all together – a summary

Education and training C20th	Lifelong learning C21st	Action for change
(In some countries) Concentrates mainly on high academic achievers in order to enhance attractiveness to parents through position in league tables	Concentrates on both academic and personal success of all pupils as a means of enhancing the school's reputation and satisfying society's need. Invites the public to share in it	Market the school strongly. Emphasize the positive learning opportunities for all children, staff and the community at large. Create own league table of all-round achievement

Figure 22.1 Broadcasting the lifelong learning news

The time has come to put this all together and to show how schools can, and must, be the originators of lifelong learning values and attitudes for the 21st century. A quote from *Lifelong Learning* encapsulates the notion:

> Unless the nettle of adopting a new Lifelong Learning approach is grasped, schools will continue to trail behind society's need. Salvation is not to be found in going backwards; the paradigm has changed. Nor can schools carry out what needs to be done by themselves. They are the agents of society's will. They operate by consent. They have a responsibility to parents, to children, to all the members of the community in which they are situated, to the government which provides their resources, to the companies and business organizations and universities in which their issue will work and further educate themselves.

What has been discussed in this chapter is nothing less than a revolution in opening schools out to the needs of a 21st-century society. Examination success alone will not achieve that, and nor will any one of the suggestions made in the preceding chapters, by itself. As with lifelong learning in Part 1 of this book as a whole, the future comes as a package – interactive, interdependent and interlocking. Without a solid, forward-looking and implementable organizational plan covering several years into the future as suggested in Chapter 15, the measures for introducing continuous improvement programmes for staff and students proposed in Chapters 3 and 16 will not happen, and nor will parents and the community be able to play their part as implied in Chapters 5, 17 and 20. Unless the community plays its part, there will not be the heavy investment in tools and techniques which bring the school into the 21st century, as mooted in Chapters 4 and 21, and nor will the curriculum be brought into a skills-based world as Chapters 9 and 18 insist. Without the support, counselling and guidance systems proposed in Chapter 19, the school strategies will continue to be undermined by the day-to-day fire-fighting activities which hold back progress, and the more outward-looking ideals of the school described in Chapter 20, as well as the students themselves, will under-achieve. Resources, financial, physical and human, are all around, as Chapters 5 and 17 suggest, but unless there is someone to tap into them and to develop the partnerships which breathe life and meaning into school routines as Chapters 11 and 20 infer, there will be a continuing inter-departmental scramble for the meagre scraps thrown out by funding authorities.

Some constraints for schools

Of course, there are many schools with energetic staff and motivated students already pushing back the frontiers of what is possible in many of these areas, and there are equally many following the line of least resistance, simply coping with the difficulties thrown at them day after day, and unaware that there is any obligation on them to re-assess their priorities and their vision into a lifelong learning future. There are indeed many reasons why schools should take such a course. Many of the fundamental constraints within which they operate are determined by government. The mighty examination system rules in many countries and, as we saw in Chapter 8, creates a success–failure culture with its own in-built self-fulfilling prophecies for those without the means or the background to cope. In some less educationally mature countries it even gives rise to crude and inequitable league tables of schools, which present a rudimentary and inchoate view of what education is about to parents, and often demean the remarkable achievements of many individuals over adversity. Much of this is not helped by a media which clings to its negative mortarboard and punishment view of education so beloved of boys' own magazines, in which any improvement in results is portrayed as 'dumbing down', and any change to a student-centred approach as 'trendy'. It takes a courageous and a visionary head and staff to oppose the traditions and fables of educational folklore.

Handing back control to the schools

But much of that is now changing. In most countries political judgement decrees that greater control of schools should be handed back to the communities in which they operate and to the staff who work there. And this, while it is to be welcomed, imposes a heavy responsibility on the administrators and staff who will take the school into this brave new world. It combines the management skills of a captain of industry, the communication skills of a broadcaster, the articulation skills of a public relations expert, the leadership skills of a great general, the development skills of an engineer, the imagination of a dreamer, the courage of an explorer and the vision of Socrates. No small order. Above all, it requires helicopter vision, the ability to rise above the problems in order to see the solutions, and to see what lies beyond the horizon in both time and space. No one is suggesting that the lifelong learning school can be achieved overnight, or even over a few years. Some will take longer than others to be responsive to the needs of every individual and to the local, national and international learning community. These are not ideals relevant to one country. Schools all over the world are experiencing similar outlooks and grappling with similar problems. As we have seen, some countries and some schools are building better foundation stones than others. Leadership, as always, is the key, but it is not the traditional view of leadership coming from one all-powerful person. It is the more the leadership of the many, the empowerment to hand over the ownership of learning to everyone.

Achieving consensus

Most reports coming from global and national governmental organizations and from experts in the field are unanimous in their diagnosis of what it takes to create a better learning world. The following list is taken from documents produced by such diverse organizations as OECD, European Commission and UNESCO:

- pre-school programmes for disadvantaged children to combat early deprivation;
- quality programmes for secondary schools;
- lifelong learning foundations for all in primary and secondary schools;
- individualized and accredited programmes for learners;
- new curricula and new delivery methods;
- schools as community learning centres for a diverse range of students;
- more innovative schools–industry partnerships;
- new academic and vocational pathways equally valued;
- strategies for motivating pupils and building up self-esteem;
- increased parental and community involvement in the school;

- learner-centred approaches to learning;
- networks with other schools and educational organizations;
- non-threatening support-based assessment systems.

Most of these are also mentioned above. They are part of the bigger picture developing around the globe to meet the needs of an uncertain and often hostile world. The educational emphasis is now on cooperation and understanding, rather than confrontation and destruction, whatever behaviour the politicians may exhibit. Europe, North America, Australia, parts of Asia, they are all moving towards the creation of a learning society within their boundaries. Learning towns, cities and regions contain learning schools, colleges, universities and businesses and interact with each other across learning countries and continents. *Learning Cities for a Learning Century* quotes 15 different characteristics within which cities are becoming more holistic and interdependent. The TELS project identified 10 domains and 28 sub-domains by which a municipality or region could identify progress towards becoming a 'learning community'.

The school's role in a learning city

Physical or virtual, geography, common interest, purpose or values, what is common to all of these learning communities is that they exist to mobilize the totality of available physical, economic, social and intellectual resources to advance personal fulfilment, social development and create economic prosperity and resilience through lifelong learning for all. In this, schools are a vital component. Their pupils are, after all, the future citizens and should have a significant role to play in its development. The Pallace project, described in Appendix 1, is the first step towards understanding that role and how it can be fostered at local and global levels. Figure 22.2 brings together all the suggested activities which can act as a beacon for those schools willing to make the effort, and acts as a summary for this whole section. The last word will be left with Denis Ralph, Chief Executive of the South Australian Centre for Lifelong Learning and Development: 'I would argue strongly, that it is learning communities that have the potential to recapture our lost ideals, it is learning communities that have the potential to bring forth our best human virtues, it is learning communities that can unite us in a sense of respectful, synergistic communion and it is learning communities that offer us the greatest vehicle for the manifestation of an ideal place to live, to work and to be.' What a vision for schools to help create.

Figure 22.2 encapsulates the recommendations for action identified in Part 2 for the creation of lifelong learning schools. All that remains is to implement them in the way most appropriate to each organization.

Education and training C20th	Lifelong learning C21st	Action for change
1. Sets narrow academic objectives and targets and works to achieve these in the present	Not only works to achieve present targets but also to impart future long-term values and attitudes to learning.	More schools/life links and partnerships – with industry, community etc construct a wider curriculum dealing with life skills
2. Rudimentary short-term business plan usually around academic matters. Little effort to keep every stakeholder informed and on-side	A full written organizational strategy, available to all, for developing the school into a lifelong learning organization, and covering all aspects of the school's activity	Develop longer-term school business plan and make it available to all. Create proactive information strategies to bring all stakeholders on-side. Adopt external quality indicators like Investors in People
3. Some teachers go on educational courses according to need or desire. Occasional seminars in schools for teachers only	Every person in the school has a continuous improvement plan for academic and personal skill/knowledge development embedded into the management system, and part related to the school development plan	Develop written continuous improvement plans for academic and personal development of pupils, teachers and admin staff. Extend these to parents and community as desired
4. Teachers only human resource for curriculum delivery supplemented by helpers. Other resources supplied from local government and school events	School adds human resource by tapping into skills, talents and knowledge of governors, parents and everyone in the community and other resource by exploring funding and other sources in the community	Appoint someone to identify and use ALL the human and other resources in the community and beyond. Use innovative strategies to involve the community in school development
5. Curriculum based on discrete subjects, and assessed on memorization of facts with pass–fail philosophy	Curriculum based on skills and knowledge, the enhancement of self-esteem and the acceptance of lifelong values. Examinations as stock-taking part of the personal learning process	Incorporate personal skills development into the curriculum. Take the notion of failure out of the system and replace it with strategies for improving personal self-esteem
6. In-school pastoral care systems staffed by overworked teachers. Sparse support services to identify and solve individual learning and social problems early	Guidance, support and counselling systems available for all learners and their families using all available resources. Rapid identification and solution of learning and social problems	Introduce individual learning guidance systems for all pupils and update frequently. Use resources in school and community – mentors etc. Involve the family. Initiate rapid response system

Education and training C20th	Lifelong learning C21st	Action for change
7. Focus on curriculum and examination success within the school. Social curriculum dealt with on an ad hoc basis. Some social and community programmes	Looks outward to the world, learning by contributing to the community in which it exists. Strong social curriculum to promote a sense of tolerance and understanding of different races, creeds and cultures	Introduce an active social curriculum in and out of school to enhance tolerance and understanding. Use Internet networks in projects to link pupils to other pupils throughout the world
8. Teacher as a passer of information through didactic teaching methods using chalk, talk and paper exercises	Teacher as developer of learning skills using motivational power of ICT, multimedia, networks etc in individualized active learning programmes	Train all teachers in the many uses of technology as learning tools. Invest heavily in ICT through innovative programmes with industry etc
9. Parents invited to school to discuss child's progress once a term. Occasional public information meetings	Involves the family in the life of the school through increased home–school cooperation and active participation in school events	Write a family participation guide outlining all the things parents etc can do for the school. Open an e-mail line. Establish a contact point
10. In some schools a play or a show once a year. Out-of-school activities led by enthusiastic teachers. Annual School Fair and Presentation Days	Enhances confidence, creativity and the cultural vision of staff, parents, children and the community through a wide range of extra-curricular activities	Establish an impressive programme of school societies, out-of-school activities, cultural events etc and involve the community where appropriate
11. (In some countries) Concentrates mainly on high academic achievers in order to enhance attractiveness to parents through position in league tables	Concentrates on academic and personal success of all pupils as a means of enhancing the school's reputation and satisfying society's need. Invites the public to share in it	Market the school strongly. Emphasize the positive learning opportunities for all children, staff and the community at large. Create own league table of all-round achievement

Figure 22.2 From education to lifelong learning in the school

Appendix 1

City-rings and the Pallace project – creating active links between cities and regions globally

---

Imagine, if you will, a system of linked learning cities and regions around the globe, each one using the power of modern information and communication tools to make meaningful contact with each other:

- school to school to open up the minds and understanding of young people;
- university to university in joint research and teaching to help communities grow;
- college to college to allow adults of all ages to make contact with each other;
- business to business to develop trade and commerce;
- hospital to hospital to exchange knowledge, techniques and people;
- person to person to break down the stereotypes and build an awareness of other cultures, creeds and customs.

And so on – museum to museum, library to library, administration to administration.

Imagine that these links include both the developed and the developing world so that, say, Brisbane, Seattle, Southampton, Shanghai and Kabul, to pick five at random, form one learning cities ring among a hundred similar networks…

Imagine that one-tenth of the money used to develop military solutions to human and social problems were to be spent on people and tools to make these city rings work effectively…

Imagine that such links had started ten years ago…

- Would it have contributed to the creation of a better world?
- Would world hatred and poverty be as great as it is now?
- Would terrorism have been as prevalent as it is now?

Isn't this one of the key challenges to us in the Learning Cities movement? Isn't this a worthy objective?

OK – so it's a stupid, hopelessly idealistic, idea, BUT... **imagine** the advantages:

- Thousands more people and organizations in the cities contributing to the solution of social, cultural, environmental, political and economic problems.
- A giant leap in mutual understanding and a transformation of mindsets through greater communication between people and organizations.
- Profitable economic, trade and technical development through contact between business and industry.
- Active interaction and involvement, and a huge increase in available resource through the mobilization of the goodwill, talents, skills, experience and creativity between cities and regions.
- Fewer refugees – developing problems can be anticipated and addressed through cooperation between the cities.
- It's sustainable – because it's so much more dispersed. Governments and NGOs are no longer the only initiators of aid to the underdeveloped. Action is now shared with the cities and, through them, the people.
- Organizations and institutions in the city/region have a real world-class focus and *raison d'être*.
- Again – understanding – understanding – understanding leading to solution – solution – solution.

What an opportunity to make a real difference! Which world leader dares to take it on?

(Keynote Address by Professor Norman Longworth to the Lifelong Learning Communities Conference of Australian Universities, Central Queensland University, Rockhampton, June 2002)

Of course, in the present condition of world politics it is indeed a hopelessly idealistic notion. It puts a burden on cities they would perhaps rather not have. And yet, cities do already make contact with each other frequently for many purposes. And there is nothing here that the technology is not already doing.

Certainly this kind of thinking is at the root of the Pallace project, a European Commission initiative to link learning cities and regions in Australia, New Zealand, Canada and Europe. In Pallace the interaction between partners will be at many levels of the learning city, engaging a variety of individual stakeholder groups in collaborative pilot activities, and increasing knowledge of their roles in learning city and region development. Each of the six partners will be responsible for leading the development of a learning module on the contribution of a stakeholder in a learning city or region, working with one or more of the other partners to test it.

Thus children, teachers, parents and community leaders connected with *schools* from South Australia will link with schools in Espoo, Finland, Papakura, New Zealand and Mt Isa, Queensland in a joint exploration of what a learning city means, how it changes the lives of its citizens and how schools and schoolchildren can help develop and maintain it in their own cities. Insights into different cultures and creeds will be strengthened by the inclusion of children from indigenous communities.

Such cross-cultural innovation is continued through ICT links between *adult education colleges* in Papakura and the Auckland Region of New Zealand with France. The result of this will be a learning module on the characteristics of a learning city usable by adult education institutions everywhere to help them understand the nature of the learning city and how they can help contribute to its development.

In another Pallace stakeholder project creative links will be established between City and Regional *Cultural Services Departments* in Finland, Edinburgh and Queensland to design, develop and test exhibitions and projects that bring learning city ideas to the notice of citizens through libraries, museums, galleries and special interest groups.

The Centre de Formation des Elus, an organization for providing training for municipal councillors in France, will work with learning city leaders (elected representatives, teachers, community leaders etc) in Sannois, France and with the City of Marion in South Australia to create a self-learning module for *councillors (elected representatives)* on lifelong learning in cities and regions.

The role of *technology providers* in learning cities will also be explored. Learning modules will focus in on the effective uses of ICT for collaborative learning within and between learning municipalities. This project will be led by the Alberta partners, in collaboration with Papakura, New Zealand.

The Queensland partners will build upon the work already being done in public/private partnerships in the Brisbane area to incorporate lifelong learning concepts into the structural fabric of a new community. It will work with Alberta on this. The results of this exciting work will be published in a learning module developed for municipalities throughout the world.

In China, the city of Beijing will combine with all cities to bring an added cooperative dimension from a non-anglophone country.

Together these seven sub-projects within Pallace constitute a powerful contribution to our existing knowledge about how stakeholders within cities can interact for the benefit of each other. It remains to expand the width and scope of these activities into the city-ring concept described above, including cities in the less developed parts of the world into a mutual aid circle. To do this requires an expanding global network of learning cities and regions promoting interaction. Such a network will be launched at the last of the four regional seminars initiated by Pallace, in Edmonton, Canada in 2004. Here the seminar will be part of a global conference on learning cities and regions organized by the World Initiative on Lifelong Learning.

Further information can be obtained from:

Professor Norman Longworth
Napier University
Department of Lifelong Learning
Craighouse Road
Edinburgh EH10
E-mail: norman_longworth@csi.com

Appendix 2

The World Initiative on Lifelong Learning (WILL)

Readers will know that many governments in both the developed and developing world are producing strategies and policies to promote lifelong learning. This is because lifelong learning is known to be at the heart of the future, and one of the most powerful influences on their development in education, society and national economies. But readers are also close enough to the action to know that most of the real development will take place at local and regional level, where organizations are situated and where people live. This explains the recent massive growth of 'learning cities, towns and regions' throughout the world at large.

WILL – the World Initiative on Lifelong Learning – is a major organization for encouraging and assisting the development of lifelong learning in countries, cities, towns, regions and organizations as vibrant, innovative and exciting places whose people accept learning as a part of life. Lifelong learning has huge implications – for the administrators, public servants, managers and teachers who will have to implement the new strategies, and for the people themselves who are on the receiving end of new structures and ideas (but who are also encouraged to participate in developing them). The range of activities and ideas for our lifelong learning future is both limitless and confusing.

WILL is a relatively new organization. It fills a vacuum at global level for the interaction and exchange of ideas, knowledge, expertise and projects between organizations in all aspects of lifelong learning. We know that the 21st century will be different and that the development of a culture of learning for life is the way to prepare for it. We know too that people and organizations will be the well-spring of action. We invite readers to join us in creating that future. It could be the best investment you will make this century. And of course there are the links to all parts of the globe through the WILL organization.

What is WILL and what is it for?

What is WILL? It is *the* lifelong learning organization offering knowledge, debate, support and action across the board at global level. This includes research and advice into the lifelong learning needs of schools, universities, companies, professional associations, cities and regions. This breadth of vision and the activity of its membership are WILL's strength and is available to the WILL member network.

WILL initiates the dissemination of information, the coordination of projects and studies, the mobilization of actions, people and organizations to bring them into the Lifelong Learning Age. It covers all sectors of society and all countries. It will appeal to:

- **Business, industry and commerce** – where lifelong learning can be a survival strategy. WILL provides examples of good practice from around the world and empowers its industry and commerce members through collaborative partnerships for developing implementable lifelong learning strategies to create learning organizations.
- **Higher education** – higher education is in a position to provide the intellectual and practical leadership for the development of lifelong learning programmes locally, nationally and internationally. WILL mobilizes universities to take this leadership position through cooperative projects and programmes, and workshops, seminars and conferences.
- **Schools and teacher training establishments** – lifelong learning begins in childhood, and schools are crucial organizations for shaping those attitudes and values which prepare future adults for a world in which flexibility and adaptability are essential. WILL exists to help and encourage teachers, teacher trainers, parents and others on how to create habits of learning that will last throughout life.
- **National governments** – which play a leading role in providing vision and setting standards. WILL members have helped to put together government strategies for lifelong learning. WILL acts as a link between governmental organizations on good practice from which good strategies and policies emerge.
- **Vocational education organizations** – which influence the creation and maintenance of employment for the future. WILL believes that lifelong learning skills and practices are crucial for effective vocational education and training. It offers its members ideas, actions and solutions through which they can maintain employability as well as employment.
- **Adult education and cultural organizations** – Second-chance colleges, leisure and sports education, continuing education, organizations in all areas with responsibilities to their constituencies, museums, libraries, women's groups, local societies. The list of people and organizations in and outside the formal education system which become involved in the lifelong learning

process is endless. They are crucial at all levels of human potential development and WILL acts as a clearing house for information and activities in these areas.

- **Professional associations and non-governmental organizations** – WILL offers information and participation opportunities to member NGOs and professional associations, whose members must keep themselves up to date and who need to know how the concepts of lifelong learning can be applied within their own organizations and for their members.

And of course:

- **Towns, cities, regions, communities** – WILL exists to provide a forum for all municipalities or regions wishing to become learning communities.

Above all, WILL believes that only through the integration of many of these sectors will a lifelong learning society become reality.

Legally, WILL is a non-profit-making organization registered in Alberta, Canada with a Board of Directors from all continents. This comprises distinguished people from industry, professional associations and universities throughout the world.

WILL addresses a reservoir of global needs and demands, including:

- the creation of learning communities in every city, town and region, and linking them to a global network of like-minded municipalities;
- the development of learning organizations in every company, school, university and government department;
- advice to governments on lifelong learning strategies for all and how to implement them;
- the development of a society in which the habit of learning throughout life is a part of everyone's personal growth and culture;
- the use of learning techniques and tools of the 21st century – technology, personal learning plans, audits, mentors, purposeful learning partnerships etc;
- the development of new skills and values to enable individuals to cope with a rapidly changing workplace and world;
- defining, measuring and monitoring progress to the acquisition of lifelong learning skills, values and habits in schools, universities, government departments, companies, communities, individuals.

Each one is a mammoth task. Each one, and more, presents challenges to those organizations with an awareness of the needs of the 21st century.

If ever we thought that lifelong learning could be implemented easily, the (initial) task list should make us stop and think again. Everywhere and for years to come, there is much to be done. It demands insight, wisdom, energy and commitment – and leadership through a professional organization like WILL.

The WILL organization comprises a president, five vice-presidents concerned with marketing and development, strategy, membership and operations, and of course a secretary and treasurer. But it is the members who are the executive arm of WILL. They help to organize the learning development groups, conferences, workshops and seminars, participate in global educational programmes and working groups, and develop reports on various aspects of lifelong learning.

WILL involves itself in and leads funded action research projects. The Pallace project is an example. Here seven cities and regions in four continents are involving their stakeholders in collaborative projects to explore how they can help each other and others in developing a learning city/region. This will lead on to a series of city rings which we hope will transform the way in which cities and regions interact with each other worldwide. Appendix 1 gives further details of this.

WILL's vision is of a professional association relevant and necessary to all global organizations, communities, governments and individuals, serving its members with the ideas, information and action which will enable them both to learn from each other and to contribute to the development of lifelong learning of others, both nationally and at global level.

Please write to or fax:

Sylvia Lee
President
World Initiative on Lifelong Learning (WILL)
Knowledge Management International
1206 Park Plaza, 9740–106th Street
Edmonton, Alberta
Canada, T5K 2P8
Tel: +1.780.488.4848; Fax: +1.780.401.3271
E-mail: kmi@kmintl.biz

References

Abbott, J (1997) 21st century learning: beyond schools, *Training, Education, Employment*, November, '*t*' magazine ltd, London

Ahmed, F (2002) *Turning failure into success, Observer* newspaper, 13 October, p 3

Armadillo Web site: http://www.teachnet.com/lesson/internet/poem.html

Ball, C and Stewart, D (1995) *An Action Agenda for Lifelong Learning for the 21st Century*, report from the 1st Global Conference on Lifelong Learning, N Longworth (ed), World Initiative on Lifelong Learning, Brussels

Ballarat (2000) *Ballarat, a Learning City – A Lifetime of Discovery*, Promotional leaflet available from PO Box 210W, Ballarat, Victoria 3350

Bannockburn Primary School: www.sofweb.vic.edu.au/lt/casestud/bannock.htm

Bayliss, V (1998) Redefining schooling: a challenge to a closed society, *RSA Journal*, **cxlvi** (5468), London

Beernaert, Y (1995) L'ecole adopte un monument, *Lifelong Learning for Schools*, ELLI, Brussels

Beijing Academy of Educational Sciences (2002) *Education in Beijing, New Developments, New Achievements, New Perspectives*, Beijing Academy of Educational Sciences, China

Bexley Business School (2002) a report broadcast on LTN local news BBC television, 10.30 pm, 10 September

Black, J (1998) Lifelong learning – the economic imperative, in *Launchpad for Success, Conference Papers and Case Studies from Europe*, ed Fitton, C, Soper, C and Sutherland, R, Edinburgh City Council, Edinburgh

Botkin, J et al (1979) *No Limits to Learning*, report of the Club of Rome, New York

Bournazel, A (2001) *L'Education Tout au Long de la Vie – Une Nouvelle Education Nationale*, Ellipses, Paris

Brennan, J (Editor) (2002) *Lifelong Learning for Equity and Social Cohesion – a New Challenge to Higher Education*, Draft Report of Final Conference, Council of Europe, Strasbourg

Bryce, J (2002) *Ways of Orienting Secondary Schools to Becoming Learning Communities*, paper presented at CQU conference on Lifelong Learning Communities, 16–19 June, Yeppoon

Campaign for Learning (1998) A learning organisation mindmap, *Learning to Live*, issue 9, Campaign for Learning, London

Campaign for Learning (2001) Learning at work days, *Learning to Live*, issue 18, summer, Campaign for Learning, London

Campaign for Learning (2000) Learning to learn, *Learning to Live*, issue 16, autumn, Campaign for Learning, London

Candy, P, Crebert, R G and O'Leary, J (1994) *Developing Lifelong Learners Through Undergraduate Education*, National Board of Employment, Education and Training Commissioned Report Number 28, Australian Government Publishing Service, Canberra

Chapman, J D and Aspin, D N (1997) *The School, the Community and Lifelong Learning*, Cassell, London

Chapman, J and Aspin, D (2001) Schools and the learning community, in *International Handbook on Lifelong Learning*, Kluwer Academic Publishers, Dordrecht, Holland

Clarke, A C (1986) *Prelude to Space*, Ballantine, New York

Cochinaux, P and De Woot, P (1995) *Moving Towards a Learning Society*, A Forum Report by European Round Table of Industrialists (ERT) with Conference of European Rectors (CRE), Brussels

Comenius, J (Jan Amos Komensky) (1987) *Pampaedia* (trans) AMO Dobbie, Buckland, Dover

Commission of the European Communities (1991) *Skills Shortages in Europe*, Industrial Research and Development Advisory Committee of the Commission of the European Communities (IRDAC), Brussels

Commission of the European Communities (1997) *Meeting the Challenge of Change at Work*, Employment and Social Affairs Directorate, EC Publications Office, Luxemburg

Commission of the European Communities (1998) *Territorial Employment Pacts, Examples of Good Practice*, EC Publications Office, Luxembourg

Commission of the European Union (2000) *Memorandum on Lifelong Learning for Active Citizenship in a Europe of Knowledge*, DG Education and Culture, Brussels

Commission of the European Union (2002) *Realising a European Area of Lifelong Learning*, DG Education and Culture, Brussels

Crichton, S and Kinsel, E (2002) The importance of self and development of identity in learning, in *Papers for the International Lifelong Learning Conference 2002*, Central Queensland University, pp 143–8

Crick, B (1998) *Education for Citizenship and the Teaching of Democracy in Schools*, Report of the Advisory Group on Citizenship, London

Cruse, H (1997) Du Kan schools, in *Lifelong Learning in Schools*, ELLI, 1997

Davis, T (2001) *Global Research on Innovation*, speech at Ericsson conference on creativity and innovation, London, reported in *EFMD bulletin 13*, February, EFMD, Brussels

Day, C (2001) Innovative teachers: promoting lifelong learning for all, in *International Handbook on Lifelong Learning*, Kluwer Academic Publishers, Dordrecht, Holland

Department for Education and Employment (1998) *Learning Communities: A guide to assessing practise and processes*, Learning City Network Secretariat, 111 Grantham Road, Bingham, Nottingham, UK, NG13 8DF. Phone/Fax: 01949 841171

Department for Education and Employment (1998) *The Learning Age, A Renaissance for a New Britain* (Green Paper on Lifelong Learning), DfEE Publications Centre, Sudbury

Department for Education and Employment (1999) *Adur Industry First*, Case Study 2 of SRB Case Studies and Thematic Good Practice, DfEE Publications, Sudbury

Department for Education and Employment (1999) *Digital Learning Partnership*, Case Study 19 of SRB Case Studies and Thematic Good Practice, DfEE Publications, Sudbury

Department for Education and Employment (1999) *Durham Looked After Children Project*, Case Study 16 of SRB Case Studies and Thematic Good Practice, DfEE Publications, Sudbury

Edinburgh City Council (1997) *Building Strong Communities*, City of Edinburgh Council, Edinburgh

Eger, J (2001) *Cyberspace and Cyberplace: Building the smart communities of tomorrow*, [online] www.smartcommunities.org/wf/cyberspeech.htm

Ellis, W N (2000) in *Creating Learning Communities*, ed Ron Miller, Foundation for Educational Renewal, Washington

Espoo City Council (2000) *Good Practices in Espoo the Learning City*, leaflet distributed by the Espoo Learning City project, Kamreerintie 5, 02770 Espoo

Espoo City Council (2002) Etalukio project, in *Good Practices in the Learning City*, leaflet distributed by the Espoo Learning City project, Kamreerintie 5, 02770 Espoo

Eurich, N (1985) *Corporate Classrooms. The Learning Business*, Carnegie Foundation for the Advancement of Teaching, New York

European Foundation for Management Development (2001) Knowledge ecology university programme, *Bulletin Number 13*, February, EFMD, Brussels

European Round Table of Industrialists (1996) *Investing in Knowledge, Towards the Learning Society*, ERT, Brussels

European Round Table of Industrialists (ERT) (1989) *Education and European Competence*, ERT Education Policy Group, Brussels

European Round Table of Industrialists (ERT/CRE) (1995) *Education for Europeans*, ERT Education Policy Group, Brussels

Eurostat (2001) *14th CEIES Seminar, Parma*, European Commission, Brussels

Field, J (2002) *Lifelong Learning and the New Educational Order*, Trentham Books, Stoke-on-Trent

Finland Ministry of Education (1997) *The Joy of Learning, A National Strategy for Lifelong Learning*, Committee Report 14, Helsinki

Frye, N (1988) *On Education*, Fitzhenry and Whiteside, Markham, Ontario

Fryer, R H (ed) (1997) *Learning for the 21st Century*, First NAGCELL Report on Lifelong Learning, NAGCELL, London

Fryer, R H (2001) *Next Steps in Achieving the Learning Age*, Second NAGCELL report on Lifelong Learning, NAGCELL, London

Gardner, H (1993) *Multiple Intelligences: The theory in practice*, Basic Books, New York

Gardner, H (1999) *The Disciplined Mind*, Simon and Schuster, New York

Glasgow Development Corporation (1999) *Attitudes to Learning in Glasgow*, Glasgow Development Corporation

Goleman, D (1998) *Working with Emotional Intelligence*, Bloomsbury, New York

Handy, C (1992) *Managing the Dream: The learning organisation*, Gemini Consulting Series on Leadership, London

Hazlewood, P (2001) Towards a 21st Century Curriculum, *RSA Bulletin*, **cxlviii** (5499, 4/4), RSA, London

Heatherwood School, example on Sofnet: ww.sofweb.vic.edu.au/edtimes/1997pdf/vsn19.pdf

Hock, D (2000) Udaipur as a learning city, *Vimukt Shiksha*, March, pp 56–62

Holt, J (1965) *How Children Learn*, Penguin books, Harmondsworth

Holt, J (1976) *Instead of Education*, Dell, New York

Huxley, A (1978) *The Human Condition*, lectures at Santa Barbara 1959, Triad Granada, St Albans

Industry Canada (1997) *Schoolnet, Plugging Kids into the World*, publicity literature from Industry Canada, Ottawa

REFERENCES

Industry Canada (1999) *Key elements of a Smart Community*, publicity literature from Industry Canada, Ottawa

International Association for Volunteer Effort (2001) *Universal Declaration on Volunteering*, IAVE, Washington

International Commission on Education for the 21st Century (1996) *Learning: The treasure within*, UNESCO Publishing, Paris

Jilks, B (1998) Interview with Bruce Jilks (online) http://www.designshare.com/Research/Jilk98/JilkInterview.htm

Kennedy, H (1998) Education for all: an impossible dream?, *RSA Journal*, **cxlvi** (5485), pp 76–80

Kent County Council (1996) *Kent Learning: Our future 1996–2006*, Kent County Council, Canterbury

Larsen, K (1999) Learning cities: the new recipe in regional development, CERI paper in the *OECD Observer*, No 217, June, OECD, Paris

Lee, S (1992) *In search of education*, Journal of the Alberta Association for Continuing Education, Edmonton

Longworth, N (1980) *The Woodberry Down School/IBM Basinghall Street Twinning Scheme*, IBM United Kingdom Ltd, London

Longworth, N (1999) *Making Lifelong Learning Work: Learning cities for a learning century*, Kogan Page, London

Longworth, N (2000) *The Local and Regional Dimension of Education, The TELS (Towards a European Learning Society) Project*, DG Education and Culture, Brussels

Longworth, N and Beernaert, Y (eds) (1995) *Lifelong Learning in Schools*, European Lifelong Learning Initiative, Brussels

Longworth, N and Davies, W K (1996) *Lifelong Learning: New Visions, New Implications, New Roles – for Industry, Government, Education and the Community for the 21st Century*, Kogan Page, London

Longworth, N, Weimer, W, Frisk, T and Paris, E (1993) *CCAM, Investigation into Common Operational Environments for the Implementation of Telematics based Training Infrastructures*, EuroPACE, Paris

Luker, P (2001) *Lifelong Learning, Rising to the Challenge*, School of Computing Sciences, De Montfort University

Maconaquah School Corporation (2001) *Project Turnaround*, Maconaquah School Corporation, Bunker Hill, Indiana 46914

Markkula, M and Suurla, R (1998) *Passion to Learn, Benchmarking Good Lifelong Learning Practice*, IACEE Report no 9, Helsinki

Muirhead, B (2002) '*Communicate*', *Projects and Activities of University of Queensland Community Service and Research Centre*, Ipswich, Queensland,

Musto, F (1989) Distance learning in industry, *European Journal of Education*, **24** (1), European Centre for Education, Paris

Naisbitt, J (1985) *Megatrends*, Organization for Economic Cooperation and Development, Paris

Naisbitt, J and Aburdine, P (1986) *Re-inventing the Corporation*, Futura, London

National Service Learning Cooperative: http://www.servicelearning.org/

Odyssey of the Mind (1995) – reference taken from awareness video sent to schools by Odyssey of the Mind Inc, Newark, NJ

Okamoto, K (2001) Lifelong learning and the leisure oriented society, in *International Handbook on Lifelong Learning*, Kluwer Academic Press, Dordrecht, Holland

Organisation for Economic Cooperation and Development (1973) *Recurrent Education: A strategy for lifelong learning*, OECD/CERI, Paris

Organisation for Economic Cooperation and Development (1996) *Lifelong Learning for All – Meeting of the Education Committee at Ministerial level*, OECD/CERI, Paris

Organisation for Economic Cooperation and Development (1998) *Competitive Strength and Social Cohesion through Learning Cities and Regions: Concepts, developments and evaluations*, Centre for Educational Research and Innovation, Paris

Petrella, R (1996) *Sustainable Cities: Toward a new alliance for solidarity among the generations and across cities*, [online] www.uee.org/fr.petre.htm

Ralph, D (2001) *The Return of Camelot*, address to Ministerial meeting on Vocational Education and Training, Adelaide 2001

Ranson, S, Rikowski, G and Strain, M (2001) Lifelong learning for a learning democracy, in *International Handbook on Lifelong Learning*, Kluwer Academic Press, Dordrecht, Holland

Rezenghani, D (2002) Unpublished address to seminar of Brisbane Educationists, 20/6/2002, University of Queensland

Rigler, I (1997) European Regional Education network inaugural conference, DG EaC, Brussels

Roddick, A (2000) Companies that care, *RSA Journal*, **cxlviii** (5495), 4 April

Romer, R (2002) Governor of Colorado on http://books.nap.edu/html/techgap/navigate.cgi

Rose, C and Nicholl, M J (1997) *Accelerated Learning for the 21st Century*, Piatkus, London

Rover Learning Business (1994) *Learning Organisation* (booklet), Rover Learning Business, Birmingham

Royal Bank of Scotland (2001) Corporate social responsibility, in *Observer* Business section, 11 February, p 5

Sanderson, B (2000) Speech to WEA/NIACE conference (online), last accessed November 2001, http://www.lsc.gov.uk/news_docs/wea_niace.doc

Schools Curriculum Industry Partnership (1994) *Bringing Business into Learning, a Practical Guide for Schools*, Centre for Education and Industry, University of Warwick

Scottish Office (1998) *Opportunity Scotland, Green Paper on Lifelong Learning*, Stationery Office, Edinburgh

Scottish Power Learning (1998) *Personal Development Plan*, Scottish Power Learning, Cumbernauld

Simpson, S (1994) Profiting from business in higher education, in *Capacity Building for the 21st Century*, UNESCO, Paris, pp 115–22

Smith, P (1995) *Reinventing Schools – The Technology is Now*, National Academy of Sciences, Washington

Southampton City Council (2002) *Even Better Learning for All*, Southampton Lifelong learning development plan 1999–2002, Southampton City Council

Speke Garston school (1999) *Case Study 4* of Case Studies and Thematic Good Practice, DfEE Publications, Sudbury

Stockton's Learning towns (2001) *Learning for Life*, booklet describing the learning and skills festival for the residents and workforce of the borough of Stockton-on-Tees, available from Startford House, Ramsgate, Stockton-on-Tees, UK

REFERENCES

Teichler, U (1999) *Higher Education and the World of Work*, UNESCO paper ed-98/conf202/cld.17, UNESCO, Paris

Tersmette, E (2001) *Second Chance Schools: from pilot project to shared responsibility*, Newsletter of the Second Chance Schools, third edition, May, E2C Europe, Brussels

The Independent (2002) Special supplement on the launch of the new citizenship curriculum, issue 27 September

The Scotsman (2002) Mentor scheme helps children to help themselves, 9 October, p 11, Glasgow

Toffler, A (1980) *The Third Wave: The revolution that will change our lives*, Collins, London

Tommila, L (2002) *The Learning City Project – a Report on the Procedure of the Learning City Project in Espoo*, available from City of Espoo, Kamereerintie 5, 02770 Espoo, Finland

UNESCO (1973) *Objectives for the Future of Education (Fauré report)*, UNESCO, Paris

UNESCO (1991) *The Coaction Project in the Belfast Model School for Girls*, *UNESCO Associated Schools Project Bulletin*, no 61–2, UNESCO, Paris

UNESCO (1994) *International Understanding at School*, ASP Bulletin, no 61–2, UNESCO, Paris, pp 4–8

UNESCO Commission on Education for the 21st Century (1996) *Learning: The Treasure Within* (Delors report), UNESCO Publishing, Paris

UNESCO (1998) *Mumbai Statement on Lifelong Learning, Active Citizenship and the Reform of Higher Education*, UNESCO Institute for Education, Hamburg

UNESCO Institute of Education (2001) Reflecting on lifelong learning discourses and practices across the world, the Beijing conference highlights, in *Reports on International Programmes*, Beijing Academy of Educational Sciences, China

Universities Scotland (2001) *Submission to Enterprise and Lifelong Learning Committee Inquiry into Lifelong Learning*, Universities Scotland, Glasgow

Visser, J (2001) Integrity, completeness and comprehensiveness of the learning environment: meeting the basic learning needs of all throughout life, in *International Handbook for Lifelong Learning Part 1*, Kluwer Academic publishers, Dordrecht, Holland

Weimer, W A (1999) *Learning to Manage in a Complex Organisation*, Twente University Press, Enschede, Netherlands

Wen Zhu (2001) Creative education and education for creativity, in Reports On International Programmes, Beijing Academy for the Educational Sciences, China

Wong, S (2002) *Examples of Learning Communities in the UK*, report for Geelong City Council, Australia

Wyse, B (1999) Home–school agreements, *RSA Journal*, **cxlvi**, 1 April, RSA London

Yule, R and Salmon, R (2002) *The Monteney Community Workshop Trust* – found on www.monteney.org.uk

Zhang Cuizha (2001) Theories and practices on learning communities in China, in *Reports on International Programmes*, Beijing Academy for the Educational Sciences, China

Zohar, D and Marshall, I (1999) *SQ – the Ultimate Intelligence*, Bloomsbury, London

Index

2 3 3 1